Pornography

Key Concepts in Media and Cultural Studies

Reality TV, June Deery
Pornography, Rebecca Sullivan and Alan McKee

Pornography
Structures, Agency and Performance

Rebecca Sullivan and Alan McKee

polity

First published in 2015 by Polity Press

Polity Press
65 Bridge Street
Cambridge CB2 1UR, UK

Polity Press
350 Main Street
Malden, MA 02148, USA

ISBN-13: 978-0-7456-5193-4 (hardback)
ISBN-13: 978-0-7456-5194-1 (paperback)

A catalogue record for this book is available from the British Library.

Typeset in 11/13 Sabon by
Servis Filmsetting Limited, Stockport, Cheshire
Printed and bound in the United Kingdom by CPI Group (UK) Ltd, Croydon

The publisher has used its best endeavours to ensure that the URLs for external websites referred to in this book are correct and active at the time of going to press. However, the publisher has no responsibility for the websites and can make no guarantee that a site will remain live or that the content is or will remain appropriate.

Every effort has been made to trace all copyright holders, but if any have been inadvertently overlooked the publisher will be pleased to include any necessary credits in any subsequent reprint or edition.

For further information on Polity, visit our website:
politybooks.com

Contents

Acknowledgements

The authors would jointly like to thank the wonderful staff at Polity who first envisioned this project and gave us unlimited support and freedom to express ourselves. Special thanks to Andrea Drugan, the one who made it all possible. We also extend our gratitude to all the Polity reps with whom we had the pleasure to work: Joe Devanny, Elen Griffiths, Lauren Mulholland, Neil de Cort and Susan Beer. Thanks as well to our book designer, David Gee. Our two peer referees gave thoughtful, supportive feedback that strengthened the final work and gave us renewed confidence in our arguments. We also acknowledge, with deep gratitude and respect, our incredible editorial assistant, Tiffany Sostar. She spent long hours and sleepless nights poring over our manuscript, not only correcting technical faults but also offering sharp insights into pornography activism. A more professional and passionate collaborator we could not have imagined.

I would like to extend personal gratitude to the students at the University of Calgary who have enrolled in my courses on pornography and taught me more about this subject than I think I taught them. The Women's Studies and Feminism Club, Consent Awareness and Sexual Education Club, the Q Centre for Sexual and Gender Diversity, and the Women's Resource Centre have given me the gift of an intellectual and activist community, from which I draw sustenance and courage.

Acknowledgements

Special thanks to colleagues near and far who have inspired this work and provided support: they include Feona Attwood, Alison Beale, Karen Boyle, Paul Johnson, Catherine Murray, Katharine Sarikakis, Clarissa Smith, Lisa Tzaliki, and Thomas Waugh. Although in many instances our paths cross infrequently and briefly, you have all been a unique part of this journey. I especially want to thank my gracious and generous co-author, Alan McKee, without whom this project may never have been completed. I must also extend an additional thank you to Tiffany Sostar for introducing me to the world of feminist queer pornography and making it possible for me to begin my own discovery of the field. What I once believed impossible has now exceeded my wildest (political) dreams.

Finally, I wake up every day grateful for my loving husband, Bart Beaty, and our amazing son Sebastian. Just because.

Rebecca Sullivan

I would like to thank first of all Professor John Hartley – my first and best mentor, and a profound thinker whose democratic approach to culture radically challenges traditional academic thinking. His work has helped to make it possible for downmarket, trashy and vulgar people like me to work in the academy.

The writing-up of this book was made possible by the Creative Industries Faculty at Queensland University of Technology through a Long Professional Development Leave grant. My ten years at QUT were inspiring and exciting and I learned a lot. Thank you to everybody there.

I'm profoundly grateful to the colleagues who helped me develop my thinking about culture and sex – Rebecca Sullivan (of course), Anne-Frances Watson, Johanna Dore, Christy Collis, Jerry Coleby-Williams, Catharine Lumby, Kath Albury, Brian McNair, Feona Attwood, Clarissa Smith, Emma Jane, Sarah Tarca, Claire Starkey, Anthony Walsh, Clare Moran, Michael Dunne, Sue Grieshbaber, Ben Mathews and Juliet Richters. Any mistakes or eccentricities remain my own.

And finally, I send my love to my husband, Anthony John Spinaze – without you I would not be so sane. Thank you.

Alan McKee

Introduction

Pornography and Porn Studies

What is pornography? Who is it produced for, and what sorts of sexualities does it help produce? Why should we study it, and what should be the most urgent issues when we do? These are the questions that frame our analysis of how pornography is conceptualized as a sexual practice, a media form, and a social issue. This is a book about pornography as a concept, one that is charged with numerous political, social, and cultural concerns about gender roles and sexual relationships more generally. As such, we are largely interested in the debates and discourses that circulate about pornography – how they are organized, what sorts of assumptions lie behind them, who is most deeply implicated in them. The goal of this book is to situate those debates and discourses within networks of competing gender and sexual politics in globalized cultural systems, and to suggest new frameworks for the understanding of pornography. We treat pornography as an integral part of commercial media industries, national and international regulatory discourses, gendered social structures, and subaltern sexual praxis.

Pornography is notoriously difficult to define, and overburdened with assumptions concerning – at the very least – gender, sexuality, power, globalization, desire, affect, and labour. Yet that should not allow us to sidestep this demanding task: it is not good enough merely to repeat the famous dictum by United States Supreme Court Justice Potter Stewart, 'I know it when I see it' (Jacobellis v. Ohio, 378 US 184 (1964)). At stake in the

1

definition of pornography is the recognition that sexual pleasure is a highly contested and politically fraught concept, and that media and popular culture have a long history of perpetuating deep-set gender and sexual inequities and making them appear pleasurable. At the same time, we also appreciate that many of us create and consume media entertainment to enhance our sexual freedoms and pleasure-seeking. In so doing, the boundaries of what can and cannot be seen, spoken, or performed are challenged and redrawn. That is why pornography is such an important concept for anyone concerned with the role of media and popular culture in everyday life. It deserves to be studied in ways that take into consideration its multiple possibilities and in the context of who is making it, who is watching it, and how.

This book engages with some of the most well-known and current strands of public debate on pornography. We pay particular attention to Anglo-European countries including Australia, Canada, Great Britain, and the United States. At the same time, we recognize that, like all media, pornography is being transformed by forces of globalization: industrialization, labour migrations, technological advancements, and the mingling of cultural forms and symbolic systems. Analysis unfolds across six major vectors: industry, technology, violence, pornification, governance, and performance. Our attention is, unless otherwise clearly stated, on pornography produced in legal contexts by adults for adult consumption. Our reasons for this focus are that this is the most prolific and profitable sector of the pornography industry, and is also the most hotly contested in determining the gender and sexual politics of pornography. While we make reference to child abuse materials (the preferred criminological term for what some call 'child pornography') and to criminal acts such as 'revenge porn', our attention to these is in the context of their outright unethical and illegal practices. As such, the issues they raise are substantially at odds with consensual adult pornography and require a radically different approach from the one we take in this book.

We approach the concept of pornography from our positions as media and cultural studies scholars with passionate commitments to feminist, queer, and pleasure-positive politics. One of our goals is to reveal the historical and political underpinnings of contemporary concerns about pornography's place in the media entertainment matrix. That term refers to the wide range of production, distribution, and consumption practices of entertainment content – commercial, amateur, and anywhere in between – occurring on multiple and intersecting media platforms. We further seek to position pornography within a larger network of cultural and sexual politics that draws attention to and claims greater rights and freedoms for non-normative, pleasure-based sexual performances and practices. To that end, we insist that pornography is neither inherently good nor bad, neither necessarily transgressive nor oppressive. Rather, we acknowledge media's ability to inform ideas about gender and sexuality, and to provide or withhold resources that assist audiences in making sense of their own media consumption. We are therefore interested in the ways that pornography is produced, obtained, consumed, debated, and defined; and how these practices help shape attitudes about gender and sexual roles and relationships more generally.

We emphasize pornographic performances and practices in this book for two reasons. The first is to draw attention to the ways that performers make sense of and gain value from their labour. Second, we seek to conceptualize the theoretical potential for some pornography to inspire consumers to expand their interests beyond personal sexual pleasure to a politicized embrace of new public sexual cultures. Performance and practice are acts of agency and skill, rarely fully empowered nor fully exploited but negotiated and self-determined based on existing contexts of everyday life. While the former term is particularly relevant for the analysis of labour and production and the latter helps frame how audiences engage with pornographic materials, they are not exclusive to either production or consumption. Rather, they reference a cycle of mutually reinforcing engagements with pornography that foregrounds the real bodies at stake.

We challenge any argument that regards pornography solely as a social ill to be eradicated by giving primacy to performers and sexually marginalized groups in our analysis. We draw awareness to the perpetuations of racist, sexist, homophobic stereotypes in much commercial pornography (as is common in most media entertainment). We also note similar attitudes in some anti-pornography discourses. Too often, warnings of pornography's destructive force are encumbered with assumptions that a 'normal' or 'healthy' sexuality proceeds from heterosexual romantic relationships between two individuals committed to both monogamy and (eventual) child-rearing. This, we refer to as 'heteronormativity'. In an early salvo against anti-pornography feminism, radical pro-sex feminist Gayle Rubin harshly critiques the 'sexual essentialism' of heteronormativity. She outlines the ways that psychology, biology, and even cosmology have been marshalled to prove that such human sexual behaviour is innate, and that outside influences such as pornography are dangerous contagions to be resisted (1984, 275–6). Rubin distinguishes between the 'charmed circle' sex based on the heteronormative principles outlined above; and 'outer limit' sex, a presumed 'bad, abnormal, unnatural, damned sexuality' that includes pornography (1984, 281). We share her critique of this arbitrary sex hierarchy, and examine the ways that different contexts for pornography can either reinforce or disrupt it in imperfect and uneven ways. Thus, while we write pornography in the singular, we see it more as a complex set of media engagements that can help force a reckoning with the concept of pleasure in our gender and sexual politics.

Pornography and pleasure

At its most fundamental, pornography refers to the graphic depiction of sexually explicit acts made available for public consumption on a media platform. Moreover, those acts are deemed pornographic because their intention is understood to be primarily for the sexual pleasure of the audience member. These three criteria – explicitness, public mediation, and pleasure – require some unpacking. First, we recognize that pornography incorporates explicit sex. We do not insist that the sex on display be 'real' because even if the acts on display did actually occur, they were created in a context of performance. Too often 'real' is used to refer to pornography as if it is a documentary or even clinical recording of sex and not a highly constructed act by individuals with varying levels of skill, mindfulness, self-determination, and experience. We recognize that the sex on display has been created with differing attention to both artistry and artifice, dependent on its industrial and labour contexts, and its intended audience. We therefore define 'explicit' as offering a high level of graphic depiction of the genitals or primary sexual characteristics of any given body engaged in acts that are represented as providing sexual pleasure. We think this is a workable definition which captures the majority of material that is understood by its producers and consumers as being pornography, although it may exclude some rarer sexual fetishes where pleasure is taken from non-genital interactions – sneezing fetishes, balloon porn, or an attraction to women's shoes, perhaps.

Second, pornography is mediated and available for public consumption. By that we mean that pornography is experienced through some kind of cultural technology that makes it available to a vast potential audience who is, through various and diverse means, physically separated from the act on display. That can be through asynchronous time, as in a pre-recorded film or image, or published text. Or, it can refer to the spatial limitations placed on live performance in streaming or social media. Regardless, the point is that pornography is offering a sexual experience but one that constructs a physical distance between performer and audience. Some claim that mediation renders the performer 'two-dimensional' and therefore objectified and somehow dehumanized (Mason-Grant 2004, 125). Such arguments rest on psychoanalytic claims that the viewer enjoys a sadistic, voyeuristic gaze over performers, reducing them to spectacular, desired objects (Mulvey 1975). Treating the performer as something less than human because they work within a mediated environment is, we contend, problematically dismissive of creator and consumer alike. We appreciate the skill required by performer and audience to produce meanings and values out of media – good and bad and mostly somewhere in the middle – that are then used in the work of individual identity formation and collective social practice. In that regard, pornography is no different from any other media practice.

Finally, we readily acknowledge that a major intent of pornography is to incite sexual pleasure. That can be for the performer but it is predominantly for the consumer. In legal definitions, pornography is often accused of being 'solely' for the purpose of inciting pleasure, as if that is an uncivil act that negatively affects the social good. We do not consider pornography to be 'solely' about sexual pleasure because we refuse the idea that bodily and sexual pleasure are divorced from either a sense of social accountability or intellectual self-understanding. Mind/body dualism is a hallmark of patriarchal thought that denigrates and denies the body as a source of knowledge and power. It then aligns the body with the feminine and then rather dubiously claims that as proof that women and non-normative sexual subjects are sexually deviant and intellectually feeble. While bodily and sexual pleasure may be foremost in pornography, there is no justification to claim it as therefore a lesser or debased form of pleasure. Additionally, we recognize that many pornography producers, especially contemporary feminist/queer performers, clearly include activist and educational intentions within their work that merit critical exploration. Thus, we define pleasure broadly and inclusively to recognize it as integral to gender and sexual politics.

We frequently use variants of the phrase 'publicly mediated forms of sexual expression' to refer to what some may call pornography. In doing so, we are raising awareness that much anxiety over pornography is intricately related to a more permissive and open-ended attitude towards sex in media and popular culture. Not all publicly mediated forms of sexual expression bring with them the level of explicitness or sexual arousal associated with pornography, yet some critics insist that 'the pornographic' is becoming ubiquitous in even mainstream media. Certainly, increased levels of sexual openness and what Anthony Giddens (1992) has termed more 'plastic' attitudes about sex have blurred the lines between pornographic and mainstream media. Pornography's increased prominence in the media entertainment matrix, and the concomitant concerns about that, demand questions about what forms of sexual pleasure are deemed acceptable for public consumption. For some, the answer is to hive pornography off from the rest of media and popular culture and regard it as anything that goes 'too far' with its sexuality. That kind of othering fails to take into account how pornography is deeply interconnected to other forms of media entertainment at all levels from the industrial to the symbolic.

Pornography in the media entertainment matrix

In this book, we focus on those discourses concerned predominantly (but not exclusively) with visual forms of pornographic production, both live and pre-recorded. These are the most prevalent forms of pornography in circulation today and therefore form the bulk of our examples and examinations. We readily admit that, in the interests of focus and clarity, we are perpetuating a neglect of explicit sexual representation in literary or non-visual forms. Helen Hester further notes that any affectual representation of disgust and excess is often called pornographic: 'food porn', 'trauma porn', and the like (2014, 14). She argues that 'pornography' has been appropriated as a rhetorical device to the point that it actually displaces sex from its own descriptor. Such a claim is provocative and intriguing. However, we argue that sexual pornography itself is alive and well, offering up explicit sex primarily intended for sexual pleasure, and that is our interest here.

Pornography is often called the 'driver' of technological and industrial innovation in the media. As we discuss in both Chapters 1 and 2, it is frequently the testing ground for new business models since production values tend to be much lower, thus dropping barriers to entry for new producers, and its subcultural status allows for more flexibility in the trial-and-error stages. With enhanced convergence and concentration of media, it is increasingly difficult to treat pornography as distinct from other parts of the media entertainment matrix. For example, the television industry includes service providers that offer pornographic channels, which are often subsidiaries of large media conglomerates, and purchase content from production houses that employ individuals who work on both pornographic and non-pornographic sets. Consider that Internet and cellular data service providers are also usually connected to television providers, and it would be nearly impossible to determine where the line separating pornographic from mainstream media begins, at least from a technological or industrial standpoint.

Yet, pornography is usually studied as something unique from any other media form. It is treated simultaneously and often incoherently as a genre, industry, ideology, and subculture. No other element of the media entertainment matrix receives quite the same treatment. We point this out as something that can potentially reinforce pornography as outside regular or 'mainstream' media practices. At the same time, its convoluted status offers some interesting opportunities to examine the dynamics between text and contexts, production and form, politics and practice that are transforming the media landscape of gender and sexuality. Pornography does have distinct aspects to its industrial organization, the occupational status of its performers, its representational and generic schema, and its audience engagement. Thus, we regard pornography as a particular set of media practices operating within social structures that position 'individuals in relations of labour and production, power and subordination, desire and sexuality, prestige and status' (Young 2005, 420). As Iris Marion Young notes, such positions are multiple, varied, and changeable in accordance with interconnected social structures and the individuals contained therein (421). Thus pornography deserves its status as unique but not to the point that it can be regarded as qualitatively different from other forms of media and culture.

Media and cultural studies of pornography

This book contributes to the growing field of media and cultural studies of pornography. What distinguishes the field is its interest in both the generic and formal qualities of a pornographic text, the social and historical conditions of its creation, and the meanings and values it engenders among varying audiences. Feona Attwood claims that media and cultural studies has helped produce a 'paradigm shift in pornography research':

> It represents a new interest in contextualizing pornography by situating particular texts in relation to issues of cultural categorization and classification, cultural value and hierarchy, and to the articulation of sexual discourse in a variety of genres, forms and media. (2002, 102)

Media and cultural studies presume that any given text is open to diverse (but not endless) interpretations and meanings. They therefore take into consideration the ability of both producers and audience members to make certain interpretations and meanings more possible than others (Duits and Van Zoonen 2011, 492). At the same time, they recognize that media production and consumption takes place in the context of large, interconnected social structures that impose hierarchical and inequitable relations of power that are felt and reiterated by individuals in their everyday lives.

As Attwood readily points out, advances in feminist theory and increasing attention to both gender fluidity and sexual agency also have had enormous impact on the way pornography can be studied (2002, 93). While the earliest feminist concerns about pornography were overwhelmingly pessimistic and saw pornography as emblematic of women's oppression by men, such claims were quickly and vociferously opposed by activists and scholars who saw in pornography the potential to liberate sexuality from patriarchal, misogynist, and heteronormative social structures. The advent of queer studies in the 1990s transformed the way that both gender and sexuality are studied. This academic approach insists that the articulation and experience of gender and sexuality are neither fixed nor co-dependent but are instead open-ended and interrelated. Queer studies was heavily influential on contemporary feminist theories of sexual agency and pleasure. Still, feminism brings to queer studies reinvigorated attention to the oppressive and inequitable ways that sexual pleasure is valued when experienced by differently defined bodies.

It is now unexceptional to claim that neither gender nor sexuality is innate but rather that both are socially and historically conditioned. It is also now common to pay attention to the ways that certain forms of gender and sexuality are relegated to the outer limits of the 'normal' and 'acceptable'. Pornography's attention to bodies and desires that are otherwise deemed distasteful or even grotesque is cheered by some feminist/queer studies as an expansion of a gender and sexual politics of the media, and a direct challenge to the gatekeepers of heteronormative privilege (Kipnis 1996; Penley 2004). Nonetheless, as Linda Williams insists in her landmark book, *Hard Core: Power, Pleasure, and the Frenzy of the Visible*, a feminist 'coming to terms with pornography' isn't about liking it, but is about asking what it does to and for us and why it persists in multiple forms and dimensions (1989, 5). Finally, contemporary media and cultural studies insists that consumption and pleasure – for all media forms, not just pornography – cannot be thoroughly problematized without also taking into consideration the contexts of production, labour, and the circulation of capital.

As our chapter on violence discusses in detail, the first iteration of pornography studies focused on what Attwood calls the 'text and effects model', an effort to determine the precise workings of pornography on the susceptible mind of its consumer (2002, 91). This was in keeping with media studies' early association with social psychology's interest in measurable effects, and aesthetic-philosophical disdain for popular culture (Beaty 2005). The 'texts and effects' model is still widely used by public intellectuals, legislators, and activists with an anti-pornography agenda. In this model, pornography is a direct route to all kinds of social ills, ranging from the destruction of marriages and families, to sex addiction, rape culture, and human trafficking. It sees pornography as a discrete object – a text, a speech-act, a material thing – that has embedded within it the power to cause harm to its user (Boyle 2000, 189). Anti-porn feminist scholars and activists from both the early radical and contemporary neo-anti-pornography movements are emblematic of this model. These include Andrea Dworkin, Catharine MacKinnon, Susan Griffin, Robyn Morgan,

Sheila Jeffreys, and Kathleen Barry, and later Gail Dines, Robert Jensen, and Ann Russo.

By contrast, and in response to the popularity of the 'texts and effects' model, the 'visual pleasure' model also emphasizes the consumer/user of pornography but is interested in the specific ways and means of that use and how pleasure is defined. Deriving from feminist and queer film studies, this model was pioneered by Linda Williams, Peter Lehman, Richard Dyer, Chris Straayer, Carole Vance, and Pamela Church Gibson, among others. In much of this work, pornography is treated as a cinematic genre like any other, with unique attributes and audience attractions. As Lehman wrote in his landmark book, *Pornography: Film and Culture*, 'Undoubtedly the academy is now adjusting – or not, as the case may be – to the . . . hypothesis that pornography should be studied in exactly the same way that film has been productively studied' (2006, 2). To that end, for example, Williams has explored connections between pornography and the musical (1989), as well as between pornography and 'body genres' like horror and melodrama (1991). The 'visual pleasure' model is interested not merely in the aesthetic but also in the ideological: representations of gender, sexuality, race, class, and other modes of difference and power. The emphasis on close textual analysis may be a defence mechanism to avoid the heavy moralizing that characterizes the media effects approach. However, as John Champagne provocatively argues, pornography is a great example of a form of cinema that can help move film studies beyond its dominant methodology of close reading and incorporate 'the social and historical conditions in which certain kinds of texts circulate and the everyday uses to which subjects put such texts' (1997, 76).

The kind of porn studies that Champagne and others champion might be called, after Ang and Hermes (1991), the 'radical contextualism' model. It is the approach that is most often taken by media and cultural studies scholars of pornography. As Attwood states, the paradigm shift in pornography research derives from a radical contextualism that includes at the very least the contexts of labour and industrial organization, circulation and access, legal and social restrictions, embodiment and desire in order to

investigate 'the ways in which sexuality is articulated in practices of textual production and consumption' (2002, 104). Such
research brings with it a range of methodologies including ethnographic and field research, empirical studies of industry and political economy, critical ideological analysis of texts, and oral and
cultural histories. It treats pornography as something more than a
text. Again, as Attwood insists, 'the meaning of pornography, like
other cultural forms and artefacts, lies not only within those *things*
but has "symbolic dimensions" (Morley 1995, 314) at the level of
cultural categorization and social regulation' (Attwood 2002, 97).

By now it is clear that we are in deep agreement with Attwood
that there has, indeed, been a paradigm shift in pornography
research. Moreover, we contend that this derives from a change in
attitude towards the problematic of pornography itself. No longer
is it adequate to state that one is 'for' or 'against' pornography
any more than one is for or against musicals. Rather, we recognize
that the pleasures offered by pornography for both producers and
consumers are not unfettered by social structures of inequity and
outright oppression. Second, pleasure is not understood as *only*
a practice of individual self-fulfilment. It is that, to be sure, but a
contemporary feminist/queer politics of pleasure realizes how the
social and historical contexts of naming and creating pleasure in
turn reproduce specific conditions of legal, political, and cultural
legitimacy.

In this book we also interrogate the ways that power has been
defined in relation to pornography. The 'texts and effects' model
sees in pornography the materialization of 'male power' over
women and its ability to exert a 'power-over' its consumers to
reinforce misogyny and patriarchal control in society. By contrast,
the 'visual pleasure' model generally develops a theory of power
that is less monolithic and more subjectively based. It suggests that
pornography has the 'power-to' resist and transform dominant
hierarchies of gender and sexuality embedded in heteronormativity (Allen 2001). Most scholars of pornography working within
the 'radical contextualism' model argue both that power operates
structurally to dominate and oppress certain forms of publicly
mediated sexual expression; and that individuals and collectives

have the ability to recognize those structures and resist, transgress, or even outright transform them (Brickell 2009).

As we were writing this book, Routledge launched the journal *Porn Studies*. The editors of this journal argue:

> We need a dedicated space to explore the complexities and potentials of research into pornography. This is the right time for a journal for porn studies. We need to develop our methods and theories, and to talk about the importance of different technologies, their particular employment as platforms for distribution, and the contributions these make to the kinds of pornographies that are available. We need to be able to engage with and examine the variety of legislative moves against pornography and how those might be tied to concerns about the spread and accessibility of other forms of information, and we need to recognize where regulation is being lessened or loosened and why this is so. (Attwood and Smith, 2014)

Importantly, work such as this journal (on whose editorial board we both sit), the recent *Feminist Porn Book* (2013), and the annual Feminist Porn Conference and Awards in Toronto have broken down the barriers between porn scholars and porn workers. This is sometimes used as evidence to discredit such studies. As Gail Dines fumed, 'Have a journal but you've got to have a plurality of voices on the editorial board and there simply isn't. There's a pornographer on it, for God's sake' (Cadwalladr 2013). Bringing in the voices of people like Tristan Taormino – an individual who has worked in pornography, publicly criticized some of its facets, and is constantly pushing the boundaries towards better ways of making it – keeps scholars accountable to our arguments and the impacts we can have on more vulnerable subjects. Additionally, the journal itself publishes the work of sex workers and activists, further integrating scholarship, activism, and practice, and providing critical dialogue between discourses that have, until now, been divided by institutional and intellectual hierarchies of knowledge. We therefore draw heavily on the writings of practitioners and listen attentively to the voices of those currently working in pornography. Without advances in integrated, collaborative discourse such as the *Porn Studies* journal and *The Feminist Porn*

Book, the field of porn scholarship would not be as rich and nuanced.

We argue that pornography is key to a contemporary gender and sexual politics of pleasure precisely because its valences of oppression and liberation are complex and deeply felt at the level of the body. There are genuine risks and potential harms in pornography production. There are also ethical constraints to what can be consumed for pleasure even if the pornography is produced by and for adults. Issues of consent, respect, privacy, and stigma affect everyone invested in pornographic relations and can result in very real repercussions on people's lives. This book grapples with all of these issues in order to formulate new frameworks of analysis on the cutting edge of contemporary porn scholarship and activism.

Key concepts in pornography

This book is an effort to unravel some of the complexities surrounding the study of pornography by organizing analysis around six key vectors, and investigating in detail the arguments and evidence marshalled by those invested in pornography debates, while bringing our own political and intellectual commitments to bear on the analysis. Although we rely largely on secondary data, we nonetheless insist that any critiques of pornography must be grounded in well-validated evidence that prioritizes the security, integrity, and wellbeing of performers and non-normative sexual subjects who experience higher levels of risk in their societies. In that sense, we use pornography to raise serious issues about how our public sexual cultures are organized and valued and to whose benefit. This book is not the complete picture, but it is a comprehensive one about pornography as a key concept in the quotidian experiences of sexual identities and relationships.

In the first chapter, 'The Global Creative Industry of Pornography', we situate pornography as part of the vast global creative industry in media entertainment. Our focus is primarily on the industry model of large commercial pornography companies that produce most of the mainstream product that tends to characterize pornography in public debates. We review changing conditions of labour and profit for these companies as the media entertainment matrix shifts and expands. We seek to centralize the experiences of porn workers and to compare and contrast their stories with reports on creative labour in non-pornographic media entertainment businesses from both 'above' and 'below-the-line'. Those terms refer to two categories of labour, the first referring to the financial managers and creative talent: producers, directors, writers, and performers. The second refers to production crew and administrative staff who make the creative work possible. We draw further connections between legal commercial pornography and the creative industry sector by outlining important differences with illegal and outright criminal activity in pornography, including child abuse materials and the non-consensual circulation of sexually explicit media. The goal here is to articulate the situatedness of pornography within the media entertainment matrix while also demonstrating its unique forms of industrial organization.

Chapter 2, 'Pornography and Communication Technologies', contends deeply with an oft-repeated claim that pornography is the main driver of technological innovation in the media entertainment matrix. It examines how content and medium intersect in ways that expand the boundaries of publicly mediated sexual expression and push for new frameworks of understanding. The Internet, in particular, has been a source of great anxiety about the proliferation of pornographic material and its easy accessibility. We look at some of the significant problems inherent in online pornography, including piracy, invisible labour and industry practices, and illegal trafficking. We also explore how advances in social media, streaming video, and other aspects of the Web 2.0 (DiNucci 1999) have helped to facilitate community building through the visibility and diversity of sexual practices available, while also outing illegal and unethical behaviour. That is not to say that the Internet has caused any of these practices. We eschew such simplistic causal models and are instead concerned with the interconnected discourses of pornography and the Internet in conceptualizing new modes of sexual expression and their value to society.

Having laid out a map of where and how pornography can be found, the following chapter, 'Pornography and Violence', provides a detailed overview of arguably the most dominant conceptual framework for pornography: that it constitutes an act of violence against women. Examining both the historical context for this claim, and its contemporary iterations, we challenge its simplistic and overbearing approach and draw attention to its inconsistencies and contradictions. We look at the two most prevalent theories of pornography as violence and their key points of intersection: social scientific claims of media effects, and radical antipornography feminist claims of social harm. Our goal is not to disclaim any possibility of wrongdoing in pornography practices but, rather, to suggest other ways of approaching these problems through better definitions of violence and harm via the important conceptual tool of consent.

Following from this critique of the 'violence' framework, we then explore its most current reiteration. In Chapter 4, 'Pornification and Sexualized Bodies', we examine the problematic displacement of sexism from the centre of pornography debates and its supplanting with the conceptual framework of 'sexualization'. Three key national reports from the United States, Australia, and the United Kingdom provide a foundation upon which to explore how pornography is treated as a pathology that preys upon the ignorant and vulnerable, leading to a host of social ills. Our greatest concern about the 'sexualization/pornification thesis', as we call it, is its unproblematized alignments with heteronormative ideals about gender roles, its racial and class-specific assumptions, and its limited view on sexual expression. We question the privileging of social psychological models of sexuality that underscore concerns about pornography use and its undue 'sexualization' of young girls and note the vastly more complex analyses offered by feminist and queer media and cultural studies. This latter scholarship foregrounds a belief in the multiplicity and variety of textual practices available to anyone negotiating their sexual identity in part through pornographic and non-pornographic media consumption in equally varied social structural contexts.

Our attention to these two related conceptual frameworks of violence and pornification, despite our own serious misgivings about their efficacies, is due to the fact that pornography governance remains heavily invested in them. Chapter 5, 'Pornography Governance and Sexual Citizenship', looks closely at three prevalent models for the governmental control of pornography, including regulatory, criminal legislative, and juridical oversight. They are the 'community standards' model, the 'harms' model, and the 'extreme pornography' model. Key to our analysis of how pornography is conceptualized as an object of governance is a consideration of sexual citizenship. Through it, we interrogate the reasons governments give for controlling how sexuality is practised in public and private, and how pornography is then defined as an object of governmental surveillance and control. Our examination relies mostly on Western Euro-American countries, including Australia, Canada, England, and the United States. We see in them the perpetuation of a global hegemonic model of heteronormativity that diminishes women's sexual agency while outright denying non-normative sexual subjects their citizenship rights. That is not to say that pornography practices are not specific to their historical and geographical contexts, but to draw attention to the ways that state networks of control seek to generalize and homogenize 'good' sexuality towards specific interests.

The final conceptual framework we offer in this book is a more optimistic and, we argue, progressive one. Chapter 6, 'Performing Pornography, Practising Sexual Politics', takes seriously our critiques of other frameworks and grounds analysis in the experiences and self-analyses of feminist/queer pornography producers, performers, educators, and activists. With reinvigorated attention to the moniker of the 'porn star' and its political potential, we examine the lived conditions of pornography performance labour from three key positions: exploited, self-determined, and one of diminished choice. The close scrutiny of pornography performance along such a continuum avoids the all-or-nothing politics that have plagued pornography debates in the past, and helps articulate an always-evolving framework where we can distinguish between pornography practices that inform a progressive pleasure-based sexual politics, and those that still need to be resisted and challenged at every possible moment.

We conclude this book with some ruminations on what we would like to see happen in pornography studies for the future. The reader may note that each of our chapter conclusions offers some direction towards a future where new approaches to the conceptual framework under exploration are taken. Here, we offer some altogether new frameworks for the study of pornography, including more robust comparative analyses with other media industries and forms, better understanding of pornography as entertainment, and the usefulness of pornography to the discourses and practices of healthy sexuality. We also argue that such frameworks demand different methodological approaches that gather empirical and ethnographic evidence from current pornography practitioners. As the Introduction has outlined, such work has begun but there is still much to do and so we offer this book as a road map for where we've been and where we can most positively proceed. Pornography can be a polarizing topic and is one that continues to be hotly debated in academic and activist circles. Thus, we offer our thoughts in the spirit of academic engagement with other scholars, and take seriously our responsibility for the very real consequences of theory on the lives of individuals who contend daily with regimes of gender and sexual oppression.

1

The Global Creative Industry of Pornography

How does pornography get made? What institutions are involved and how are they structured? Who pays for pornography to be made and consumed? How is money distributed to those involved in its production? Pornography is big global business and a significant player in the media entertainment matrix. Every year, tens of thousands of people around the world produce millions of pornographic images and videos for hundreds of millions of consumers. We start this book by focusing particularly on the production and distribution of pornography, and its relationship with other media entertainment industries. It is our contention that pornography is, like almost all other media entertainment, transforming into a global creative industry. What that means in terms of profitability, organizational structure, and labour relations are important questions, made more so by the stigmas many porn performers face.

Pornography can be produced within either professional or amateur systems of production and consumption. It is not a form of culture that is commonly state-produced. Governments typically provide funding for the production of particular kinds of culture – ballet, opera, visual arts and so on – but there is little state-produced pornography (McKee 2001). Usually, when it is revealed that a state-run cultural fund has provided support to pornography production, a moral panic erupts and the state must quickly claw back funding or promise to review its programme to ensure that no public money goes into explicit sexual media. For example, after the Canada Council funded the 1999 film *Bubbles*

Galore, a feminist soft-core porn film starring Nina Hartley and Annie Sprinkle, then Culture Minister Sheila Copps vowed to ensure no more such 'ridiculous grants' would happen. Similar outcry happened in Sweden over the film *Dirty Diaries*, a feminist porn film funded by the Swedish Film Institute in 2009.

In this opening chapter we look at the business of producing commercial pornography, that is pornography produced for profit. As the production of pornography is an important issue, we revisit it at various points in the book. In Chapter 5 we discuss the governance of pornography production. We consider amateur and not-for-profit pornography in more detail in chapters on performance and technology. But to begin our story, we focus on the commercial world of pornographic production as a global creative industry – the mainstream, traditional, 'legacy' materials (a term for 'old' media before the Internet) that many people think of when they hear the word 'pornography'.

Estimates of the global worth of the pornography industry range widely. In the United States alone, in 2010, some quoted the size of the pornography industry as ranging from $8 billion to $13 billion (Szalai 2010). Globally, in 2002, the worth of the pornography industry on the Internet was calculated as $31.2 billion (Perdue 2004, 263); while in 2007, it was estimated at a substantially smaller $4.9 billion (Jeffreys 2009, 66). *Forbes* magazine claimed the entire global pornography market in the early 2000s, across all sectors, was $56 billion (Whisnant 2004, 16). As Coopersmith notes, 'many of the numbers proffered are estimates, often by people or institutions with a vested interest – or an axe to grind' (Coopersmith 1998, 120n24; see also McNair 2002, 6).

Both producers and critics of pornography have an interest in making it seem as big as possible. Porn companies seek to position themselves as mainstream by arguing for their importance to the economy. Critics of the industry, such as Sheila Jeffreys, Diane Russo or Gail Dines, look at the financial profits as proof of a crisis overwhelming modern societies. We say that the actual size does not matter as much as understanding how the pornography business actually operates as industry. In this chapter, we examine multiple forms of industrial organization to produce and distribute pornography, distinguishing between large commercial enterprises and smaller DIY efforts. We are particularly interested in the organization of creative labour on the pornography set, including for non-performers, and in the unique occupational health and safety issues that affect performers.

Pornography as a creative industry

Globalization of labour is growing. Right or wrong, governments increasingly commit to free trade agreements and see the globalization of markets as a desirable way to raise living standards in countries around the world. Innovations in communication technologies have increased the globalization of the production, distribution and consumption of a wide range of products and services, including pornography. Despite the widening network of capital exchange, it currently remains the case (although maybe only in the short term) that supply and distribution are mostly controlled by a small network of Western-dominated companies and concentrated in major global urban centres like Los Angeles and Amsterdam (Jacobs 2007, 30). We start this chapter therefore by looking at what Melinda Tankard Reist and Abigail Bray call 'Big Porn Inc.' (Tankard Reist and Bray 2011) – large-scale commercial pornography producers who distribute transnationally but are still often based in wealthy Western countries. These companies prioritize profits and growth, the same as any vast commercial media enterprise.

For example, Vivid Entertainment LLC is one of the biggest pornography producers in the world, with an estimated annual revenue of $100 million (Reuters 2006; Szalai 2010). For a period from about the mid twentieth century (the launch of *Playboy*) to the early twenty-first (the maturation of the Internet), commercial pornography companies like Vivid were able to work with high profit margins from the production and distribution of sexually explicit materials across a wide range of platforms. The business model was simple. Pornographic materials were produced as physical objects – first as photographs and magazines, then as film loops, then video cassettes, and then DVDs. These would be sold to a distributor, who could either distribute them by direct mail, or sell them on to a wholesaler who would then sell them on to a retailer. Every step of the process saw a substantial mark-up and every agent in the supply chain made a profit. There was little paid advertising, or subscription models. It was a straightforward model of selling a product for more than it costs to make with lots of middlemen along the chain (Coopersmith 1998, 104).

However, as digital technologies become increasingly accessible and interactive, the situation is no longer so rosy for these legacy pornography companies. New business models have emerged with smaller economies of scale: direct sale or hire of product (videos and DVDs), advertiser-supported websites, and website subscriptions. Internet pornography has also led the way in business model innovations such as 'affiliate networks, performance-based advertising, traffic sharing and even those pop-up console advertising windows that are annoying but highly effective' (Perdue 2004, 262). Furthermore, the Internet makes possible virtual hubs so that independent performers can upload their work and receive payment based on 'clicks', the number of times their work is viewed either by streaming or downloading. For example, the PornHub network includes PornHub, YouPorn, Tube8, PornMD, SpankWire, XTube, Extreme Tube, Peeperz and others. Much of the work on these sites is available free of charge. The company earns its revenue through advertising and premium memberships. Furthermore, there are persistent allegations of pirated material and poor payment systems that have severely compromised the earning potential of performers and producers. We discuss this emerging landscape in more detail in the Technologies chapter of this book. At this point we note that the traditional business models of 'Big Porn Inc.' are facing severe challenges from these new competitors

Who works in pornography, and what are their experiences of the industry? Those questions tend to be sidetracked when dealing with the size or profitability of the industry. Whether we are talking about major corporate enterprises, or about one of the alternative business models promoted by technological

innovation, pornography – like all of the so-called 'creative industries' (film and television, publishing, music, advertising and so
on) – involves a delicate balancing act between creative performance and industrial labour. In pornography – as in Hollywood,
and indeed all entertainment media systems around the world –
most of the money in pornography is made by the producers and
distributors (Spark Tech Talk 2012). Between them they make
the biggest money in the pornography industries (Jacobs 2007,
12; see also Jeffreys 2009, 67; Russo 1998, 23; Reeve 2010; Ray
2010). The exception is a tiny margin of performers or media
personalities who achieve stardom and command extraordinarily
high salaries. Producers are the people who come up with ideas,
raise finance, put teams together and oversee the production of
content (Collis, McKee and Hamley 2010, 922). Distributors
'solicit content from companies and prepare it for global distribution'. Coopersmith notes that in the days of legacy media, both
producers and distributors could easily make 100 per cent profit
on every tape sold (Coopersmith 1998, 104). Several large-scale
commercial pornography companies continue to make profits
– although in increasingly challenging circumstances (Campbell
2014). But it is rarely performers, and almost never the rest of
the crew, who make good money working in pornography. Thus
it is worthwhile to investigate the working conditions of both
performers and ancillary workers in trying to make a living from
the pornography industry.

Working hard for the money:
Support players in the pornography industry

It is important to recognize the host of different workers engaged
in pornography to see it as one sector of the creative industries,
albeit a particularly unique and occasionally fraught one. More
attention is being paid to those who work in the pornography
industry not as performers but as technical and administrative
support staff. Their stories help to reveal the way that pornography is either celebrated as a liberating and progressive career

or denounced as exploitative and abusive. As Laura Agustin points out, the sex industry includes large numbers of 'non-sexual employees': 'drivers, accountants, lawyers, doctors . . . newspaper and magazine editors [and] Internet entrepreneurs' (Agustin 2005, 618). In our consideration of the pornography industry in particular we can add to that list camera operators, sound engineers, designers, advertising sales people, office managers and so on. These are either administrative support staff or 'below-the-line' workers – a film and television industry term that includes all production workers except for actors, producers, directors and writers. The labour of below-the-line workers is often nomadic, casualized, demanding and poorly compensated. Once again, this is true across the creative industries and not only in the pornographic industry. Vicki Mayer's ethnographic account of camera operators who produce footage for 'soft-core reality video' shows like *Girls Gone Wild* emphasizes the precariousness of this work:

> Typically men spent twelve to eighteen hours on their feet . . . Spilt beer, flying confetti and whizzing beads . . . potentially damaged equipment . . . Given levels of intoxication on the streets, fights and shouting were common . . . [and t]he actual material compensation for this labor was also questionable. Men talked about receiving far less than they were promised or expected. (Mayer 2008, 104)

For Mayer, the situation of these camera operators is not specific to pornography – in fact, she argues that their situation is typical of television more generally. In John Caldwell's account of mainstream film and television 'production culture' he similarly notes that key elements of creative labour are lack of job security, periods of intense overwork, and lack of overall creative control on projects. In a 'more flexible post-Fordist industrial economy' (Caldwell 2008, 156), the creative industries tend to 'outsourc[e] . . . creative work' (Caldwell 2008, 119). A lack of job security – or 'Nomadic labor systems' – means that 'even after a [creative] worker has obtained employment . . . they must still hustle for every new production they hope to work on . . .' (Caldwell 2008, 113).

Mayer notes that many of the camerapeople she spoke to emphasized that despite the lack of material reward the work was their 'dream job': 'I mean, I love tits'; 'I just wanted to be part of the action'; 'I thought, wow, this is going to be fun' (Mayer 2008, 102). This sort of hyperbole is generic across the creative industries. In order to compensate for the lack of material reward, these jobs tend to oversell the idea of intrinsic benefits such as gratifying labour, career flexibility, democratic management, and workaholism as creative forms of self-fulfilment (Caldwell 2008, 33). For example, PornHub's FAQ ends with the question, 'Is working for PornHub the coolest job ever?' and answers, 'Yes. Yes it is'. This is not to say that such rewards are unimportant. For example, weighing up the pros and the cons of working as the managing editor of online pornography site Danni's Hard Drive, Taylor Marsh emphasizes the pleasure of working in the creative industries:

> Although the time I spent at DHD was often chaotic, and even though our business relationship would never be stable, one of the things that kept me enthused about being managing editor for DHD, especially in the beginning, was my periodic creative meetings with Danni . . . For hours we would hash out ideas and possibilities for new content, both of us excited about what was happening on the site. (Marsh 2004, 255–6)

It cannot be denied that some workers may find working in the pornography industry creatively and professionally satisfying. Yet, with the popularity of 'docuporn' – documentary and reality series offering behind-the-scenes peeks at the making of pornography – the idea of working in pornography as a pathway to an authentic, fulfilling work life is increasingly oversold. The Canadian documentary television series *Webdreams* (2005–8), or the German documentary film *9 to 5: Days in Porn* (2008), provides insight into the everyday lives of workers and performers, while companies such as Playboy and Vivid offer their own soft-core documentary series on their business with *The Girls Next Door* (2005–10) and *Pornovalley* (2005), to name a few. All these examples draw on pre-existing genre work in contemporary docu-entertainment and reality television that seeks, in essence, to shift political and economic critique of the creative industries into the realm of subjective experience and personal validation. You might have no job security and the pay might be terrible – but see how much fun the work is!

We discuss pornography as performance in more detail in Chapter 6, but in this chapter we look specifically at pornography performance as a job. A study by Sharon Abbott found that performers enter the industry for a number of reasons: money, fame and glamour; freedom and independence; opportunity and sociability; and being naughty and having sex (Abbott 2010, 50–8). The first seven of these are generalizable for aspiring actors across the creative industries; this is less the case with the desire to be naughty or to have sex. In terms of the desire for money, the vast majority of pornography performers do not make as much from their work as do producers and distributors. For professional pornography actors, Abbott finds that 'annual incomes generated . . . typically approximate middle-class earnings'. Usually, performers are paid by sexual act. So, for example, 'actresses receive between $300 [for masturbation or girl on girl] and $1000 [for anal sex or double penetrations] for an individual scene' (Abbott 2010, 50). Women in the industry can also earn substantial extra money by doing outside work such as 'erotic dancing and modeling' (Abbott 2010, 51).

As we note earlier in this chapter, it is true that a very small number of porn actors do go on to become genuine stars. Vivid Entertainment, for example, began its company by 'recreat[ing] Hollywood's old studio system in the pornography business' (*Economist* 1999, 56), and offering a small number of 'superstars' (Canyon, quoted in Rutter 2009) exclusive and well-paying contracts. But only a very small number of actors become stars – in pornography or in mainstream film and television. Their experience – just as in mainstream (i.e., non-pornographic) film and television – is so rare as to be statistically unrepresentative from an industrial analysis point of view, and is covered more completely in Chapter 6.

Thus, for the majority of actors in pornography the experience is more like that of 'supporting artists' or extras in mainstream film and television. These on-screen workers lack the star power that makes the experience of working in film and television so lucrative for the successful few. Extras are the 'least powerful' people in the film and television industry (Johnson 2009) and are often treated like objects, their bodies discussed as though they are not there:

> 'Quite often you get talked about as if you're merely an inanimate prop', says Chloe Franks, a fellow extra. 'I remember some costume ladies bustling around me as I was standing timorously in corset and knickers, saying, "Well, she is very small isn't she? With incredibly big feet!"' (Johnson 2009)

Most pornography actors suffer from the same casualization of labour that affects mainstream film and television supporting artists: lack of job security, short periods of intense hard work, lack of creative control, and discriminatory casting practices based on race, age, ability, and other factors can shorten and/or limit careers. Indeed, some pornography performers say they experienced even worse working conditions in mainstream film and television. Well-known porn performer and sex activist Annie Sprinkle recalls:

> Once I tried out for a part in a 'straight' big budget feature film, *48 Hours*, starring Eddie Murphy. They were looking for someone to play a bit part as a hooker. Dozens of women showed up for the casting call, and we had to wait for two and a half hours. They treated us like children and were very disrespectful. That ended my interest in a straight movie career. I decided to stay in pornography, where I was treated with more respect. (Sprinkle 1998, 28)

Sprinkle's comments are illuminating because of the kind of stigma often associated with pornography performers. Many comment on the difficulty they have in 'crossing-over' into mainstream production (something below-the-line workers do not claim to experience), and having their work experience valued outside the pornography industry in general.

Stereotypes and discrimination

Another way in which pornography resembles mainstream film and television is in the continued existence of stereotypical representations. Pornography is one of the most highly classified genres, where every slight difference in race, ethnicity, age, body size, etc., is exaggerated and sold as a fetish. Those performers who do not conform to a rigidly narrow definition of 'typical' (young, white, able-bodied, thin, conventionally attractive, etc.) have a more difficult time accessing the more lucrative and sustainable jobs. They may also be expected to engage in on-screen performances that are insulting, abusive, and derogatory to their identity; such as having plus-sized women force-eat or representing petite Asian women as servile. Mireille Miller-Young critiques the proliferation of pornographic 'cybertypes', mimetic reproductions of fetishized Others whose depictions perpetuate racist, discriminatory attitudes in a sexualized form (2005, 206; see also Nakamura 2002). Siobhan Brooks, in her analysis of the exotic dance industry, states emphatically that the erotic capital of women of colour is presupposed to be less than that of white women, repeating longstanding labour discrimination across economic sectors (2010, 5–7).

In their 2014 keynote to the Feminist Porn Conference, genderqueer performer, director and activist Courtney Trouble advocates for an intersectional framework to guide ethical porn production that promotes open casting calls. They insist that part of changing the labour practices within the industry requires calling out exploitative and discriminatory marketing practices that tout 'ghetto bitches' or 'big tit creampies'. Trouble notes that the AVN and X Biz Awards – two of the biggest promoters of the mainstream industry, have added Plus Size Performer, Lesbian Performer, and Feminist Porn Movie to their awards rosters, while the Tranny Awards changed their name to the Transgender Erotica Awards. More respectful dialogue within the industry can lead to greater diversity and inclusion on the screen, Trouble argues (2014a). The result can be a healthier and more sustainable workplace where diversity and inclusion are standard practice, and labourers are treated with respect and integrity.

Of course, diversity brings its own problems regarding ethical representation, particularly in a business where niche marketing is everything. In 2014, Chelsea Poe, a trans woman, sought to be cast in one of Lily Cade's films. Cade specializes in lesbian porn and is often recognized as a member of the ethical porn community in Southern California. When Cade declined, she was accused of discrimination and transphobia by many of her peers, including Trouble. Cade's response was that her business model depended on particular body types and performances to which her audience base was accustomed, but that she fully supported others interested in making trans-inclusive porn. Controversy ensued in what Cade called 'the great Twitter War of June 2014' with Cade making some flippantly transphobic, fatphobic, and insensitive comments (Cade 2014). The case offers interesting perspectives about the balance between the business of ethical porn production and the politics of ethical porn discourse. Pornography is at its core a commercial (or at least publicly accessible) product developed with specific creator and audience tastes in mind. No one film can cater to all desires. A cisgender lesbian porn producer claiming that her work targets an audience that is not attracted to people with penises seems pretty uncontroversial in a cisnormative cultural climate. However, it is important to realize the sublimated transphobic discourse contained therein that equates genitalia with gender and as the ultimate object of sexual desire. Social media has become an important marketing tool for ethical porn producers, creating a vibrant online community that is always testing the boundaries of both performance and the language used to describe it. There is indeed a niche for cisnormative lesbian porn, or any kind of normative porn, but there is also a need to recognize the ongoing hierarchies of gender representation and identity within sexually explicit media. In other words, there is a difference between niche marketing and exclusionary politics in describing the porn product and production practices.

Social media uproars bring to light the vested interests pornography workers have in maintaining a safe, welcoming environment among themselves, especially considering the kinds of stigma they face from those outside the industry. While we have taken some measures to outline the ways that pornography is similar to related creative industries like film and television, there are several areas where they diverge. One of the most important of these is the issue of stigma facing performers. A number of studies have demonstrated a correlation between people's perception of pornography and their beliefs about pornography performers; in particular women-identified performers. In what has been called 'the damaged goods hypothesis', those who see pornography as a social ill regard actresses as abused, exploited, or otherwise desperate victims (Griffith et al. 2013, 622). However, when scholars take the time to interview and study workers themselves, they find high levels of social, sexual, and spiritual support within the industry. One of the biggest areas of frustration and anxiety reported by actresses actually comes from their treatment by those outside the industry (Abbott 2010; Griffith et al. 2013). Baseless prejudice from outsiders who insist that working in pornography reflects poor moral character and low confidence in oneself is regarded as a significant occupational hazard.

In a study of female sex workers in Australia, the issue of 'community attitudes towards the industry' (47%) was more of a worry for them than 'their personal safety' (38%) (Groves et al. 2008, 393). In another study, sex workers talked about having to live a 'double life' where they felt:

> they were forced to lie about their job to family and friends, they had a 'working' name and a 'real' name. Participants described it as 'hard work' maintaining their double lives and that it could lead to feelings of guilt and anxiety. (Begum et al. 2013, 95)

The degree to which this stigma survives for female porn stars in 2014 can be seen in the case of Belle Knox, a student at Duke University who was 'outed' as a porn performer by Thomas Bagley, a Duke freshman. He demonstrated no shame in watching her films but deliberately sought to shame her for being in those films. Knox became the focus of a heated controversy, including online 'slut shaming' and death threats (O'Connor and DeJohn 2014). Some commentators worried about her lost reputation and diminished opportunities for future happiness and prosperity, oblivious to the fact that it was their own judgementalism and prurience that would create such a situation. Ironically, Knox was able to capitalize on her rather unwelcome fame, earning enough from her work on porn sets and in strip clubs that Duke University withdrew her already modest ($13,000) student aid package. Thus, she announced that she will be have to take on even more sex work to cover the $62,000 a year costs of attending the prestigious institution. This is indicative of the problem porn actresses and other sex workers face when trying to find other ways of earning a living. If her detractors sought to shame her out of sex work, their tactics succeeded in forcing her even deeper into the industry. She admits that she almost dropped out of university since 'my choice to finance through porn has meant intense ridicule and harassment' (Gupta 2014). In October 2014, the popular American television show *Law and Order SVU* aired an episode based on the Belle Knox case in an effort to showcase what Knox calls 'the chilling rape culture entitlement that comes along with men discovering that I'm a porn star'. As the fictionalized character states to the detectives when they ask why she will continue in porn after a brutal gang rape, 'At least here, when I say "no", they stop' (Knox 2014).

The example of Knox demonstrates how social stigma affects individuals' post-sex work career decisions. As we noted above, it is the case that for most actors across the creative industries – and particularly women – careers are of a limited length. Young women working in mainstream porn must contend with over-exposure and audience fatigue at a much higher rate than men. One actress interviewed for a study on porn workers notes:

> Girls have a shelf life of nine months to two years, unless you are different. Like me, I am Asian, so it helps. Men stay forever. It is different for a man. If he can perform, he can stay in. There are guys that have been in the business ten or fifteen years. (Abbott 2010, 129)

Ageism and sexism within the industry lead to the problem of what to do when a porn-acting career dries up long before the end of the employment life-cycle. Monica Foster warns that 'many employers out there . . . will not hire you (and possibly fire you) if they find out you've worked in the porn industry' (Foster 2010, 16; see also Abbott 2010, 60; Jeffreys 2009, 77; Begum et al. 2013, 92). Something as simple as having a personal bank account becomes a problem, as when Chase Bank decided to refuse all clients who were associated with the pornography industry (Alptraum 2014). Even high profile figures such as Courtney Trouble admit that 'outside of porn, I have presented myself as nothing more than a housewife or a fast-food worker on many occasions, because the stigma behind what I really do makes most conversations with most strangers unbearable' (Trouble 2014a). This kind of stigma spills over into areas of governance including occupational health and safety, where the experiences and opinions of sex workers are discounted when drafting legislation on making their workplace better.

Perhaps because of the limitations that such stigma places on switching careers, increasing numbers of actors – including women – are moving into the more lucrative producer roles after (or as well as) their performance work. Candida Royalle, Nina Hartley, and Danni Ashe are among the more famous actors-turned-producers in pornography (Marsh 2004, 246). And there now exists a genre of books on how to be a pornography small business person (Brown 2010; Spriggs 2008; West 2005; Miller 2009) – including those written by female porn actors-turned-entrepreneurs (King 2009; Sharlot 2003). Of course, such books are neo-liberal in their focus on social mobility and individual entrepreneurship. They offer ways of navigating a porn career through an existing system, rather than inspiring industry members to work collectively to change that system.

Lynn Comella's research on 'remaking the sex industry' argues that increasing numbers of women involved as producers in pornography has in fact led to structural changes: a focus on women's pleasure, and on more ethical and even environmentally aware production models (Comella 2010). Furthermore, as Chapter 6 discusses in detail, performers committed to social, educational, and political goals around sex positivity and gender fluidity have made surprising inroads into the labour and marketing practices of mainstream pornography. The social mobility and financial security of individuals need not be separate from collective identities and awareness – especially when dealing with individuals already marginalized from the centres of socio-economic legitimacy. The example of occupational health and safety and the advocacy that happens among workers to minimize the risks associated with the job underscores how many porn performers treat their work seriously with respect for their community.

Workplace health and safety

Clearly, there are unique bodily risks associated with pornography performance. Most obviously, the risk of contracting STIs and HIV is acutely high in the pornography industry compared to other workplace situations. That said, medical risk of illness, injury, or even death is not exclusive to pornography but is a concern of any workplace that includes demanding physical labour and high bodily risk. As Caldwell notes, film and television sets are always potentially dangerous places where physical limits are tested, and sometimes lives are lost (2008, 43). It is best practice to conduct a risk assessment in the mainstream film and television industry, although this is not always the case on low-level cheap, pro-am productions. Indeed, on the major feature film *Black Swan* (2010), when star Natalie Portman injured herself on set, she discovered that the producers had not hired any paramedical staff to attend to emergencies. This despite the fact that many of the actors on set were engaged in rigorous physical performance with a high risk of injury. As she herself pointed out, 'I don't even think that's legal' (*Los Angeles Times*, 2010).

The most dangerous jobs on film sets are those of stunt performers, and Kath Albury refers to pornography actors as sexual stunt performers (McKee, Albury, and Lumby 2008, 173). Their job definition is to do visually spectacular things that are outside the boundaries of everyday practice, which risk physical injury and even death. In addition to STIs and HIV, other physical risks such as eye infections, chafed or torn skin and exhaustion should not be underestimated. Especially on lower budget pornography sets, there is generally less protection for these performers, and less attention to occupational health and safety than there is in high-end professional film and television production. In part, this is a vicious cycle of stigmatization whereby individuals working in porn are assumed to tolerate high risks and 'get what they bargained for'.

To the extent that the industry pays attention to occupational health and safety the focus is HIV prevention, with occasional panics of an 'HIV epidemic' affecting workers. In the United States, the Adult Industry Medical Health Care Foundation (AIM) was launched in 1998 to provide HIV testing and health counselling to sex industry workers. 24-hour hiatuses are called for to verify a 'false-positive' test on a relatively frequent basis. AIM oversaw a shutdown in production in 2004 when it was revealed that an HIV positive performer had infected four other people. In 2010, they helped initiate another temporary shutdown when another worker tested positive. Both these instances were heavily reported in the media and spurred the County of Los Angeles to introduce the so-called 'Measure B', the County of Los Angeles Safer Sex in the Adult Film Industry Act in 2012. This legislation requires all pornography production companies within the county to obtain a licence before they shoot sex scenes, and mandates the use of condoms in productions. Some journalists claim that pornography production in the county declined by up to 95 per cent following the introduction of the Measure, and suggested that companies were moving to Las Vegas, which has cheaper permits, no health checks and no condom law (Dreier 2014). This raises further issues about performer health and safety, the disruption of a tight-knit labour community, and the uprooting of individuals in order to continue working. The problems of governmental intervention in a climate of stigmatization is discussed in Chapter 5.

While condom use offers specific debating points in terms of governmental regulation, what is clear to most at least within the legally operating industry is the need to keep workers safe and healthy. It simply makes business sense. Unfortunately, the industry lost one of its most visible health and safety agencies following a nasty scandal in 2011. Adult Industry Medical Health Care

Foundation shut down after its database was hacked and the personal information of over 12,000 pornographic performers was released on a website called Porn Wikileaks. It is a virulently homophobic and misogynist wiki site that seeks to remove 'the homosexual criminal scumbags out of straight porn' by releasing both their names and the 'whores' who work with them. Also released were their legal names and home addresses. AIM provided medical testing to people who do not work in the pornography industry, but the leak made no distinction. Subsequent lawsuits over privacy infringement forced AIM to file for bankruptcy and cease its work of coordinating HIV testing for the industry. Porn Wikileaks celebrated its closure, and no other agency has stepped forward to do the vital work that AIM once did. It is distressing to see that the ongoing stigma faced by pornographic performers – which made the leaking of their private details so dangerous – led directly to the closure of their main health support service.

Many of the larger companies have implemented their own health and safety standards. Vivid offers their workers salaried contracts with health care and other benefits. Wicked Pictures has a mandatory condom policy – the only straight porn studio to maintain it. The BDSM (bondage and discipline; domination and submission; and sadomasochism) site Kink.com posts its 'best practices' guidelines to ensure the safety and wellbeing of its workers. However, it is important to note that these efforts are often undermined by accusations that they do not follow their own guidelines or that these initiatives are publicity gimmicks more than ethical practices. Often, these attacks come either from those working outside the industry or former workers now agitating for 'porn abolition'. More worthy of attention are those performers who are willing to speak out against what they see as unsafe working conditions without condemning the industry as a whole. A former performer with Kink.com, Maggie Mayhem, detailed her experiences working in The Armory – Kink.com's headquarters in San Francisco – that included unsanitary equipment, unsafe work environments, abusive employers, and worker intimidation (Mayhem 2013). Her claims were sometimes greeted with anger and accusations that she was contributing to the anti-porn accusations that call the industry inherently harmful. Yet, others argued that it is important for people working in the industry to hold their employers to account in order to ensure safe, healthy, and sustainable working conditions and prove that it is not only possible but necessary and expected from pornography companies as it is from any other industry (Trouble 2014a). It is worth noting that other performers, including Aurora Snow and Lori Adorable, have also criticized Kink.com for unsafe and coercive treatment of its performers (Snow 2014).

AIM was one of the few examples of coordinated industry-based regulation of the health and safety of porn workers anywhere in the world, partly due to the fact that there is a large geographic concentration of pornography production in the San Fernando Valley of California, and that the California porn industry enjoys the support of the larger mainstream film and television industry in nearby Hollywood. However, for other regions where pornography is more ad hoc, localized, and individuated, it is difficult to coordinate such efforts. Many porn sets are not covered by federal occupational health and safety regulations and workers can be isolated and pressured into unsafe conditions. Thus, workers have sought to organize into collectives on their own behalf. Gregor Gall identifies sex workers' unions in the UK, Germany, the Netherlands, the USA, Australia, New Zealand, South Africa, Eire, Argentina, and Trinidad and Tobago, and notes that:

> Where a relatively stable union presence and union recognition has been established . . . significant advances have been made in winning better terms and conditions for sex workers. (Gall 2007)

The countries identified by Gall as having successful collective organizations of sex workers are predominantly developed and wealthy. While there are increasing numbers of sex worker advocacy groups around the globe (see The Global Network for Sex Work Projects), the issue of occupational health and safety is not so easy to determine in poorer regions.

Criminal involvement in pornography

A major and ongoing concern relating specifically to the pornography industry is the question of organized crime's involvement. Certainly, there were once deep ties within a now legalized industry in America. Coopersmith notes that in the 1960s:

> Despite its illegality, pornography continued to attract producers and distributors, because of the high profit margins, profits which were associated with high legal risks and organized crime. (Coopersmith 1998, 99; see also McNeil, Osborne, and Pavia 2005, 192; Jeffreys 2009, 73)

The US Attorney General's Commission on Pornography ('the Meese Commission') wrote in 1986 that:

> According to Chief Daryl F. Gates of the Los Angeles Police Department, 'Organized crime infiltrated the pornography industry in Los Angeles in 1969 due to its lucrative financial benefits. By 1975, organized crime controlled eighty percent of the industry and it is estimated that this figure is between eighty-five to ninety percent today.' (Hudson et al. 1986)

One pornography distributor testified to the Commission that 'the mob' controlled what could be sold in American adult stores, and if a store owner stocked material they did not approve of 'they're gonna break your legs' (Hudson et al. 1986). *Deep Throat*, the pornographic film that broke into the mainstream, was funded by New York mobster Anthony Peraino (Hudson et al. 1986). The Commission found that organized crime's involvement in the pornography industry in the 1970s included narcotics distribution, money laundering, tax violations and murder:

> During the late 1970s a number of persons involved in the pornography business were murdered in what were believed by law enforcement agents to be pornography turf wars. The son of Joseph Peraino, one of the producers of *Deep Throat* along with an innocent woman, was murdered 'gangland style'. (Hudson et al. 1986)

It is not clear to what extent criminal control is still the case in relation to large commercial pornography production companies in America. This point is not made lightly. The legalization of pornography in 1989 has, as is often the case with legalization and decriminalization, lessened the ability of organized crime to control the industry (see California v. Freeman (488 US 1311 (1989)). Most accounts of the industry in the 2000s emphasize the increasingly mainstream and legitimate nature of the pornography industry in America. Legs McNeil, in his detailed oral history of the development of the pornography industry, describes the story as 'the porn industry's rise from a marginal criminal enterprise of starving hippie actors and mob-sponsored back-alley loops to the multi-billion-dollar juggernaut it is today' (McNeil, Osborne, and Pavia 2005). Vivid Entertainment has been the focus of much mainstream economic journalism, and works 'in the bright glare of the public spotlight rather than the shadows of the Hollywood backstreets' (Vivid Entertainment 2009). Its business practices are discussed in the *Economist* magazine and major national newspapers. Some pornographic production and distribution companies are now even listed on Stock Exchanges (*Economist* 2011; Jeffreys 2009, 65). In a legitimized pornography environment the role of organized crime is less clear. However, the picture is not as positive for industries operating in economically and politically fraught regions.

To this point we have focused on 'Big Porn Inc.' – large commercial producers of pornography, and in particular the American examples that are still at the centre of the global capitalist pornography industry. But the world is changing – it is becoming increasingly globalized and decentralized, and so is the pornography industry. And in relation to occupational health and safety, and to the importance of organized crime to the industry, this movement away from regions with high levels of democracy, human rights, worker enfranchisements and gender and sexual freedoms has important implications.

The global pornography circuit

As we noted at the start of this chapter, in a world of globalized markets and government policies, innovations in communication technologies have increasingly led to the globalization of the production, distribution, and consumption of pornography. Even before the advent of the Internet there existed international markets in pornographic magazines, including illegal imports into nations with more restrictive censorship systems. International phone systems supported the development of complex networks of oral pornography performance whereby companies owned in the Netherlands could route telephone customers to small countries like Guyana, the Dutch Antilles, Niue or Moldova – or even to more economically advanced urbanized centres like Toronto, Canada, 'where operators speaking English, French, Spanish, Greek, Italian and Swedish deal with the callers' (Coopersmith 1998, 115–16). However, the advent of the Internet and the accelerated ease of access to distribution networks that it brought has made possible flows of pornographic material on a truly global scale – with challenging effects on cultural centres and margins alike.

Los Angeles remains 'the most lucrative porn space in the United States' (Jacobs 2007, 28). But some reports claim that the Canadian city of Montreal has become the world's third largest site for the production of pornography, after Los Angeles and Amsterdam (Murphy 2008). For the time being Western companies still dominate the provision of content for the Internet, although there exists:

> an emerging network of people and places outside the major metropolitan areas. Places like Hungary and Thailand are becoming new centres for the creation of pornographic materials because of the easy availability of sex workers. (Jacobs 2007, 30)

When it comes to the hosting of pornographic websites:

The Global Creative Industry of Pornography

The vast majority of adult websites are hosted on computers within the United States, but other clusters can be found in the Czech Republic, Russia and Bulgaria. (Jacobs 2007, 30)

These clusters in non-Western countries have raised concerns about the ethical standards of pornographic materials:

There are hundreds of pornographic films and videos produced each year in Budapest. Budapest is now the biggest centre for pornography production in Europe, eclipsing rivals such as Amsterdam and Copenhagen. Most Western European producers of sex videos use Eastern European actors whenever possible. An executive at Germany's Silwa production company explained 'they cost less and do more. Even excruciating and humiliating acts usually cost only two or three hundred dollars.' (Hughes 2004, 111)

Indeed, some activists worry that trafficking of women and children from poorer countries in order to be used in the production of pornography is becoming a worldwide epidemic (Cole 1992, 30; Baldwin 1989; Sarikakis and Shaukat 2008, 109). Antitrafficking crusaders claim that there are 'hundreds of thousands' of victims worldwide (Baldwin 1989, 335), while US government figures have ranged from 600,000 to four million per year (Weitzer and Ditmore 2010, 335).

Some researchers caution that trafficking figures are 'totally unreliable' and that 'most of the statistics being circulated are probably "false" or "spurious"' (Weitzer and Ditmore 2010, 335–7), used for political effect rather than in an attempt to understand what is actually happening. The International Labour Organization estimates that of the 20.9 million people in forced labour ('trafficked for labour and sexual exploitation or held in slavery-like conditions'), twenty-two per cent are sexually exploited. Seventeen per cent are domestic workers, another seventeen per cent are in agriculture, fishing, or forestry; ten per cent are held in state-imposed slavery; and thirty-four per cent are in construction, mining or manufacturing (ILO 2014, 7). No matter what, any number for enslaved sex work is too high and the issue of workplace conditions in the global pornography industry must be addressed. America and other wealthy countries demonstrate increasing concern for the ethics of pornography production, distribution and consumption at both local and global levels (Mondin 2014). A positive sign is that more developing countries are also organizing sex workers into collectives and unions. In Africa, countries with sex-worker coalitions include Nigeria, Mali, Uganda, and South Africa. India, Bangladesh, Cambodia, Hong Kong, Taiwan, and Thailand all have organizations, and an Asia Pacific Network of Sex Workers is underway. In Europe, the Sex Worker Advocacy Network organizes among less wealthy countries in the eastern, central, and southern regions. TAMPEP advocates on behalf of migrant sex workers across Europe. The Global Network for Sex Work Projects maintains a comprehensive data base to coordinate groups who seek 'to uphold the voice of sex workers globally and connect regional networks advocating for the rights of female, male, and transgender sex workers. It advocates for rights based health and social services, freedom from abuse and discrimination, and self determination for sex workers' (http://www.nswp.org/page/who-we-are).

In globalized markets for pornography – as for other products and services – questions of occupational health and safety and of slavery in supply chains are increasingly recognized as critical human rights issues (Doherty 2012; Burke 2013). A decentralized global network of pornography production and distribution makes research on the conditions of employment in the pornography industry increasingly difficult. We tend to rely on old models of 'national cultural industries' or the mainstream/independent dichotomy to try to understand the systems embedded in the media entertainment matrix. But the bottom line is we don't know where a lot of pornography is produced, by whom, and what labour laws (if any) are followed. Furthermore, the stigma still attached to sex work and the political efficacy of an abolitionist approach to pornography makes it harder for researchers to gather necessary data on global industry practices and to seek input from sex workers themselves.

One response that has been proposed to this dilemma is the concept of 'fair trade' pornography following standards of labour and environmental ethics developed for a vast range of globally sourced products (Bussel 2013). As one advocate argues:

> The sustainable food movement hasn't eliminated factory farms or our inexhaustible craving for junk food. But it provides an alternative model of consumption that we can aspire to. Organic and fair trade practices are leading us, gradually but inevitably, to a better relationship with food. Maybe Fair Trade porn could reconnect us to a better relationship with the human body. (Christakis 2012)

Most easily accessible, currently existing examples of 'fair trade' porn exist in the developed Western countries. The Bay area arguably has the highest concentration of 'fair trade' performers and companies. For example, Pink Label TV, a feminist on-demand website with an explicit 'fair trade' label, guarantees 'queer feminist porn produced by fair-trade studios ... respecting the rules and regulations of the trade and valuing all the agents involved in the production' (Mondin 2014, 189). Jiz Lee offers a comprehensive, but always evolving, guide to best practices for content trading and labour-sharing among independent ethical porn producers where finances are tight and resources limited. They argue that such arrangements 'can create unique content that has the potential to elevate careers, provide income, and birth new production studios with new, inspired filmmakers' (Lee 2014). Fair trade or ethical porn is not necessarily feminist or queer in the sense of attending to women's or queer desire foremost. As Pandora Blake, the owner-operator of *Dreams of Spanking* explains, 'I think it's possible to produce male-gaze porn in an ethical and fair trade way. That means complete respect for performers, for their boundaries and consent. If someone says no, you don't ask again, you don't ask last minute in the middle of a scene. You don't trick them into doing stuff. You pay them. It's not only all of those principles, but also communicating that to your audience' (Williams 2014).

The example of the fair-trade porn movement indicates that workplace standards tend to be higher in wealthy countries than they are in developing countries. Thus, Western countries have an additional responsibility to ensure that their supply chains avoid slavery and provide sufficient guarantees of workplace health and safety and of living wages (Young 2013). The concept of 'fair trade' pornography offers at least one possible way to expand the gains that have been made for pornography performers in Western countries to other parts of the globalized pornography production industry. In the UK, journalist and sex educator Nichi Hodgson has launched the Ethical Porn Partnership (ethicalporn. org), to champion those producers who adhere to 'best practices', and:

> to channel funds to anti-trafficking, anti-sexual violence and sex education initiatives, as well as taking an unequivocal stand on condemning child abuse imagery, and all non-consensual sexually explicit material, such as so-called 'revenge porn'. (Hodgson)

Importantly, without recognition and support from governmental and international NGOs to remove the stigma of sex work, the grassroots efforts of ethical, 'fair trade' pornographers and sex workers could remain marginalized.

Global porn and the child abuse industry

The problem of child abuse materials – the preferred term by law enforcement agencies for what is colloquially known as 'child pornography' – has been exacerbated by globalization. Commercial child abuse materials tend to be produced in developing countries, including former Soviet bloc nations (McKee, Albury, and Lumby 2008, 151). By contrast, in wealthy countries the production of child abuse materials tends not to be commercial, but to be the result of organized networks of paedophiles who produce and circulate images 'for no material gain . . . solely motivated by a sexual interest in minors' (Liptak 2014; US Department of Justice 2010, 26). There are also instances of Western-based international distribution hubs, facilitating the sharing of images produced in other countries within a covert network (Cribb 2013; US Department of Justice 2010, 25). The production and circulation of commercial child abuse images is enabled by the fact that '[p]articularly in very poor countries, laws against the sexual exploitation of children may be nearly non-existent or poorly enforced' (Association of Sites Advocating Child Protection 2010, 16).

The international nature of these systems of production and distribution of child abuse materials – both commercial and underground shared communities – creates significant challenges for law enforcement agencies. The material might be produced in a developing country, hosted (often unknowingly) on a server in the US or another developed country (Association of Sites Advocating Child Protection 2010, 14) and then downloaded by a consumer in yet another country:

> Search engines and directories are . . . 'tricked' into indexing [child sexual abuse material] websites. Meanwhile, the feeder, doorway, billing and paid access content pages are often all hosted in different locations, utilizing different servers, under different legal and national jurisdictions. This 'decentralization' makes it more difficult to track and detect [the materials]. (Association of Sites Advocating Child Protection 2010, 6)

For this reason national governments are increasingly cooperating with other nations and with transnational NGOs in their attempts to stop the production and distribution of child abuse images (Akdeniz 2008, 2–3).

The Virtual Global Taskforce, established in 2003, is an international organization of law enforcement agencies and private sector partners dedicated to combating child sexual abuse materials online, including members from Australia, the UK, Italy, Canada, New Zealand, and the USA as well as Europol and Interpol (Virtual Global Taskforce 2012). The VGT has undertaken a number of large-scale 'Operations', including 'Operation Rescue' (March 2011):

> A global paedophile network consisting of thousands of online members was shattered, resulting in more than 200 children being safe-guarded and 184 offenders arrested across the globe. This operation started in 2007 and involved cooperation between seven of the

VGT member agencies, including the Australian Federal Police, the Child Exploitation and Online Protection (CEOP) Centre in the United Kingdom, the New Zealand Police, US Immigration and Customs Enforcement, The National Child Exploitation Coordination Centre, as part of the Royal Canadian Mounted Police, the Italian Postal and Communications Police Service and Europol. (Virtual Global Taskforce 2012)

The VGT is also drawing awareness to the problem of defining child abuse materials and bringing those standards to the enforcement agencies of less developed nations. While production may take place in regions where human rights abuses are more common, the financing and distribution can often come from countries that pride themselves on their human rights legislation and their record of stopping child abuse materials. A recent international sting operation called Project Spade discovered one of the largest child abuse production companies was operating in Toronto, Canada. Brian Way, the operator of a production and distribution company called Azov Films, had earned approximately $4 million from the trafficking of child abuse materials until his arrest in November 2013. The films were mostly produced in the Ukraine and Romania; yet, of the 348 people arrested worldwide, 108 were from Canada (Mehta 2013). Police estimate that nearly 400 children were rescued.

Another approach to attacking commercial producers of child abuse images is by targeting their financial systems. Commercial producers of child sexual abuse materials 'make fraudulent use of legitimate websites and the services of online billing companies', using money laundering, credit card loading mechanisms, or hijacking affiliate programmes (Association of Sites Advocating Child Protection 2010, 15). Groups like the Financial Coalition Against Child Pornography – which includes law enforcement agencies, banks, credit card companies, online payment processors and Internet service providers – have promoted more stringent content review policies by billing companies, and greater oversight by financial institutions, making it more difficult for those seeking to profit from child sexual abuse materials to process online payments (Association of Sites Advocating Child Protection 2010, 16). In an increasingly decentralized environment the production and distribution of commercial child abuse materials is a global problem – and one that requires coordination across multiple levels of governance and human rights agencies. It is rightly treated as a criminal problem, not an industry regulation issue.

Conclusion: The future of the business

Pornography is a massive global industry, worth billions of dollars. But it is not a homogenous one. In this chapter we have focused on 'Big Porn Inc.' – major corporate players in legacy media like Vivid Entertainment or Playboy Enterprises that employ hundreds of people, release products with high production values, follow existing labour laws and regulations, and actively seek legitimation as a mainstream cultural industry. Like other parts of the creative industries pornography promotes the casualization of labour, and a lack of job security or even decent remuneration often justified in terms of the 'creative' satisfaction of the work. Furthermore, the ongoing stigma attached to the industry limits workers' abilities to organize for fair employment standards and have their experience in pornography treated as valued labour. As pornography expands into a decentralized, global enterprise, the question of organized crime returns to the industry and concerns of serious human rights violations must be treated urgently.

The pornography industry is an increasingly heterogenous one. While criminal operations do exist, they are not necessarily endemic to the industry any more than other industries with close ties to trafficking and abusive work conditions (ILO 2014). Increasingly, those seeking to benefit from the commercialization and profiteering in legally produced pornography are challenged by sex-worker coalitions to respond to ethical concerns of working conditions, discrimination, occupational health and safety, and post-career support. Such discussions take place within problematic social constraints that treat sex work with deep scepticism, distrust, and contempt. Thus, what draws together all of these forms of production – from the biggest corporate giant to the queerest independent performer – is that they produce their material in a context of heightened state oversight, where lawmakers and public commentators have strong feelings that any kind of explicit sexual labour – performance, representation or service – should be monitored and controlled in a way that is quite different from most other creative industries. In a sense, then, these systems of governance produce pornography – or at least the category of pornography. We examine these frameworks of governance in greater detail in Chapters 4 and 5.

Pornography as an industry is now confronted with greater competition and lower profit margins, enabled by innovative communication technologies. This competition has brought to light issues relating to the working conditions for pornography performers. There now exist other models of pornography production that are far less coordinated and easy to track. Yet they also open up opportunities for independent and self-controlled work. Departing openly and dramatically from these corporate giants are individual sex performers and producers operating collectively through subcultural networks. They tend to place more emphasis on sex activism than profits or company growth, while insisting that fair compensation for sex work is a necessary part of that politics. In between the two polar extremes of big business and indy activism are niche operators who provide distribution hubs and adult entertainment ISPs with some industry support and worker assistance, but more from a neo-liberal model that often puts profit maximization ahead of ethical business models. To understand better the changing landscape of pornography, it is necessary to investigate how technological innovations are transforming all aspects of the industry.

2

Pornography and Communication Technologies

How have developments in communication technologies expanded the audience for sexually explicit materials? Is a commercial, for-profit pornography industry feasible in an era of free and on-demand content? What is the historical relationship between communication technologies and pornography? Take for example the printing press, one of the most important communication technologies in the history of the modern world. Despite the massive impact this invention would have on all aspects of Western culture and society (Eisenstein 1979), for the first few decades of its existence it didn't produce material for a wide audience. Instead, it was mostly used to reproduce theological, legal, and scientific works for already-literate cultural elites. It was in 1524 that the printing press began to 'popularize print and bring literacy to the masses' (Johnson 1996, 219), with the publication of Pietro Aretino's *Postures*, a 'series of engravings of sexual positions, each with a ribald sonnet', which became '*the* underground porn classic for centuries' (Johnson 1996, 219–20).

The invention of photography was similarly an important moment in the history of communication technologies, and it was even more quickly associated with pornography. On 9 January 1839 the French Academy of the Sciences announced the invention of the daguerreotype – the first commercially successful photographic process. Within two years the first nude photograph was produced. It was the start of a whole new world of representation:

The practice of producing and selling 'artistic studies' . . . was so successful that less than three years after the invention of the daguerrotype, the United States Congress passed the Customs Act of 1842, which specifically forbade the import of 'obscene or immoral . . . pictures'. (Lane III 2001, 43)

In contemporary Western countries we see ongoing concerns about communication technologies and the proliferation of pornography. The birth of the Internet, of mobile devices, and of social media, have all led to concerns about the accessibility and the variety of sexually explicit material (Tedeschi 2012). But there is more to the relationship between technology and pornography than simply the impact of the Internet. Every new communication technology brings new affordances to cultures, but this is not to say that these technologies have some predetermined form that must change a culture in a particular way. Raymond Williams critiques such 'technological determinism' and argues instead that technologies develop within 'a crucial community of selected emphasis and intention' (1975, 11). In other words, a need or desire and the belief that it is possible and even laudatory to fulfil it presupposes any technology. Thus, the ready appropriation of new technologies into the practice of publicly mediated explicit sex says something about the long history of human desire and pleasure in textual forms.

Pornography as a driver of technology

According to historians of technology, the desire for pornography has driven the development and uptake of communication technologies (Coopersmith 1998, 112–13). While it may not be the case that many inventors of new communication technologies have set out to create new ways of producing and distributing pornographic material, in the history of new communication technologies it is clear that demand for, and take-up of, new technologies has been consistently driven by the desire of audiences to access pornographic material more easily and more privately. This in turn has created a feedback loop that has led to the development of technologies in ways that serve the needs of pornography. For example, in 1950s America:

> Camera stores also quietly stocked [pornographic] films to rent. Not only did the films provide clear profits . . . but they 'also served as a catalyst for the rental or purchase of movie projectors, screens, cameras and other equipment'. (Coopersmith 1998, 101, quoting US Commission on Obscenity and Pornography)

As another example, Peter Johnson suggests that printed pornography helped to 'bring literacy to the masses' (Johnson 1996, 219). Pornography drove the uptake of VCRs in the late 1970s and early 1980s, 'providing customers with a product, and, at the same time, justification for acquiring an expensive piece of equipment'. They also led the way in developing a market for video cassettes. During the early days of VCR consumption 'X-rated tapes constituted over half of all sales of pre-recorded tapes in the late 1970s' (Coopersmith 1998, 104, 105). Porn has been the 'deciding factor' (Donenfeld 2008) in technological format wars – the triumph in the 1980s of VHS video tapes over the technologically superior Betamax 'is attributable to Sony's refusal to cooperate with the pornography industry' (Waskul 2004b, 3). Similarly, the porn industry's decision to favour Blu-Ray over HD-DVD led mainstream entertainment companies to invest in the former early in the twenty-first century (Mearian 2006) (and the fact that Sony owns the Blu-Ray format suggests that they learned their lesson from that first format failure).

Porn audiences are a particularly important demographic group because they are early adopters of new technologies, and they are willing to pay a premium for the privilege of gaining easier and more private access to sexually explicit materials. Thus, they bear the additional financial burden of testing new technologies that are later adapted into mainstream media at substantially reduced cost (Coopersmith 1998, 95). That this is the case can be seen in the development of the World Wide Web. As one writer has put it, 'sex shaped the Internet' (Perdue 2004). At the very least, pornography was instrumental in the development of CD-ROM software, financial verification software for online payments, digital watermarking, computer based videoconferencing, video streaming, software, e-commerce payment systems, third-party counters that measure 'traffic and signups', exit consoles (new windows which launch when you leave a site), technologies for 'fraud scrubbing' (which 'detect fraudulent transactions before they are processed'), digital file tracking, the 'double opt-in system' that requires email confirmation, paid video on demand, live streaming video, commercial applications of video conferencing, Webcam hardware and software (Perdue 2004, 260–89). Considering that list of innovations, it is hard to disagree that pornography created the Internet as we currently know it.

Most significantly, pornography has been the testing ground for the business models that have made Internet companies viable and kept them solvent while developing other markets in less stigmatized areas. In this sense, pornography is a key node in the e-commerce matrix because it allows for market maturation 'by testing technologies and concepts to attract customers and their money' (Coopersmith 1998, 112–13). Among other innovations, pornography companies are behind the development of pay-per-click-through programmes (where 'a site pays the referring affiliate site a small amount, typically $0.05 to $0.10, for every visitor who clicks through') and 'conversion base performance systems' (where 'payments are made only for click-throughs that result in a purchase') (Perdue 2004, 260–89).

Lewis Perdue also argues that a whole range of Internet companies have relied on the pornography market to keep them afloat including Cisco (routers), Sun Microsystems (servers), Yahoo (advertising from sex sites), web hosting companies, and AOL (sex chat rooms) (Perdue 2004, 260–70). Indeed:

> Web sex provided the only income stream to the nascent World Wide Web, revenues that developed the technology, and the market and funded innovation out of real profits. (Perdue 2004, 260)

Thus, the development of new communication technologies has been intimately linked with the demand for sexually explicit materials. That relationship has sparked deep cultural anxieties about the limits of sexual expression in moments of rapid social and technological change.

Online pornography and media moral panics

The image said it all: a blue-eyed, blond-haired little boy, his face a ghastly, ghostly blue from the computer screen, his eyes bulged out and his mouth agape in horror. What could possibly be haunting his innocence? Cyberporn. *Time Magazine*'s now legendary 1995 cover story helped set the stage for an ongoing media moral panic about how to simultaneously 'protect our kids – and free speech' when it came to online pornography (1995, cover). Media moral panics are not new and social scientific studies of media effects are a by-product every time a new communication technology rises to dominance. In the United States, for example, the Payne Fund Studies from 1933–5 sought to quantify stimulation effects on children watching films, including sexual arousal (Jowett et al. 1996). A moral panic is a sudden instance of public distress over a presumed threat to the social order. Gilbert Herdt argues that, increasingly, moral panics are tied to fear of dissident sexualities undermining the moral authority of heternormativity. Yet, he points out, that threat is constructed by those with the power to combat it easily and deploy governmental strategies to further marginalize, ostracize, and stigmatize individuals who fail to conform (Herdt 2009, 3). Public concern over intricate and convoluted bonds between pornography and technology are only the latest in a long line of media moral panics.

Walter Kendrick argues that the first attempts to regulate pornography, in nineteenth-century Britain, were driven by concerns about the technologies of popular printing. In the eighteenth century, sexually explicit images were available – but only to the wealthiest men in society. The discovery of 'lascivious' frescoes in the ruins of Pompeii, for example, did not cause a major social problem because only the wealthiest and most educated citizens could gain access to view them:

A gentleman with appropriate demeanor (and ready cash for the custodian) would be admitted to the locked chamber where controversial items lurked: women, children and the poor of both sexes and all ages were excluded. (Kendrick 1996, 6)

The problem emerged with popular printing, when books that reproduced such materials began to escape such careful management. Books, as Kendrick notes, are 'sluttish' (Kendrick 1996, 15) – they can be read by anyone who is literate and who can access a copy of them. With books, moral guardians could not exercise 'the case-by-case surveillance exercised by Neapolitan gatekeepers' to keep pornography a privilege of the elite (Kendrick 1996, 15). As books about sexual subjects began to circulate, concerns emerged about their effects on 'the sensual, the vicious, the young and inexperienced' (Kendrick 1996, 27). These readers might not bring to bear the appropriate level of educated discrimination, and might rather use sexually explicit books in the wrong way, 'converted into mere guidebooks to vice, or to afford amusement to the prurient fancy of the depraved' (anonymous reviewer, quoted in Kendrick 1996, 27).

Kendrick notes that during the nineteenth century a strategy of 'expurgation' and a 'bowdlerizing sensibility' (Kendrick 1996, 51) took place to ensure that sexually explicit materials did not fall into the hands of those who were not properly trained to manage them – the working classes, women, and children. The Obscene Publications Act of 1857 in England formalized this process, for the first time legally defining obscenity and restricting its distribution. This was a direct result of the democratization of access to sexually explicit materials brought about by popular printing (Kendrick 1996, 99). The enfranchisement of the working classes in Britain through the Reform Act of 1867 meant that they could now represent themselves politically. It thus reduced the discursive power of claims that legislators were protecting the unprotected. Similarly, the People Act 1918, initiating the process of giving women the vote, made it less possible to campaign against pornography on the premise of protecting women. Yet children have remained a powerless group throughout political history who cannot speak collectively against any efforts to deny them cultural access. Thus, concerns about 'delinquency' and corruption of minors have been a cornerstone of media moral panics about pornography in this and the past century, coinciding with rapid advancements in communication technologies.

The spectre of pornography reaching children is never far from the minds of contemporary moral gatekeepers. In the 1950s and 1960s, the American-based organization Citizens for Decent Literature raised alarms about cheap colour printing and what materials this would make available to children:

> A floodtide of filth is engulfing our country in the form of newsstand obscenity. It is threatening to pervert an entire generation of our American children. We know that once a person is perverted it is practically impossible for that person to adjust to normal attitudes in regard to sex. Yet much of this material has been described as an illustrated, detailed course in perversion, abnormal sex, crime and violence . . . no matter who buys this material, 75–90% of it ends up in the hands of our children . . . never in the history of the world have the merchants of obscenity, the teachers of unnatural sex acts, had available to them the modern facilities for disseminating this filth – high speed presses, rapid transportation, mass distribution – all have combined to put the vilest obscenity within the reach of every man, woman and child in the country. (Keating 1965)

In later decades similar concerns were raised about the accessibility of pornography on cable television (Coopersmith 1998, 102), and through home video cassette rentals (Jeffreys 1990, 253). From this perspective, it is clear that contemporary fears about Internet and mobile pornography are nothing new and remain bound to hegemonic orders of social control and privilege.

Concerns about the possibly damaging effect of Internet pornography on children have fallen into four broad categories. The first concern is that young people are using Internet pornography for sex education and thus learning rough or kinky sex, anal sex, or casual sex. There exists a tradition of quantitative social science research investigating the question of whether 'unrestrained' access to pornography is damaging to young people (Zillmann 2000). As we discuss in the chapters on violence and on sexualization, this work tends to find a correlation between sexual adventurousness and the consumption of Internet pornography – although it proves nothing about causality (Braun-Courville and Rojas 2009).

The second concern is that pornography on the Internet is addictive. Jennifer Johnson argues that online commercial pornography is a 'spider-like network' that preys on 'vulnerable' men who are 'a ripe target for economic exploitation' (2010, 153). The debate over porn addiction or compulsive viewing of porn continues among psychologists, but there is not as much attention paid to actual increases of porn consumption because of the Internet. Ley et al. point out that:

> In contrast to frequent claims in the popular media about an epidemic of porn use, no change in the last four decades has been noted in more detailed longitudinal data since Internet access increased. (Ley, Prause, and Finn 2014)

The third concern is that the Internet has facilitated the production and distribution of child abuse materials (Endrass et al. 2009, 2). It is certainly the case, as we discuss in Chapter 1, that the Internet has made the existence of child abuse materials more visible. It also appears to have facilitated the capturing and prosecution of the perpetrators of such material through a network of international treaties and regulatory cooperation (Association of Sites Advocating Child Protection 2010).

The fourth concern is that Internet pornography is more violent than previous forms:

> Today's porn is not your father's *Playboy*. Type porn into Google and you won't see anything that looks like the old pinups; instead, you will be catapulted into a world of sexual cruelty and brutality where women are subject to body-punishing sex and called vile names. (Dines 2010)

This raises the first important point discussed in this chapter about the change in the nature of pornography brought about by the Internet. Each new communication technology has in turn brought about an increase in the variety and accessibility of pornography to audiences. The Internet may now have brought this logic to an extreme. The range of pornographic materials that is now easily accessible to a computer user is indeed much wider than has been the case at any time in the past – but what are consumers actually looking at?

Rule 34

'Rule 34' is a familiar Internet meme which states that 'If it exists, there is porn of it' (Urban Dictionary 2006). Using Google you can quite easily find things that look like old-style pinups (see, for example, http://weheartit.com/entry/25064928#). You can find 'extreme' pornography of the type described by Dines in the quote above. You can find balloon sex and fluffy sex and foot fetishism and food sex and a whole range of other sexual possibilities. What you will see, in short, is variety. As we noted in Chapter 1, the Internet has massively lowered the costs of entry into pornography and so now it takes only one person to have a particular sexual interest for that to be available on the Internet. Nose licking porn? http://www.pornhub.com/view_video.php?viewkey=1681229695. Sneeze porn? http://fapdu.com/sneeze.porn. Cartoon porn of the Flintstones? http://cartoongonzo.net/cartoonmovie016_flint stones/index.html?id=tabascoandtr=scp. It's all there. Pornography on the Internet is certainly more 'diverse' and 'eclectic' than magazine or DVD pornography (Jacobs 2007, 16). However, it would be going too far to make the historical claim that porn 'in the good ol' days' was much cleaner, more innocent and lighthearted, than it is today. While it is true that the most easily purchased mainstream commercial porn had a limited aesthetic (think the numbing sameness of the Playboy Bunny), as any history of early twentieth century stag films will prove, the Internet did not invent kink or BDSM.

This wide range of pornographic material is spread across an equally wide range of sites and networks. Unlike adult stores in the physical world, the online world is less easily managed by zoning laws. A local council in the physical world can require an adult entertainment store to be a certain number of metres from residential zones, schools, or churches; but there is no equivalent online, where every site is potentially only ever one click away from every other site. Take the example of 'xxx' domain registration. It was introduced in 2012 by the Internet Corporation for Assigned Names and Numbers, under pressure from the United States government, in an effort to corral all pornography sites into one location. This had an effect – but not the one that was hoped for. The result was actually a new kind of moral panic, which one reviewer called the fear of 'Your Brand Name in Porn'. Internet registration companies charged as much as 500 per cent mark-up on 'defensive registration' costs to decidedly non-pornographic companies like Pepsi or Nike. The University of Kansas paid $3000 in an effort to licence every possible *.xxx name that might be associated with them. Meanwhile legitimate porn companies who count on the 'curious clicker' (Johnson 2010) accidentally stumbling onto their site had no business incentive to comply (Ulanoff 2011). In May 2012, it was reported that forty per cent of the approximately 216,000 *.xxx registered domains were defensive registrations, and that the highest ranking porn site with the *.xxx domain stalled at 51,549 (Matyszczyk 2012). The *.xxx domain moral panic was a clear example of how pornography serves as a spectre within Internet regulatory and business practices with little adverse effect on Internet pornography itself.

The business models of Internet pornography

As we noted in Chapter 1, digital distribution of pornography is challenging legacy pornographic media and, in particular, traditional business models of selling units of product directly to consumers. The cutting edge technologies developed by porn companies online are experimenting with new ways of getting Internet users to consume explicit material. The ability to compile aggregate user data has made possible a matrix of affiliate networks to turn the potential porn user into a paying consumer, using 'click manoeuvres and marketing gimmicks' (Johnson 2010, 148). Pornography has been a key organizer for both innovative e-commerce models and networked community building, challenging and transforming the understanding of both porn producers and consumers – with significant effects on the bottom line.

Just prior to the opening of the 2012 Adult Entertainment Expo, the largest porn convention in the world, speculation was high that finally the recession-proof industry was succumbing to the vicissitudes of its own success. Rampant digital piracy and advertising-driven porn hubs that specialized in free, amateur-produced shorts were driving down the profit margins of commercial enterprises. The larger 'prestige' companies like New Sensations were producing less long-form content and diversifying their business into subscription sites, live events, and branding commodities (Morris 2013). The Internet, still the engine of pornography's proliferation, was now the cause of its economic downfall (Theroux 2012; Rosen 2013). Yet, just as in other media industries caught with the problem of monetizing Internet content, pornography producers are pioneering online subscription models that may result in smaller-scale audience reach and profit margins. This in turn provokes important questions for scholars and activists regarding ethical creative labour practices in the age of accessible, DIY digital culture. While there may exist a huge variety of pornographic materials on the Internet, not all of them are created equal in either aesthetic quality or ethical practice. There are structures and patterns to the material that is available. To put it simply, different kinds of websites offer different kinds of material, which is accessed and monetized in different ways.

Subscription sites

In the face of Internet piracy it is increasingly difficult for capitalist models of pornography profiteering to continue at the levels previously enjoyed (Campbell 2014). One model that appears to be at least lessening the loss is subscription-based services offering 'premium' and regularly updated material. Traditional large-scale pornography companies can survive by using this model. For example, Bel Ami (http://tour.belamionline.com/tour.aspx), an internationally successful Slovak-based gay porn company, has a successful subscription website. The company was established in 1993 and now produces not only pornographic audio-visual material but also a whole empire of brand extensions and merchandizing including calendars and photo books, as well as organizing performance and signing tours by its stars. Subscription sites like this one – the new online face of legacy porn companies – sell themselves on the basis of 'quality' and, to a lesser extent, legitimacy and sometimes ethical practices as outlined in Chapter 1. They tend to feature actors who are conventionally good looking, and their production values are consistently high. Under this model, traditional models of 'high-end' pornography can survive on the Internet, albeit at a lower profit margin.

Because the Internet has lowered barriers to entry for the production and distribution of pornography, the subscription site model has also worked for smaller operations and sole-traders. It allows a wider variety of material to be produced, and, importantly, a wider variety of people to become producers of pornography, and to maintain control over, and make money from, their own productions. Before the invention of the Internet it was certainly possible to create videos on home video cameras, to duplicate those one at a time on a home video cassette recorder, to put a small ad into a specialized publication offering copies of the video for sale, and then to post them through the postal service (Coopersmith 1998, 107). All of this was possible – but it was, at the very least, cumbersome. By contrast the Internet has made it possible to upload material to potentially millions of customers in the space of minutes, using a standard domestic technology that the majority of Western consumers now have in their homes. Of course there remain questions about the structural factors that impede access to these technologies and the ability to use them – primarily socio-economic class and age – but by comparison with previous regimes of media production and distribution, the Internet is undoubtedly more democratic.

Of particular interest is the fact that women are heavily

represented among those taking up the possibilities of the subscription site model to generate income from their own pornographic performances (Perdue 2004, 292). Some of these
are in the mainstream of pornographic representation, with an
aesthetic indistinguishable from major commercial sites – such
as Jenna Jameson's *Club Jenna* (http://tour.jennajameson.com/
home/). Yet, increasingly, others promote themselves by representing different body types, sexualities, and interests (Jacobs 2007,
27). Amazon Amanda's subscription site (http://www.amazona-
mandaandfriends.com/) is run by, features material of, and earns
money for a woman who is, according to her FAQ, 'Amazon by
height, BBW by size, and Goddess by nature'. Vanessa Blue, one
of the pornographic industry's most influential women-of-colour
performers and directors, runs her own site (http://www.vanessa-
blue.com/tour/index.php). These sites do not rely as much on high
production values to sell their material; rather they sell themselves
as a brand that may be related to a particular sexual niche, or
the personality of the sole trader. More importantly, as discussed
in Chapter 6, many of these porn entrepreneurs link with other
similar sites to form a networked community committed to ethical
labour practices and progressive gender and sexual politics. Once
defined as 'amateur', these sites now take care to distinguish themselves from hub sites that rely on user-generated content, citing
concerns about intellectual property and fair pay, among others.
What remains in the domain of amateur, therefore, raises important issues about ethical porn practices in online distribution and
consumption.

Aggregate sites

The business of Internet pornography offers important insights
into the ethics of distribution and consumption. Dominating
Internet porn are aggregate network sites that are a combination
of user-generated content, creator-uploaded professional content,
and pirated professional content. At the highest end are ethical
porn coalitions that merge gender and sexual politics with pornog-

raphy and market themselves as independent and alternative to mainstream porn media. At the lowest end are revenge porn sites and child abuse networks.

The most popular of aggregate sites sit in the middle – between progressive and abusive. Often with the moniker 'hub' or 'tube' (PornHub, Porn Tube, XTube, RedTube), these sites are not that dissimilar to the Internet juggernaut youtube.com, except that they specialize in explicit sexual content – precisely what YouTube does not allow on its site. Clips are short and not necessarily of the highest quality, organized around the usual kinds of fetish categories found in any online porn video store. The free material is generally supported through advertising, with various subscription packages available to access longer clips or better produced content. According to the web analytics company Alexa Internet Inc., on 1 October 2012 the most popular adult site in the world was xhamster.com (Alexa 2012). This site relies on user-generated material. Some of this is 'amateur' in the everyday sense of having no commercial intent. Such material is commonly created by men. Women rarely post material to these mainstream aggregate sites without any commercial intent. This low-end user-generated material is often grainy, badly framed and need not feature conventionally attractive body types. This material is generally not promoted highly within the site and, unlike the work of ethical feminist and queer porn entrepreneurs, which we discuss below, remains more invested in conventional forms of voyeurism than in transgressing hegemonic gender and sexual roles. It makes up only a small amount of the material on aggregate sites.

Another category of available content comprises shorter segments of full videos that are available at other paid subscription websites – XHamster users can watch a few minutes for free, but then the video ends with the URL for the subscription site where the full video can be watched. This is not 'amateur' material – it is advertising for professionally produced material. Other user-generated materials are essentially advertisements or audition reels for performers hoping to break into a crowded market and achieve mainstream success. This material is neither fully amateur nor professional, but more like aspiring professional.

Some of these aggregate sites have become increasingly controversial within the porn industry, not only because of accusations that they steal copyrighted material, but also because they provide little to no oversight into what porn they accept, how it has been produced, and who enjoys the profits earned by it. The issue of piracy is critical for professional pornography producers. In some instances, the pirated material consists of old videos that are digitized and uploaded without permission from the original producers or performers. It is sometimes argued that those individuals cannot be located but that does not justify presuming consent. Similarly, contemporary material that is behind paywalls is ripped illegally from other sites and uploaded. This, of course, has a more immediate impact on the livelihoods of performers currently seeking to earn a living from their work. As with all other entertainment content producers, those who wish to earn a living from their work in pornography are engaged in an ongoing war against such piracy, with associated technological breakthroughs such as digital watermarks, or automated search tools that claim to be able to detect copyrighted material (Campbell 2014). In 2014, independent feminist porn producer Jacky St James publicly criticized Belle Knox, the porn actor mentioned in Chapter 1, who made headlines when she was outed by fellow students at Duke University, for accepting a summer internship at PornHub, named as 'a piracy-based tube site' (Dickson 2013).

In pornography, as in other areas of the entertainment industry, it seems that for the moment at least the pirates are winning. A recent article about MindGeek, a 'global industry-leading information technology firm', revealed that it is also the largest owner of online aggregate pornography sites including PornHub, YouPorn, and RedTube. They also own numerous porn studios and have content deals with many others. 'Since then, industry workers have been in the difficult situation of seeing their work pirated on sites owned by the same company that pays them – imagine if Warner Brothers owned Pirate Bay' (Auerbach 2014). Independent performers have been fighting against porn piracy for years, with increasing urgency. In 2011, genderqueer porn performer Jiz Lee stated clearly on their website, 'the only time

I've felt exploited in porn, is through piracy' (Lee 2011). In 2014, performers and companies launched PayForYourPorn.Org. It not only increases awareness of the harm piracy causes workers, but also reflects on how the industry itself can rebalance its business models for fairness and sustainability (Hern 2014). Unfortunately, it seems as if stigma against sex workers is keeping regulatory agencies from cracking down on porn piracy. Yet, as our chapter on industry noted, once this model of predatory centralized control takes hold of the porn industry, other online entertainment sectors could be affected. Thus, regulators ignoring this issue due to a prurient disregard for porn workers' labour rights may realize too late the widespread damage it could cause (Auerbach 2014).

Community user websites

The last Internet pornography model we explore is the network of websites that do not contribute to mainstream aggregate sites in favour of creating their own online communities. The best of them feature material produced by users not only for profit but also with explicitly stated artistic, political, and educational goals. We discuss in the chapter on performance a growing international network of feminist and queer pornography producers and activists. Here, we focus on the centrality of the Internet to this coalition building. These sites are mostly subscription based and/or keep all but a small sample of their material behind paywalls. While their investment into a capitalist system of commercial exchange may seem at odds with their sexual and gender politics, it actually turns the tables on the complacency of certain forms of Western critical thought that rely on a general suspicion of commodity capitalism as inherently bad – and expects the least advantaged in that system to eschew its allures (Smith 2010, 107). These activists reject such vulgar Marxism by insisting that they have the right to earn a living and be fairly compensated for their labour. At the same time, through small-scale economies where more immediate interaction between producer and consumer is possible, new forms of sexual–political alliances can occur (Jacobs 2007, 45). In an era where creative workers are increasingly threatened by piracy, lower pay, and precarious employment – conditions often blamed on the Internet – paying people for their creative, cultural labour seems to be the better politics (www.culturalworkersorganize.org).

Courtney Trouble has been a leader in online porn community building (and fair pay politics), beginning with No Fauxxx (since renamed Indie Porn Revolution) in 2002. Their Troublefilms Web Network now includes Queer Porn TV, Real Queer Porn, Trouble Films, FTM Fucker, TransGrrrls, Lesbian Curves, and their personal site CourtneyTrouble.com. The sites are professionally designed but also intellectually driven, with blogs, commentaries, statements about labour practices and the need for increased visibility of marginalized bodies and sexualities. On their own performer bio page, Trouble argues that the Internet has made possible an 'anti-oppressive safe space for all genders, sizes, and races. Let's strive to make it that way and keep it that way.' In addition to the websites, Trouble, like many of their colleagues in feminist queer porn, is active on major social media sites. Through Twitter, Facebook, and other such venues, they are building a global community of producers and fans. In so doing, they are able to draw as much attention to their politics as their pornography. As Trouble writes:

> Many of us do other kinds of work that is much more financially rewarding or career-making, but queer porn is our preferred process, and through it we are able to search for something beyond financial gain: knowledge, power, acceptance, visibility, desire, justice, love, to name a few. (Trouble 2014b, 200)

There are other forms of user-generated websites that are not merely unethical but downright criminal. The openness of the net has led to concerns about 'revenge-porn', sexually explicit images or videos of ex-partners posted for revenge and without the ex-partners' consent. The Internet did not invent this despicable practice. *Hustler* Magazine used to run a regular feature called Beaver Hunt, where men submitted photos of naked women taken without their consent. Nonetheless, as with other practices, online distribution has made it more visible. Some websites have found a particularly vicious and unethical new business model to exploit this trend, inviting members to submit sexually explicit images of individuals to be posted without their consent, and then charging the harmed individuals to have the images removed (Musil 2014). The target market for these sites is usually spurned lovers and ex-boyfriends exacting revenge on women. The first porn site dedicated to revenge porn was Is Anyone Up?, run by Hunter Moore. By 2012, he was facing numerous civil and criminal investigations. In 2014, he was arrested and faces federal charges of Internet hacking (Hill 2014). Regulation is now catching up with these sites. In January 2014 Israel became the first country to make it illegal to post sexually explicit material without the subject's consent (Frizell 2014). Other countries are signalling their readiness to introduce legislation against what is sometimes termed 'the non-consensual distribution of intimate images,' and some American states have already passed legislation (CCSO 2013).

In a more neutral register, consumers of pornography have also become their own distributors, using social media to share favourite material. Facebook is notorious for controlling sexual – or even naked – photographs on its site, to the point where pictures of breastfeeding have been taken down (Hern 2013), while facing criticism for allowing sexist and misogynist content to remain (Gross 2013). As a result, in 2013, Facebook announced new protocols targeting 'sexist hate speech'. Examples of noxious sexual content online are important to highlight, but what can also be noted is that the high visibility of these networks – unlike the underground, below-the-counter, or mail-order networks of before – makes civil and criminal action against them more possible. Of course, there is always a lag between technological developments and governmental response. Sexting, the sharing of sexually explicit images through mobile devices, is the latest media moral panic around pornography. Concerns are being raised that minors, especially teenagers, may find themselves caught in a web of child pornography laws ill-suited to deal with this practice. This new form of publicly mediated sexual expression is requiring new discursive capacities to contend with the nuances of consent, motivation and harm (Crofts and Lee 2013, 85). Those concepts are addressed in greater detail in the chapters on violence and governance.

The fact that consumers will use any new communications technology to access and distribute pornography is blurring the lines between consumer-driven sites and social media networks:

> Online pornography websites are increasingly starting to behave like social networks – encouraging users to share, like, rate, comment, curate and even create content. (Perraudin 2014)

This, in turn, upsets the standard cycle of production–distribution–consumption long favoured by scholars of legacy media. Online interactivity is redefining the relationship between pornographic content and its medium of delivery. In so doing, it is challenging the way that we understand the media entertainment matrix.

Interactivity

Compared with previous breakthroughs in communication technologies, the Internet is far more interactive. Technologies like video recording or DVD burning certainly allowed for sharing, and print subscription made possible publishing fan mail. However, the Internet is interactive in real time and with far less editorial control. This has changed the form radically – to the point where clear boundaries between explicit sexual services (aka prostitution) and explicit sexual performance have become increasingly unstable.

Webcams are an important part of online pornography across all models from the most commercial to the purely altruistic. Live webcams allow viewers to watch somebody (or more than one person) engaging in sexual acts while responding to them in real time by means of typed comments or VOIP (voice-over Internet protocol). At one point, one webcam on XHamster had 853 people watching simultaneously, all able to type live comments to the participants. This kind of live mediated large-scale sex has never before been possible. It is a genuinely new form of pornography, and a new form of publicly mediated sexual expression, breaking down the line between representation and practice: cybersex is 'masturbation, mutual masturbation, erotica, pornography and sex all at the same time' (Gillis 2004, 98).

On XHamster, the distinction between amateur webcam performances and those done for commercial gain is strongly associated with gender. The overwhelming majority of men on XHamster's webcams are performing for exhibitionistic pleasure, while the overwhelming majority of women on the site are performing for money. On one site visit in September 2012 there were over forty men performing on webcams, many of them with their webcams focused on their penises as they masturbated. The way that XHamster is set up allows you to view what is happening on the webcam for free and without signing in. If you want to write a live message to the model you have to log in. But then models can also have an account with a 'Tip' button – viewers can buy tokens from the website to tip models. On this visit only one man from the more than forty who were performing offered the option to tip. These amateur men were not doing it for the money – they were doing it for exhibitionist pleasure. Fireman381, for example, is a single man, looking for a relationship with a woman. The tagline on his webcam is 'Can I show someone my cock?', and his camera shows his whole body as he masturbates his erect penis. Similarly 19yroldcckkk's tagline is 'I want to get HARD!!!!!' – and his webcam is a close up of his hard penis.

This amateur, masculine use of webcams is part of a long tradition of consumers appropriating communication technologies for their own exhibitionistic pleasure. The Polaroid instant camera, video camcorders and videotext systems like Minitel have all been appropriated by consumers for the sake of sexual self-expression (Coopersmith 1998, 106–109). What is new about this form, as noted above, is its interactivity. Interactive sex entertainment is 'both representation (or image) and presentation (or act)' (Kibby and Costello 2001, 353). As Dennis Waskul states:

Cybersex is a form of coauthored interactive erotica . . . only marginally related to pornography and . . . more squarely situated in a specific kind of interactive erotic *experience* . . . a hybrid form of erotica – part pornography and part live erotic entertainment. (Waskul 2004a, 19, 36, 44)

By contrast with the exhibitionist men, the women using webcams on XHamster were mostly employing this new model of mediated sex/pornography for commercial gain. On the same visit, every woman on the webcam had her 'Tips' button activated. For women, the exchange of money seemed to play at least some part in their exhibitionism. In XHamster's invitation to users to join their 'cams programme', it lays out their business model. Webcam models get 'about 60 per cent of the revenue' from their tips. The site has 'easy to use cam features for the models', there is a 'friendly user community' and a 'friendly and helpful support team', 'Membership is FREE. Signing up is FAST. Broadcasting is EASY' and 'PRO and newbie models are welcome for fast help and advice' (xhamster.com 2012). The women performers were embracing this apparently fast, friendly, and free business model.

As noted in Chapter 1, the question of female sex workers' motivations remains a complex one. Begum et al. interviewed sex workers in Australia and found a range of 'contradictory characteristics' – women sex workers talked about the work as 'financially rewarding but entrapping', being 'empowering and demeaning', and as 'offering both intimacy and competition' (Begum et al. 2013, 85). Thus, an either/or binary where women sex workers must be doing it either just for the money or just for their own sexual pleasure fails to recognize the diversity and subtlety surrounding pornography work. A continuum of motivations and experiences, some contradictory, is almost always in play. By contrast, when men appear on webcams it seems to offer them a more straightforward exhibitionistic pleasure.

In 2014, a flurry of reports about security breaches within webcam sites raised the important issue of privacy expectations in a fundamentally public medium like the Internet. An Australian law firm announced that gay men who engaged in private sexually explicit 'webchats' discovered that they had been recorded and uploaded onto aggregate porn sites registered in different countries and therefore under different privacy laws (Same 2014).

Even more disturbing was the realization that major national security agencies in Britain and the United States were intercepting and storing webcam footage of individuals engaged in consensual, legal activities that they thought were private (Ackerman and Ball, 2014).

The ongoing and dramatic reconfiguration of private and public sexuality is addressed in more detail in Chapter 5. Here, we suggest that such distressing reports again underscore the openness and volatility of the Internet. Some may try to use these as fear mongering to keep sex private or risk social embarrassment and reprisal. Yet, that argument carries with it again an underlying stigma against both sex work and sex-for-pleasure. What is more worthwhile is to use such examples not as arguments against publicly mediated sex per se but against *non-consensual, exploitative, and abusive* publicly mediated sex. It is also an incentive to find better models for analysing and critiquing how and by whom sex is produced, distributed, and consumed; how to combat and ultimately prevent pornographic injustices through regulatory, civil, and criminal means; how to uphold high industry standards for fair, ethical, respectful treatment of all individuals engaged in pornographic networks; and how to build respectful, critically engaged pornography communities. Such research is more possible due to the Internet.

Big porn data

To this point we have talked about what is available on the Internet. But there is a big difference between what is available, and what consumers actually look at. A third unique affordance of the Internet discussed in this chapter is the possibility of accessing so-called 'big data' for research. Although in one sense the Internet is the most private of media – you can access pornography without having to go into a shop, buy some material, and bring it home in a brown paper bag – it is also simultaneously the most public. The possibility exists that every website you visit, every picture you view, every search term you enter, and every keystroke you make can be monitored and recorded. On the one hand this is the stuff of our most paranoid fantasies. On the other hand it is a gift for researchers, and allows us to make a distinction between what is possible to find on the Internet, and what consumers actually want to look at.

Mazières et al. analysed metadata for almost two million pornographic videos hosted on the aggregating sites XNXX and XHamster. They found that the rule of the 'long tail' applies to pornography as it does to other forms of content on the Internet:

> A large proportion of items are covered by a very small number of almost universal categories, while a long tail of more specific categories still gather a large variety of content. (Mazières et al. 2014, 82)

The 'long tail' refers to the general phenomenon that while there may be a huge number of objects on the Internet, only a very small number of them are popular, while the vast majority – the 'long tail' – get little or no traffic. There remains, even on the Internet, a mainstream or dominant/hegemonic culture. In the case of these aggregate porn sites, Mazières et al. found that 'the top 5% of the most popular tags covers more than 90% of videos' (Mazières et al. 2014, 85). The top ten tags on XHamster are amateur, men, teens, hardcore, blowjobs, anal, big boobs, masturbation, mature, and cumshots; on XNXX they are blowjob, hardcore, amateur, teen, cumshot, anal, brunette, blonde, pussy, and sex (Mazières et al. 2014, 87). Similarly, neuroscientists Ogas and Gaddam, in what they call 'the world's largest experiment' (Ogas and Gaddam 2011), analysed 55 million Internet searches for erotic content between July 2009 and July 2010. The top ten most commonly searched-for categories globally were youth, gay, MILFs (Mothers I would Like to Fuck), breasts, cheating wives, vaginas, penises, amateurs, mature, and animation. The 'massively quantitative approach' (Mazières et al. 2014, 92) of these researchers reveals the mainstream of Internet pornography. Youth is in there, as are mature women and mothers. Breasts, vaginas, penises, and anuses are all present. Masturbation, blowjobs, and cumshots are popular across the sites analysed. None of them is outside what we might consider the 'mainstream' of offline pornography before the Internet.

It is also possible, using this approach, to drill down into the data to find out what particular groups or regions seek. Porn MD, for example, has released top ten lists of porn searches by country (Porn MD 2014). There are consistencies across countries – teen, mature, MILF, and amateur figure highly in many country's lists. Interestingly, for most countries, the search for their own nation's pornography tops the list – a surprising localism in this global Internet culture. There are also unique twists in some countries' search histories – for example, 'pov' (point of view) features in the top ten British searches while the Netherlands include 'squirt'. One fascinating trend that Big Data reveals is that more conservative and religious states in the USA tend to consume more online pornography than more progressive areas (Edelman 2009), and the Bible Belt states watch more gay pornography online per capita than others (Broderick 2014).

The 'long tail' analysis is useful for allowing us to identify the mainstream of Internet pornography, and to distinguish between on the one hand what is available, and on the other what consumers are actually searching for and watching. Ogas and Gaddam identify 'rape' as the thirty-sixth most popular pornographic search term, at 0.48 per cent of searches (although this includes rape fantasies, not necessarily viewers searching for real images of rape). This search comes below categories such as Grannies, Skinny, Tattoo, and Hairy in terms of its mainstream popularity (Ogas and Gaddam 2011, 252–3). Big data analysis has also shown that child abuse materials, for example, are definitely not in the mainstream of the Internet – even on peer-to-peer platforms, which in themselves are less mainstream than web pages. Latapy et al. analysed 'hundreds of millions of keyword based queries on the peer to peer system eDonkey and found that 'approximately 0.24% of queries are paedophile' and that just over '0.2% of users enter such queries' (Latapy, Margnien, and Fournier 2013, 248). Such material is certainly part of the 'long tail', but it is not the mainstream of Internet pornography. Big data gathered from the Internet can make critical analysis and even political intervention better grounded in evidence rather than moral panic.

This is not to say that there aren't useful critiques to be made about the perpetuation of heteronormativity, hypermasculinity, all forms of abuse, sexism, and objectification of women, and racism in online pornography. In addition, the normalization of coercive language and a lack of explicit consent in much mainstream pornography is a major concern. While we do not agree that the majority of porn being accessed by consumers is overtly violent in the sense of non-consensual and coercive, we do see troubling representations of gendered power dynamics in much mainstream pornography. Nonetheless, an analysis of consent in pornography that recognizes the complexity of the issue is much more useful than universally condemning all representations. We deal with the issue of consent more broadly in the next chapter.

Conclusion: The future of technology

As media and communication technologies continue to evolve and expand, it is clear that content will become increasingly mobile and platform-neutral, so you can access any entertainment content at any time, from any communications device. Internet access is now joined with cellular data networks and other modes of connecting online:

> 'Many say that mobile technology is the future. It gets to consumers in parts of the world where internet reach is patchy', says Terry Jackson of Adultmoda, an adult mobile-advertising outfit. His firm served 4 billion mobile ads in January this year; by August it was dishing up twice that number. (*Economist* 2011, 64)

Interactivity will probably become increasingly important. In a pornographic industry that is now struggling to make money from selling product, this shift to mediated sex as a service is one way to remain viable. Videos can be pirated, but the moment of live interaction, where you input a request for a performer to do as you ask, is much harder to steal for profit (although, as the case of the gay chat site proves, not for blackmail). Just as other sectors of the entertainment industries are moving towards the experiential economy to monetize brands, the pornographic industries may eventually find that recorded audio-visual content is a loss-leader that brings audiences to a more lucrative live experience that they cannot get any other way.

One thing we can say with certainty – if the history of the printing press, photography, cable TV, VCRs, the Internet, and mobile phones is anything to go by – is that whatever innovations emerge in communication technologies, audiences will be there trying to work out ways of using them to make, distribute, or access pornography. Against the backdrop of that certainty, many things remain unclear. The Internet is massively changing the ways in which pornography is made, how it is distributed and how it is consumed. New communication technologies are changing the content of pornography, the kinds of people who are represented and the kinds of sex they can have. It is leading to a greater variety of sexual practices and kinks being represented publicly, to the formation of new communities, new identities, and new ways of being sexual. In turn, it reveals significant problems in the way that pornography has been defined and debated by scholars and activists alike. In the next chapter, we explore one of the most long-lasting frameworks of analysis: that of pornography as sexualized violence. It is predicated on the 'texts and effects' model, and continues to see pornography as discrete and definable objects that lead to bad sexual practices, which therefore can and should be eradicated from society. In this model, democratizing communication technologies are viewed as dangerous pathways to social and sexual decline. It, thus, speaks to the way that 'pornography' is used to signify a sense of anxiety felt when sex is made public and pleasure-driven.

3

Pornography and Violence

Does pornography cause violence against women? Whether you think the answer to that question is yes, no or maybe, the question itself seems like a commonsense way to approach the form. But this hasn't always been the case. It is only since the 1970s that public concerns about pornography have been framed predominantly in terms of violence, often conflating this term with harm, rather than the impact of sexually explicit materials on public and individual morals. Chapter 5 explores pornography governance and looks more closely at the dominant frameworks of morals and harm. Here we are particularly interested in how violence became central to activist and scholarly arguments against pornography, and to illuminate some contemporary dissent to that argument. The claim that pornography is a form of sexual violence continues to influence political and public health policies on publicly mediated forms of sexual expression. We have reached the point where the very word 'pornography' calls up the question of 'violence' as a kind of inescapable word association. In much current debate, pornography is defined as an act of violence and violence is defined as an inescapable part of human sexual relations – creating fraught associations and naturalized hierarchical power relations that deeply impact the perceived value and threat of not just pornography but all forms of non-normative, pleasure-based sexuality.

Quantifying violence in pornography research

American quantitative social science has an important part to play in the development of the now apparently commonsensical link between violence and pornography. American media research is a very individual beast, with a history that is quite distinct from the research traditions of other countries. Historically, as the chapter on technology briefly discussed, the dominant tradition has been on quantitative research to determine media effects on individual human behaviour. 1970 marks an important turning point for the imbrication of pornography with violence. This was the year that the US President's Commission on Obscenity and Pornography released its report on the place of pornography in American life. The Commission had been formed in 1967 as part of the progressive 'Great Society' social programme of president Lyndon Johnson (Lewis 2008, 8), and tasked to:

> analyse obscenity law and recommend a useful legal definition for obscenity . . . explore the nature and volume of traffic in pornographic materials . . . study the effect of such materials on the public . . . [and] recommend legislation to regulate such volume and traffic. (Lewis 2008, 10)

As the first major review of pornographic materials by a government body, the commission garnered numerous empirical studies on pornography effects, which comprised the bulk of the final report. It found 'no evidence to date that exposure to explicit sexual materials plays a significant role in the causation of delinquent or criminal behaviour among youths or adults' (Lockhart 1970, 27). Both Congress and the Senate rejected that finding, and newly elected president Richard Nixon denounced the whole report as 'morally bankrupt' (Nixon 1970).

It is difficult to find any academic journal articles that investigate the relationship between pornography and violence published before 1970. After 1970, a small flood appears – and it has never stopped. Quantitative social scientific research into pornography was part of a larger media-effects paradigm dominant in the academy at the time, which sought scientific measurements to control and curtail any media deemed deviant or subversive (Beaty 2005). As censorship boards waned in influence, and a new morality of personal experience and authenticity usurped the authority of religious and civic leaders, political interest in maintaining some measure of public regulation over media and popular culture turned to science.

The 1950s and 1960s were a tumultuous era as new levels of economic prosperity, political activism, and cultural permissiveness took hold. Yet attitudes towards gender roles and sexual behaviour still relied heavily on conservative beliefs in a natural order of heterosexuality. In this sense, the influence of Freud and conservative neo-Freudian arguments for 'normal' sexual development are important. Freud's work on sexuality transformed the way that people thought about sex, especially in the mid-twentieth century when the American sexual revolution took hold of the Western imagination (Illouz 2008). Particularly influential was his suggestion that the individual subconscious struggles between Eros – the life principle where desires are properly fulfilled – and Thanatos – the death drive or aggression principle that leads individuals on futile quests to have immature or downright deviant desires fulfilled in ways that are ultimately destructive to the psyche as a whole. For Freud, sex and violence were intimately related. The neo-Freudian theories that took hold in the postwar era appealed to monogamous heterosexual families as the correct path to a normal, healthy psyche, and assumed conventional gender roles of active/aggressive (masculine) compared to passive/docile (feminine) to define healthy sexual attitudes (Gerhard 2001). With such assumptions at the core of public policy debates on sexuality, and growing concern that media and popular culture were not fitting this model, it is not surprising that pornography became a major subset of media effects research. The search was on to prove that pornography was the apotheosis of violence and Thanatos.

Public campaigns against pornography before this period tended to be organized in terms of morality, with 'decency' and 'family values' being preferred concerns (Strub 2006). According to public opinion surveys, the overwhelming majority of Americans assumed that individuals accused of rape, perversion, or other sexual behaviours deemed deviant (including homosexuality) were also avid consumers of pornography (Lewis 2008, 14). Yet there existed little academic research investigating this connection. It would seem that the desire to link 'abnormal' sexual desire to pornography was not much more than a fallback position to maintain rigid heteronormative values and gender roles at the heart of the social fabric. Transforming such claims from moral suasion to scientific hypothesis certainly appeared more effective in reaching a counter-cultural generation for whom social convention meant very little and sexual experimentation was at the centre of a culture of personal growth. Thus, violence did not so much supplant morality as provide a scientific sheen.

Even though the findings of the President's Commission did not conclude that there was a measurable, causal link between pornography and violence, the very fact that the question was posed cemented the link in the public's mind (Lewis 2008, 13). The Commission made the relationship between pornography and violence the central question of concern when thinking about the government's role in managing sexually explicit material. It further suggested that psychology was the most suitable academic discipline for answering this central question.

Psychologists rely on two main methods to produce quantitative data about the relationship between pornography and violence – experimental studies and surveys. Experimental studies involve artificial settings where subjects are shown sexually explicit material and then their behaviour is tested in some way (see for example Malamuth 1981). By contrast, surveys gather data from pre-existing populations to map behaviour in naturalistic settings (see for example Garcia 1986). The results of all this research are profoundly contradictory (Fisher and Barak 1991). Some experimental studies find negative effects from consuming porn (Donnerstein and Berkowitz 1981) while others don't (Padgett, Brislin-Slutz, and Neal 1989). Some surveys find negative effects (Boeringer 1994), while others don't (Davies 1997). A 'meta-analysis' that compiled the data from a large set of both survey-based and experimental studies on pornography and violence was published in 1995. It discovered that experimental studies (in the laboratory) were able to demonstrate a connection between watching pornography and being more accepting of sexual violence towards women (what is known as 'the rape myth acceptance scale'), although it cautioned that other factors were likely involved. Non-experimental studies (in the real world) were unable to prove any such connection (Allen et al. 1995, 5).

The best lesson to be learned from such a conflicting morass of numbers is that statistics have a powerful allure in simplifying and codifying something as complex as sexuality and its publicly mediated expression. Journalists in particular love a good statistic to illustrate a story – putting a number against a trend, no matter how spurious that number might be, gives a strong effect of truth. Quantitative methodologies are indeed strongly 'reliable' – which is to say that they are very replicable: if any researcher follows the same methods with the same data they will produce the same result. But this is not to say that they are 'objective' in the everyday sense of the word that suggests 'unbiased' or telling a simple truth about an object of study.

To start with, quantitative studies can only answer the questions that researchers ask. For forty years now quantitative researchers have been exploring the negative effects of pornography, with a particular focus on the promotion of violence and the objectification of women. But there are many other questions that could be asked about the effects of pornography. Does consuming pornography lead people to talk more openly about sex? Does it lead to the creation of a stronger sense of sexual agency? Does it lead to more satisfying sex lives? These are also valid questions – but not ones that have been the focus of much quantitative psychological research.

A second and related concern with the unquestioning acceptance of any quantitative survey is that there are always value judgements involved in research, even research that uses numbers. Surveys are written in the language of their culture. Across most societies, unfortunately, inequities and injustices against women and non-normative sexual subjects persist, often in oblique, subconscious, and even outright repressed ways. As will be discussed in Chapters 4 and 5, appeals to family values, middle-class normalcy, and procreative sexual practices remain the cornerstones of national and transnational policies, as well as everyday public and mediated discourses on sexuality in general and pornography in particular. There are hundreds of ways of posing a question about pornography and violence against women. Understanding how key terms are defined and research questions are phrased can provide some insight into the inherent biases that any researcher would invariably hold.

Academic studies have a 'conclusion' section, which provides a qualitative explanation of what the numbers must mean for society. For example, a recent quantitative study claimed to find a relationship between exposure to sexually explicit material and 'beliefs that women are sex objects' (Peter and Valkenburg 2007, 381). But looking at the data it turns out that the researchers measured whether or not men thought of women as sex objects through a series of questions that included 'Sexually active girls are more attractive partners' (Peter and Valkenburg 2007, 389). People who agreed with this statement were given a higher score for treating women as sex objects. That is to say, these researchers are suggesting that an interest in casual sex with a woman who shares that same interest is the same thing as treating women like sex objects. In its effort to expose objectification, the framing of the question and the interpretation of the answer actually ends up objectifying sexually active women. Such problematic questioning is a familiar line in quantitative social science research on pornography. Dolf Zillmann, one of the most prominent quantitative researchers on the effects of pornography, has written that the negative effects of exposure to pornography include 'Cynical attitudes about love . . . [where the] institution of marriage is seen as sexually confining and raising children is considered an unattractive prospect' (Zillmann 2000, 42). He is also concerned about the normalization of 'sodomy, group sex, sadomasochistic practices' and 'promiscuity', all of which he sees as negative (Zillmann 2000, 41–42). As McNeill (2013) has argued, this is a heteronormative position that disadvantages people who may be polyamorous, or simply enjoy more flexible forms of relationships, or even people who don't want to have children.

A third concern is the confusion between correlation (two things happen at the same time) and causality (one thing causes another). Many articles have shown a correlation between consuming pornography and sexual adventurousness – for example, being more sexually permissive, having more sexual partners and so forth (Brown and L'Engle 2009). But none of these articles have shown causality – that consuming pornography causes sexual adventurousness. The reverse is just as plausible – that people who are more sexually adventurous are more likely to consume pornography. Social scientists know this very well – they understand the difference between correlation and causality – and the most rigorous among them are always careful to state this in their articles. For example, Braun-Colville and Rojas find that consuming pornography is related to various other sexually permissive beliefs and sexually experimental acts. They state explicitly that they can't say anything about causality:

> We are unable to establish whether exposure to sexually explicit material leads to engagement in sexual behavior or whether those individuals who partake in more high-risk sexual behaviors also have a tendency to seek out sexually explicit Web sites. (Braun-Courville and Rojas 2009, 161)

But despite this explicit acknowledgement, they write their article using language that implies that it is pornography that is causing the other sexual behaviours. Throughout the paper they make statements about 'the Internet's impact on adolescent sexual attitudes and behaviors' (Braun-Courville and Rojas 2009, 156), claiming that 'prolonged exposure [to pornography] can lead to . . . sexually permissive attitudes' (Braun-Courville and Rojas 2009, 157).

This discursive sleight-of-hand is common throughout anti-porn quantitative literature: social scientists know that they cannot prove causality but, all the same, the idea that there is a relationship between pornography and violence is so engrained in Western cultures that it seems like common sense. The unspoken assumption seems to be that while it cannot be proven, it must be pornography that is causing 'negative' effects like consensual, casual sex, experimental sexual practices, non-monogamous sexual relationships, and the like. Such work often claims a feminist concern for women's safety and wellbeing, and quantitative scholars such as Neil Malamuth and Ed Donnerstein have been strong allies of anti-porn radical feminists since the late 1970s. Yet, many others who identify as anti-porn feminists distance themselves from these methods (Boyle 2000; McGlynn 2010). They cite the same concerns we raise about how pornography, violence, and the sexually explicit are defined in ways that are 'neither internally consistent nor compatible with a feminist politics' (Boyle 2000, 190). In place, they argue for methodologies that demonstrate the 'harm' created within the 'cycle of abuse on which much audio-visual pornography depends' (Boyle 2000, 189). The primary source of evidence for this research is testimony from individuals who have either exited pornography work (usually but not exclusively women) or made the decision to stop watching porn (usually but not exclusively men).

Radical anti-porn feminism and the harms framework

Quantitative social science has become a powerful institution for linking violence and pornography in public debates. But not everyone accepts its claims to truth. In the 1970s and 1980s, anti-pornography radical feminists were one group that powerfully challenged the truth-value of quantitative research on pornography. For example, Susan Griffin, writing of 'the difficulty with social "science"' (quotation marks in original), claims that 'even more than physical science, social science is shaped by the values, the ideologies and the perceptions of the culture from which it is born' (Griffin 1981, 104). As Susan Cole wrote in 1992, 'I have never really felt that women needed a patriarch in a lab coat to tell us what rape feels like, or whether pornography feels like an assault' (Cole 1992, 10).

One place where activists and scholars gained their insight was from consciousness-raising sessions wherein women engaged in a collective process of investigating feminine identity, including 'body image, roles, feelings, choices, and sexuality as defined by a sexist society, by feminists, and by the individual woman' (Randolph and Ross-Valliere 1979, 922). It was an important tool of sexual self-discovery for many women in multiple ways. Betty Dodson, an artist and sex educator, developed sexual consciousness-raising sessions for participants to explore genitalia and experiment with various forms of sexual self-pleasure in a supportive circle of questioning women. In other circles, women recounted their experiences with non-consensual sex and outright violent assaults, and discovered that they were far from alone. Not only that, the tactics of shame and silencing that led women to believe there was something wrong with them to have felt violated were finally exposed and condemned. Thus, consciousness-raising not only provided an important strategy in a politics of greater sexual freedom for women. It also cemented the belief among some feminists that testimonial evidence of sexual violence was key to women's liberation (Basiliere 2009, 5). The anti-pornography movement adapted this methodology of 'listening to women' (Lahey 1991, 118) for its own purposes, collecting anecdotal accounts of women who experienced sexual violence and agreed that pornography played a significant role in harming them.

Sex and violence were central to feminism in the 1960s and 1970s. As Susan Griffin wrote in 1971: 'I have never been free of the fear of rape' (1971, 26). Yet, violence emerges as a central concern for feminist anti-pornography campaigners in a strategically different way from quantitative researchers. Whereas the statistical tradition in psychology draws upon a normative Freudian model and worries about the threat of violence to traditional heterosexual families, anti-porn radical feminists were genuinely and sincerely committed to the sexual freedom of women (Gerhard 2001). They saw in pornography a pattern of violence that, in their minds, lay at the very heart of traditional heterosexual relationships. Feminists steeped in the liberal politics of Betty Friedan and others radicalized their politics as their exposure to gender and sexual inequity grew, even within New Left culture. Consciousness-raising seminars shed new light on the extent of sexual violence experienced by women heretofore in shamed silence, and it shocked the movement into action. Before this, such issues as domestic battery, spousal rape, child sexual abuse, and other crimes were kept tightly closeted and the woman who spoke up was blamed for inciting the violence against her. Rape crisis centres, sexual health clinics, women's legal aid, and other support networks were launched by radical feminists outraged and emboldened by the stories told in these consciousness-raising groups.

It was in this context that Robin Morgan's 1974 article 'Theory and Practice: Pornography and Rape' introduced the influential formulation: 'Pornography is the theory, and rape the practice' (Morgan 1993 [1974], 88). Morgan's argument was intentionally provocative but it also served a purpose for emboldening political action against pornography within the women's movement, particularly in the United States. Over the course of the 1970s, for some American feminists, pornography was granted a special place as a conspicuously dangerous form of sexist culture (Bronstein 2011). In 1975, Susan Brownmiller, a founder of Women Against Violence in Pornography and Media (WAVPM), published *Against Our Will: Men, Women and Rape*, which again claimed a link between pornography consumption by men and their propensity to inflict violence on women. She wrote, 'pornography, like rape, is a male invention, designed to dehumanize women, to reduce the female to an object of sexual access . . . Pornography is the undiluted essence of anti-female propaganda' (Brownmiller 1993 [1975], 394). In 1978, the first Take Back the Night rally held in the United States was organized by WAVPM, cementing the link between pornography and sexual violence. Andrea Dworkin's *Pornography: Men Possessing Women* (1981) presented a book-length version of this argument, and led the way for a number of books making similar arguments (Griffin 1981; Kappeler 1986; Cole 1992).

As noted above, these accounts of violence and pornography did not embrace the empiricism of quantitative social science. Brownmiller asks:

Does one need scientific methodology in order to conclude that the anti-female propaganda that permeates our nation's cultural output promotes a climate in which acts of sexual hostility directed against women are not only tolerated but ideologically encouraged? (Brownmiller 1993 [1975], 395)

Radical feminists built their case for the violence of pornography through the stories of individual women:

I hope that these readers will listen to the voices of women whose lives have been devastated by the institutions of pornography, and I hope readers will understand that knowing these things have not happened to them will not take away the pain from the women who have suffered. (Cole 1992, 9)

The relationship between violence and pornography, for radical feminists, was evident from the stories of women who had been raped or attacked by men who were said to have been inspired to violence by seeing pornography. Rather than promoting a straightforward causality of the type that sustained quantitative social science research, radical feminist anti-pornography campaigners proposed a cultural-ideological model that assumed men are innately prone to the violent domination of women and that pornography was their chief weapon. 'Pornography instills the values of male dominance and female submission' (Cole 1992, 68). Moreover:

The fundamental problem at the root of men's behavior in the world, including sexual assault, rape, wife battering, sexual harassment, keeping women in the home and in unequal opportunities and conditions, treating them as objects for conquest and protection – the root problem behind the reality of men's relations with women, is the way men see women, is Seeing. (Kappeler 1986, 61)

Under this radical feminist model the problem was not so much individual brains and how they reacted to exposure to individual texts. It was 'the overwhelming effect of culture upon the decisions of our lives' (Griffin 1981, 105), and the ways in which men learned that the sexual abuse of women was a normal and acceptable behaviour in society.

Radical feminist theories against pornography introduced some very important initiatives still in practice today that raise awareness of the systemic problems of sexual abuse and the fact that it is still overwhelmingly experienced by individuals who identify as women, and perpetrated by cisgender men. Nonetheless, the focus on pornography raises two important and interrelated issues. Why even seek a theory of causation, and why choose pornography? In her book, *Battling Pornography: The American Feminist Anti-Pornography Movement, 1976–1986*, Carolyn Bronstein charts the rise of pornography as the central concern of radical feminist politics (Bronstein 2011). As she notes, Women Against Violence Against Women, one of the first groups to protest sexist and violent images of women in the media, campaigned against the Rolling Stones' album *Black and Blue* as well as against the X-rated film *Snuff*. It was only in 1979 with the setting up of the group Women Against Pornography that the anti-pornography movement decisively broke with critiques of the wider media (Bronstein 2011, 198–9). The reasoning may have been strategic – to guarantee more press coverage, and to build the widest possible political alliance – but this shift of focus did not convince all feminists. Some groups, including WAVAW, rejected the focus on pornography rather than media in general. They felt it could negatively impede women's fight for sexual freedom while giving a free pass to advertising and other forms of popular culture (Bronstein 2011, 165).

On one level, it is not hard to understand why some feminists saw pornography as a root cause of a culture of violence against women. There was a growing realization that sexual violence was far more pervasive than previously acknowledged, and there was a genuine urgency to challenge the social consensus that it was women's fault. That realization happened to coincide with the era of porno-chic, a term coined in 1973 by *New York Times* columnist Ralph Blumenthal. Pornographic films like *Deep Throat* (1972) and *Behind the Green Door* (1972) were enjoying mainstream acceptance as a sign of both cultural and sexual sophistication. The visibility and ubiquity of pornographic materials was only growing, especially with the advent of Betamax and VHS home viewing in the late 1970s. That pornography rose in visibility simultaneously with an awareness of the pervasiveness of sexual violence against women helped incite claims to a causal relationship, but this narrow focus proved divisive within the feminist movement.

A second problem – one that had devastating repercussions for feminist groups in America – was that while radical feminists claimed to be listening to the voices of 'women' in their campaign against pornography, in practice they only listened to the voices of women who agreed with them. Many feminist groups openly rejected the anti-pornography message, and women working in pornography were often insulted and offended by the way they were treated. In a 1981 documentary on pornography, a woman recalled her experience at a Women Against Pornography rally held in New York City:

> When I went and joined their ranks and told them that I was a stripper it was like 'Oh, poor you. Gee, where do you work? Oh those guys, oh.' They were making excuses for me. They were very condescending. And when you get anyone who's condescending, they've already passed a judgment on you. (Klein 1981)

The best and most loyal allies of the anti-pornography feminists were extremist conservative Christians on moral crusades to rid their communities of pornographic materials (Bronstein 2011, 243). This relationship, unfortunately, continues to this day, albeit often in highly fraught arrangements.

The disagreements between the anti-pornography movement with anti-censorship and sex radical feminists became the basis of the 'sex wars' of the 1980s. Tensions came to a head in 1982, and have never really ended. In April 1982 the women's centre at Barnard College, New York, held a conference in their series 'Scholar and the Feminist' entitled 'Towards a Politics of Sexuality'. Organized by Carol Vance, with Ellen Willis and Gayle Rubin also on the organizing committee, the conference did not include anyone from the anti-pornography movement. Members of anti-pornography organizations were so outraged by what they called this 'rigged and dishonest' approach (Leidholt, quoted in Dejanikus 1982, 5) that they contacted the administration of Barnard College and alerted them to the existence of a conference diary, which included sexually explicit drawings by women. The administration responded by confiscating the diary.

Under the name 'Coalition for a Feminist Sexuality and Against Sadomasochism', anti-pornography feminists picketed the conference wearing T-shirts that said 'For a Feminist Sexuality' on the front and 'Against S/M' on the back. They distributed a leaflet that named individuals and accused them of refusing to challenge 'a six-billion-dollar-a-year industry that traffics in women's bodies' (Coalition for a Feminist Sexuality and Against Sadomasochism 1983, 180). They accused these women of making, using and promoting pornography – and charged some of them with being sadomasochists. The organizers of the conference in turn accused them of using 'McCarthyite tactics to silence other voices' (Abelove et al. 1983, 180). Undeterred, anti-porn feminists accused 'sex positive' feminists of putting forth arguments 'in an ongoing monologue that not only suppresses dissent, but contemptuously dismisses those who would object' (Sere 2004, 270). Chicana artist and activist Cherié Moraga perhaps summed up the crisis best when she wrote in *Off Our Backs*, 'The way the movement is breaking down around sex makes me feel that women of color are being played between two white (sector's) hands. And, I don't like it' (Moraga 1982, 23). The fallout from this event continued for years, with participants telling ongoing stories of trauma and discrimination (Wilson 1983, 35).

The Barnard Conference is a key moment in the history of radical feminist thinking about violence and pornography – and particularly about the definition of violence. Is consensual power play a reiteration of the kinds of systemic violence experienced by women in society, and thus something to be rejected by feminists? The members of the Coalition for a Feminist Sexuality and Against Sadomasochism were clear on their position:

> We acknowledge that all people who have been socialized in patriarchal society – feminists and nonfeminists, lesbians and heterosexuals – have internalized its sexual patterns of dominance and submission.

But No More Nice Girls, Samois, The Lesbian Sex Mafia, and the butch-femme proponents are not acknowledging having internalized patriarchal messages and values. Instead, they are denying that these values are patriarchal. And even more dangerous, they are actively promoting these values through their public advocacy of pornography, sex roles, and sadomasochism and their insistence that this kind of sexuality means liberation for women. (Coalition for a Feminist Sexuality and Against Sadomasochism 1983, 181–2)

By contrast, the 'sex positive' radical feminists argued that an exploration of sexual practices such as sadomasochism could contribute to feminist politics:

The net effect of consensual S/M, no matter what the content of a scene, is not to oppress people . . . S/M does not mock the oppressed. It does indeed mock the oppressors, since real-life power-trippers can't abide sexual freedom in any form. (Califia, in Vance et al. 1983, 595)

Underlying this debate was a general question about which forms of sex were abuses of power. It led to other questions about whether heterosexuality was, by definition, a form of violence against women. The radical anti-pornography side was adamant in its distrust of men. Andrea Dworkin stated categorically, 'Male power . . . is violent and self-obsessed; no perception of another being ever modifies its behaviour or persuades it to abandon violence as a form of self-pleasuring. Male power is the raison d'être of pornography; the degradation of the female is the means of achieving this power' (1980, 38). It is no surprise that heterosexuality itself soon came under suspicion. For Susan Griffin 'the basic elements of rape are involved in all heterosexual relationships' (1971, 30). In such a context, 'it is necessary for women to become lesbians if they are to develop self-love and work effectively for their own liberation' (Jeffreys 1990, 290). In short, some argued that 'the choice of lesbianism is a form of political resistance' (Jeffreys 1990, 279), but only certain forms of lesbianism could be allowed as feminist. Among these activists, lesbian sadomasochism was still infected with the violence of patriarchal heterosexuality.

Given the increasing acceptance and more nuanced discussions around pornography today, it can be said that the 'sex positive' feminists won the Porn Wars – but there has been little celebration. The so-called backlash against feminism in the late 1980s and through the 1990s hinged largely on a popular perception that feminists were for the most part racist, homophobic, and above all anti-sex. Claims that feminism was dead were trumpeted in the media as anti-pornography activism became increasingly tied to an outmoded form of sexual politics that denied women the possibility of achieving pleasure without losing political consciousness. Yet, insistence that anti-pornography is not the same as anti-sex remains compromised by continued claims that certain sexual practices are necessarily degrading and degenerate and undermine the fulsomeness of intimate erotic relationships (see Dines 2010). Or, as Gayle Rubin (1984) argued in her paper at the Barnard Conference, anti-pornography radical feminism began from an unquestioned position that bad sex contaminates good sex. However, like any war, the losing side never fully surrendered. A contemporary anti-pornography movement continues to thrive, relying on arguments of a patriarchal/masculine propensity to perpetrate violence against women.

Neo-anti-porn activists

As the first wave of the 'porn wars' subsided, a new generation of scholars took up the fight against pornography. With a few notable exceptions, such as Sheila Jeffreys, this group does not involve many of the leaders of the anti-pornography movements of the 1970s. Gail Dines and Rebecca Whisnant, and a smattering of men, like Robert Jensen, have become familiar figures, particularly in the popular media, for their re-presentation of the argument that pornography is intimately linked to violence. Like their foremothers, they largely reject empirical quantitative research (Jensen and Dines 1998, 70) and they similarly promote a testimonial approach of 'listening to women': 'I have listened to women tell me about being raped and brutalized by men who wanted to re-enact their favorite porn scene' (Dines 1998b, 163). However there are some key differences in the work of the neo-anti-porn activists.

For example, the conceptualization of how pornography produces harm has become more nuanced. Whereas quantitative social science researchers maintain models of mechanistic causality, and early anti-pornography campaigners wrote in terms of 'propaganda', neo-anti-porn activists use three main discursive clusters in their claims that pornography causes harm: teaching, legitimation, and addiction. In the first cluster of metaphors, neo-anti-porn activists claim that men use pornography as a collection of 'textbooks' that teach them how to relate to women. From pornography, 'men learn to sexualize inequality and objectify women's bodies' (Russo 1998, 19). Pornography 'teaches that men become and remain men by penetrating women or other men' (Funk 2004, 341). Gail Dines' account of women's experiences emphasizes the role of pornography as a how-to guide:

> Women have talked about being forced by their partners to watch the pornography so they can learn how to dress, suck, fuck, moan, talk, gasp, lick, cry or scream like the women in the pornography. And many of these men get very upset if their partners don't react the same way as the women in the pornography. (Dines 1998b, 164)

In the second cluster of metaphors, neo-anti porn activists claim that pornography provides a justification for sexual violence. It plays a role in 'naturalizing, legitimating and perpetuating sexualized . . . violence' (Russo 1998, 11), by 'legitimizing the objectification of women, and by training men and boys to desire and expect compliant sexual servicing from women and girls' (Whisnant and Stark 2004, xiv). They claim it 'normalizes male sexual aggression' (LEAF, quoted in Kendall 2006, 116).

A third set of arguments claim that pornography does violence to the brain of the consumer, causing addiction:

> What pornography does to the brain is terrible; it activates the same dopamine reaction that gambling or other addictive behaviour does. The more you masturbate to porn, the more you want to; it is desensitizing, so you need more and more. (Naomi Wolf, quoted in Wyndham 2012, 17)

These claims are fortified by the work of Valerie Voon, who argues that brain scans of individuals diagnosed with 'compulsive sexual behaviour' are similar to those of drug addicts – with the usual caveat that 'inferences about causality cannot be made' (2014, 9). Nonetheless, the argument that porn turns men into sex addicts holds sway. The consequences, as neo-anti-porn activists argue, are that consumers (nominally 'men') are turned into addicts and then lose interest in sex with real people: 'Healthy men are having sexual dysfunction as a result of addiction to pornography' (Naomi Wolf, quoted in Wyndham 2012, 17). Porn addiction then leads to a 'pandemic of harm' which can 'condition men to view women as objects for their pleasure and desensitize them to the real pain caused by sexual exploitation, including sex trafficking. Thus, pornography creates the demand for sex trafficking' (Trueman, 2014).

Although the models of causation have evolved and become more complex, the attitude towards empiricism remains the same. The stories of harmed women and recovering men are presented as sufficient evidence that porn acts as a kind of 'magic bullet', constituting a significant social and psychological threat to the general populace. Counter-stories that may bring more insight into how pornography consumption is implicated in a wide variety of social and sexual practices are ignored. The definition of 'violence' has also evolved in neo-anti-porn activist discourses to become more complicated. Indeed, it is often replaced with the more nebulous concept of 'harm'.

Chapter 5 discusses some of the legal frameworks for harm and the difficulty in proving its effects within the justice system, but it remains a major pillar of feminist anti-pornography activism. In some instances, BDSM practice continues to be cited as harmful to women whether they engage in it or not (Obendorf 2006, 162). Others claim that 'uncomfortable' sex is harmful (Jensen and Dines 1998, 76). Still more argue that casual sex is a form of violence against women (Jensen 2006, 23; Langman 2004, 205). Various neo-anti-porn activists condemn 'unusual' sex acts such as double penetrations (Bridges et al. 2010, 1080), anal sex (Jensen and Dines 1998, 67), ejaculation onto the body or face (Jensen and Dines 1998, 67, 73), anulingus (LEAF quoted in Kendall 2006, 116), deep throating (Jeffreys 1990, 267), 'blow bangs' (one woman giving blowjobs to multiple men) (Jensen 2004, 33), or fistfucking (Jeffreys 1990, 217). Some argue that all penetration is a form of violence (Funk 2004, 341); while for others it is only of concern if it is 'hard, repetitious pounding by the man into the woman for several minutes at a time' as this 'likely results in, at the very least, soreness if not more severe pain' (Jensen and Dines 1998, 83). Some neo-anti-porn activists argue that using dildos or vibrators turns women into sexual objects (Dines 1998a, 61). Others argue that pornography's focus on sexual pleasure is in itself harmful: it teaches consumers that sex is about 'individual self-fulfilment' when it should really be about 'social change' (Russo 1998, 34). Some neo-anti-porn activists argue that representations of enthusiastic sex are harmful as they give men the impression that they don't have to work at giving women sexual pleasure (Jensen and Dines 1998, 72).

One very productive development of the discourses of harm is that it has raised important questions around racial and bodily difference and the classification of non-normative bodies as fetish objects in mainstream pornography. Such arguments begin with the recognition that racial and ethnic identity informs the particular ways that women are objectified through their sexuality (Collins 2000; Forna 2001). Specific to pornography, non-white women are oppressed not only by gender but also by disturbing racial stereotypes such as slavery (Afro-Caribbean) or submissive torture (Asian) (Bell 1987). After that, specificity becomes less of a concern. Neo-anti-porn activist Gail Dines makes the sweeping claim that 'all pornography uses sex as a vehicle to transmit messages about the legitimacy of racism and sexism' (2009). She further states, 'pornography delivers reactionary racist stereotypes that would be considered unacceptable were they in any other types of mass-produced media' (2009).

Few people would claim that other cultural forms within the media entertainment matrix have sufficiently challenged racist imagery. Yet, some choose to see mainstream racism as the fault of pornography (McKay and Johnson 2008). Leslie Heywood (2000) argues that black women athletes were increasingly subjected to a form of 'pornographic eroticism' in which their bodily skill was reduced to a sexual desirability informed by pornographic representations of black women's subjugation. The problem with this rather neatly sewn up argument is twofold. First, pornography becomes the ideological driver of racist representation and not part of a widespread, complex, and multi-faceted system of institutionalized media racism prevalent in everything from news coverage to pornography. Second, and related, pornography therefore is the problem, not racism, and is presumed once again to be a site where nothing but harm and violence is possible. We discuss the problematic arrangement of sexism and racism in anti-pornography discourse in more detail in the next chapter.

Systemic racism remains distressingly prevalent in all entertainment media, and thus it is important to call attention to its presence in pornography. However, we note that much neo-anti-porn work has not been as attentive to ongoing oppressions of queer sexualities. A growing body of critics (with the notable exception of radical lesbian separatist Sheila Jeffreys) argue that it is queer – or 'non-normative' (Bridges et al. 2010, 1070) – acts and sexualities that are most harmful to women. This is an important departure from 1970s radical feminism. For many activists of that era, heterosexuality itself was a suspect institution, and pornography's role in promoting heterosexual pleasure was one of its key dangers. Interestingly, separatist radical feminists today are less engaged in anti-pornography work than they are in promoting 'womyn-born-womyn' solidarity and denying trans women a place in the feminist movement (Goldberg 2014; Jeffreys 2014).

With the reduced focus on pornography among radical separatist lesbians, heterosexuality seems to be rarely named as a central problem of pornography in neo-anti-porn activism. Indeed, as the next chapter shows, the 'charmed circle' of romantic, heterosexual, married love against which 1970s radical feminism protested is now held up by some neo-anti-porn activists as the ideal that is damaged by pornography. Dines argues that porn is 'not about making love' but 'In porn, the man "makes hate" to the woman' (2010). We posit that this heteronormative turn

in anti-pornography activism has something to do with its problematic affiliation with conservative Christian family values campaigns. It has now reached the point where conservative Christian
and feminist activists co-edit books about the harms of pornography (Tankard Reist and Bray 2011). As a result of such alliances,
anti-pornography feminists rarely call into question heterosexual
romance, marriage, and the nuclear family.

Neo-anti -porn responses to gay and feminist porn

Importantly, some gay activists have joined the neo-anti-porn
movement to argue that gay pornography also leads to sexual
violence. This is because 'gay male pornography maintains the
very same social oppression – of women and queer men – that
it allegedly rebels against' (Funk 2004, 344). Even in 'those scenarios where male sexual partners "take turns" being the "top"',
'the characteristics of dominance and nonmutuality remain central
to the sexual act' (Kendall 2006, 116). In watching gay porn 'the
message is sent that some people want and deserve to have sex
forced on them' (Kendall 2006, 116):

> The linking of manliness with heterosexuality and overt masculinity is
> a common theme throughout many of these materials, with masculin-
> ity often gained at the expense of a woman or ostensibly gay male's
> safety and self-worth. The misogynistic overtones in these materials
> are clear. (Kendall 2006, 112)

And so gay male pornography teaches men to 'be in control', 'be
a top' (Funk 2004, 341). From such logic, it is possible to argue
against the very possibility of feminist pornography as all representations of sexual engagement imply unequal and dominating
power.

Some neo-anti-pornography activists claim that every sexualized representation, no matter what its content or mode of
production, automatically promotes inequality because when
people masturbate with pornography this involves an unequal
relationship between a human being and a two-dimensional object

(Mason-Grant 2004, 139). Thus, claim neo-anti-porn activists, people who use pornography learn to enjoy having sex with objects (pictures) – and so, when they have sex with real people, they treat them like objects (just as they would treat a picture). Rus Ervin Funk explains from his own experiences how he believes this process works:

> While looking at pornography, I developed a way of looking at women. I developed, if you will, a pornographic ethic. After looking at pornography, I did not look at women as colleagues, potential friends, or allies, or with any kind of gaze based on justice or caring. I looked at women based on how I compared them to the man-made images of women I saw in the magazines, or on the videos. The women I saw on the street, in classes, at meetings, etc. became simply 'fuck-able' to varying degrees. I looked at them and thought about the things I would like to do to (not with) them sexually. (Funk 2004, 339)

Robert Jensen tells a similar story about his experiences with pornography: 'by making female sexuality a commodity, pornography allowed me to control when and where I used it, and therefore used the women in it . . .' (Jensen 1998, 145).

For neo-anti-porn activists, then, all forms of sexualized imagery, no matter their feminist claims, promote hierarchical forms of sexual relationships (ultimately between human beings and objects), which men then transfer onto real women. It is a classic model of voyeurism and objectification that presumes no agency for the on-screen performer, nor an ability for the consumer to discern nuances of intention, desire, and sexual politics within the pornographic text. Furthermore, such claims are only made possible if it is also assumed that consent is so impossible as to be irrelevant to any discussion on pornography.

Violence and consent

Debates around consent in pornography are not new. During the porn wars of the 1980s, anti-porn activists claimed that the pro-sex radical feminists were victims of 'false consciousness' by their claims of sexual pleasure, and perpetuated systemic gender oppressions with their sexual role-playing and BDSM fantasies (Allen 2001, 516). Thus, Catharine MacKinnon claims, these women were something less than women. For her, a 'woman' is 'a being who identifies and is identified as one whose sexuality exists for someone else' (MacKinnon 1989, 118). In other words, womanhood was reserved for only those who admitted that consent was impossible in their sexual lives. Elsewhere, Dworkin and MacKinnon argue that only women who accept their oppression by pornography are constituted as citizens (more on this in Chapter 5). This means that MacKinnon can listen to 'women' – who will only ever, under her definition, tell stories of powerlessness and harm – and never have to listen to the voices of people (even those who were designated female at birth and/or self-identity as women) who disagree with her.

Many neo-anti-porn activists have distanced themselves from MacKinnon's arguments while still insisting that consent to kink or casual sex is a categorical impossibility for women. In the case of women who speak positively about enjoying pornography or other forms of non-normative sexual pleasure, such as BDSM, neo-anti-porn activists accuse them not of false consciousness, but of outright wilful deceit. Russo notes that 'feminist sexual liberals . . . have colluded with the pornography industry' (Russo 1998, 31). Rebecca Whisnant and Christine Stark claim that 'feminists who defend pornography and prostitution' are 'harmful to women, to feminism, and to the cause of social justice' (Whisnant and Stark 2004, xiii). Christine Stark argues that '[s]ex radical women do the pornographers' dirty work . . . They front for rapists and racists' (Stark 2004, 290). They are 'complicit in the abuse of women and children' (Stark 2004, 279). The only reason to listen to these particular women's voices is because 'They must be held accountable' (Stark 2004, 290):

> Many of the sex radicals are white, privileged academics who have made their careers championing the sexual exploitation of women by regurgitating age-old woman-blaming lies . . . Some sex radical women

are tricks who buy prostituted women or otherwise get pleasure from the harm prostituted women and girls experience. (Stark 2004, 284)

A slightly different suite of arguments exists for explaining why we should not listen to the voices of the women involved in the production of pornography: it is because they tend to minimize the harms they experience out of either desperation or ignorance. There is important work that has criticized the way that the pornography industry itself underscores the abuse many women experience as a marketing ploy centred on neo-liberal logics of choice and individualism (Boyle 2011). The question turns, though, on how best to highlight these issues. What should be foregrounded more: consent or violence? If the latter is defined strictly by a typology of acts that appear oppressive, coercive, or harmful – regardless of whether such feelings actually occurred – then there is no possibility to imagine a feminist or ethical pornography since pornography is somewhat tautologically defined as acts of violence against women. For neo-anti-porn activists, consent in fact becomes irrelevant, explained away as a diversion masking either false patriarchal consciousness or wilful selfishness and privilege.

Consent is a cornerstone of contemporary feminist pornography activism, and is discussed at length in the chapter on performance. However, it is important to note here that its absence from the arguments of neo-anti-porn activists goes to the heart of the connection of pornography to violence against women. If consent is excluded from the debate, then any depiction of extreme or heavily physical sex acts is wrong because it is violent. Really, any depiction of any sex act is violent because the very act of representing it is an instance of objectification, and objectification constitutes psychological harm.

A frequently cited definition of violence comes from Elizabeth Stanko:

Any form of behavior by an individual that intentionally threatens to or does cause physical, sexual or psychological harm to others or themselves. (Stanko 2001, 316)

Larry Ray suggests this is 'a reasonable working definition' except for its emphasis on the individual that doesn't take into account collective acts of violence. Furthermore, harm need not necessarily be conventionally violent but could also derive from acts of neglect or negligence (2011, 7). His expansion of the definition is interesting in that he still fails to take into account one crucial aspect missing from the definition: consent.

Prior to Stanko's accepted definition, Robert Baron and Deborah Richardson defined violence as:

> Any form of behavior directed toward the goal of harming or injuring another living being who is motivated to avoid such treatment. (Baron and Richardson 1994, 37)

By including motivation to avoid violence on the part of the individual Baron and Richardson bring consent into play, and exclude requested actions from the category of violence.

By contrast, both radical and neo-anti-pornography feminism insist that there can be no consent to any act deemed violent as per the definitions above. The ongoing debate, therefore, isn't about consent per se but about the root causes of its absence in pornography. Early radical anti-porn feminists claimed that women who said they appreciated depictions of violent acts in pornography were in fact experiencing 'the internalized expression of sexual subordination' (Cole 1992, 124). The reason for this is that a 'subjection willingly embraced can seem more tolerable than a subjection unwillingly borne' (Jeffreys 1990, 134). Contemporary arguments against consent focus on women working in pornography. Like women consumers, they are in 'denial' or have 'post-traumatic stress disorder' (Simonton and Smith 2004, 355), or are suffering from 'selective memory' (Lee 2004, 59) or 'delusion' (62). Carol Smith – who was a sex worker and then became an anti-pornography activist – notes that:

> They [sex workers] think it's great. They think it's wonderful. I could've looked you in the eye ten years ago and told you that I loved being in pornography, was proud of what I was doing and that I was having a great time. But now I can tell you that it's so far from the

truth. I was very convincing. I could convince you. I mean, I could walk up to a porn star today and she could tell me the same story and I can remember being in that place. (Simonton and Smith 2004, 354)

An anti-porn position that denies the possibility of consent to acts and images that appear on the surface as violent must also refuse the general proposition that all of us form our identities in various ways at various times in relation to the contexts of discourses and institutions in which we find ourselves. Violence, in this regard, needs to be thought about more as a negotiated contract, not as a monolithic and unidirectional force imposed upon unsuspecting and victimized women.

Conclusion:
The future of consensual violence in pornography

It is important to restate that this chapter examines the all-or-nothing position contained within a dominant strand of anti-porn feminism. That position relies on a nebulous and one-dimensional definition of violence, often conflating it with harm, and assuming that women are perpetually in a victimized position. This is a largely American-based narrative with strong influence around the world, but it is certainly not the only story. For example, Karen Boyle offers incisive critiques of the way that members of the pornography industry present coerced violence in docuporn and porn memoirs as a mundane and predictable aspect of the business (2008, 2011). Such work is important in distinguishing problematic and outright oppressive practices in some pornography. However, when anti-porn discourse emphasizes violence as an inherent aspect to pornography, with a corresponding de-emphasis on consent, it raises significant questions about the theories of power underpinning any position on pornography. Anti-porn feminism that takes an abolitionist position (the removal of all pornography from the world) assumes that sexual violence is an inevitability unless we erase any triggers to the biologically innate part of men's sexuality that requires the oppression of women. It therefore further assumes that men's sexuality is irrevocably and even naturally violent. It then extends that argument to assume that women's sexuality is naturally passive to the point of being inescapably victimized. For gay anti-porn activists, non-heterosexual relations are read through the prism of unequal gender relations between men and women, making heteronormative gender roles natural and essential even to queer-identified persons.

As discussed in the Introduction, and revisited throughout this book, popular or public debates on pornography are heavily marked by conflicting claims that pornography represents a malevolent 'power-over' women and marginalized groups such as queer men, or grants an intriguing 'power-to' that allows these same groups to reframe sexuality on the grounds of personal pleasure, alternative gender subjectivities, and subverting heterosexual norms (Allen 2001). The better arguments consider these two forms of power in dynamic tension with each other, managed through practices of consent where everyone involved in the sexual act genuinely attempts to understand what their partner(s) want(s), and the pressures they may experience in coming to those decisions. A feminist model of consent considers the ability to openly communicate desire, while recognizing that it isn't always possible for someone to simply say what they want without impediments (Bussel 2008, 43–4). Consent does not presume complete sexual empowerment, but it does insist on the ability of individuals to self-determine their sexual practices within the contexts of their specific circumstances. It also seeks to enable individuals to better articulate their desires and ask what their partner(s) want(s) in return. Thus, at the heart of this model of consent is communication. Without our speaking up and demanding that our lovers do, too, we don't ever truly know what they are thinking, which impedes us from having the sex we could be having (Bussel 2008, 43).

Importantly, feminist practices of consent have been deeply informed by the kink community and pornography workers. The kink community, which includes BDSM, erotic power exchange, role play, and fetish, has developed a number of strategies to help practitioners reach the high level of ethical negotiation demanded by risky and even dangerous sexual practices. Rachel Kramer Bussel suggests the use of a 'Yes, No, Maybe' chart – whereby, in a non-sexual setting, each partner works through an extensive list of sexual possibilities, noting for each one whether they are interested in trying it, not interested, or might be interested under certain conditions – as a way to remove some of the pressure around sexual negotiations in the heat of the moment (Bussel 2008, 44). In 'Cum guzzling anal nurse whore: A feminist porn star manifesta', gonzo porn performer Lorelei Lee insists, 'Never in a civilian sexual encounter had I been explicitly asked what I was and wasn't willing to do with my body. Never before had someone presented me with a list of options or said, "I want to do these three things today, how does that sound?"' (2013, 209). Furthermore, she realized that in engaging in these robust conversations about what she would or would not do on camera, she began to investigate her sexual life off-camera and how to delineate between the two (2013, 209).

Lee's discussion about the centrality of consent is particularly significant since her work is most known for pushing boundaries and testing the limits of her body through intense penetrations and fetish acts. In 2010, she was at the centre of an obscenity trial against John 'Buttman' Stagliano, a controversial figure in pornography debates due to his popularization of anal sex and gonzo porn in the 1990s. The film in question, *Milk Nymphos*, included shots of cum swapping, enema play, and racially charged language. Before the case was dismissed on strictly technical grounds, Lee was expected to take the stand to explain the health and safety standards on the set, including STI testing, before and after care for the performers, discussion of scene expectations, and negotiating agreement among all performers to proceed. Lee was interested in performing in this film precisely because it showed two women as sexual aggressors towards a man, seeking to go beyond the conventionally feminine in expressing women's sexuality, and to demonstrate how that could be done in a way that not only respects the performers but exhibits that respect on camera. In an interview with *Salon*, she rejects the idea that the sexual acts portrayed in this film are inherently violent or degrading and argues

instead that such determinations should come more from an interrogation of the working conditions and less from the actual work
performed. As she puts it, 'I've had infinitely more degrading experiences as a waitress or a barista in a chain coffeeshop than I've
ever had on set' (Clark-Flory 2010).

When critics claim pornography is inherently violent – defined
broadly as harmful, degrading, and coercive – and offer no corresponding recognition of the role of consent, it assumes traditional definitions of aggressive male sexuality and passive female
sexuality. As Lee herself notes, there seems to be too much effort
within anti-porn feminism to claim that women's natural sexuality is antithetical to the athletic and adventurous performances
in which she specializes (2013, 211). However, as evidence of
women's sexuality appears more and more to contradict such
claims, anti-pornography arguments must turn to a different
subject to save. Theories of sexualization and pornification of
culture draw heavily on anti-pornography activism but with a very
specific person in mind: the girl. In her, they imagine a subject pure
of pornography's violent assaults but who is perpetually at risk of
losing her true sexuality to its perverse seductions. Interestingly,
quantitative social scientists have also picked up on the potential
of the girl to reignite their research agenda against pornography.
Evidence of causal violence and harm may be difficult to prove in
the present, but the threat of it occurring in some indeterminate
future has once again united psychologists, moral crusaders, and
anti-pornography feminists in a common cause.

4

Pornification and Sexualized Bodies

We have thus far explored concerns about the impact of digital technologies on the distribution of pornography, and worries about the potential violence and harm represented by the form. These issues are brought together in one of the most familiar current debates about sex and media: the spectre of 'pornification' and its more generalized cousin 'sexualization'. If porn is so ubiquitous now in popular culture, relocated from the fringes and into the mainstream, then what are the consequences on our sexual mores? And how will this affect young people's attitudes towards sex and sexuality? Such questions, simplistic and overgeneralized as they are, have become grounds for intense scholarly, media, and governmental debate. The United States, Australia, and the United Kingdom have all released studies on sexualization and its supposedly deleterious effects on young people. Other countries have followed suit, naming sexualization as detrimental to women's emancipation and empowerment, such as in The Netherlands' Emancipation Policy 2008–2011. Best-selling treatises on 'raunch culture' (Levy 2010) and 'the end of masculinity' (Jensen 2007) claim that increasing levels of so-called negative and unhealthy forms of sexual expression are proof that pornography 'is damaging our lives, our relationships, and our families' (Paul 2005) and 'hijacking our sexuality' (Dines 2011).

In this chapter we consider the discourses of 'pornification', and how they have evolved and been used in popular discussions of sex. While we share concerns about gender and sexual inequities in the media, we are ill at ease with the fact that pornography has become the preferred object of blame for persistent crises of misogyny, sexism, racism, and homophobia in all forms of popular culture. We see these arguments paying scant attention to differences of history, socio-economic conditions, racial and ethnic relations, and distinct subcultures of sexuality. We are unconvinced by analyses that ignore all possible alternative sources of patriarchal attitudes, such as religious, medical, or educational systems. Furthermore, we contend that pornification proponents remain fixated on young women and girls as passive objects of a virulent media bent on turning them into mindless sex toys for young men and boys who are equally helpless at navigating a mediated culture of sexual entitlement.

This chapter examines the circuitous logic of the pornification debate and its close relationship with the sexualization thesis. Examining pornification and sexualization as framing devices, not empirically established social trends, allows us to unpack some of the unspoken assumptions around gender roles, their racist and classist underpinnings, and the privileging of heteronormative sexuality embedded within them. The chapter then goes on to explore some recent debates about hip-hop and African American urban subcultures as one particularly fraught area where pornification and sexualization are claimed to have infected popular culture and damaged young women's sexuality. To be clear, as media scholars we insist that concerns should be raised about the way that sexuality is expressed and understood in all forms of media and popular culture, including the pornographic. We are strongly opposed to sexist, racist, and heteronormative representations. Nonetheless, we challenge the claims of both sexualization and pornification that it is all pornography's fault (see Gill 2012a, 746).

Sexualization and government surveillance

Ground Zero for current concerns about sexualization in Western countries is the 2007 *Report of the American Psychological Association Taskforce on the Sexualization of Girls.* A report released a year earlier in Australia had impact within that country, but not the international reach of the APA report (Rush and La Nauze 2006). The definition employed by the APA quickly became the global standard. According to the report, sexualization occurs when:

- A person's value comes only from his or her sexual appeal or behaviour, to the exclusion of other characteristics;
- A person is held to a standard that equates physical attractiveness (narrowly defined) with being sexy;
- A person is sexually objectified – that is, made into a thing for others' sexual use, rather than seen as a person with the capacity for independent action and decision making; and/or
- Sexuality is inappropriately imposed upon a person. (APA Taskforce 2007, 1)

Subsequent reports mimicked this definition, including The Standing Committee on Environment, Communications and the Arts for the Australian Senate's report, *Sexualization of Children in the Contemporary Media* (2008), and the UK government-commissioned *Sexualization of Young People Review* (Papadopoulos 2010). These three reports comprise the bulk of our analysis in this chapter. They differ according to their national circumstances, but they share a number of common features.

First, rather than exploring the question of whether sexualization actually exists, or is a real problem, they start with the assumption that it exists, that it is easily defined, and that the media – rather than any other social or cultural institution – is primarily to blame for the problem. For example, the Australian committee was mandated to: 'Examine the sources and beneficiaries of premature sexualization of children in the media' – presuming without evidence that such sexualization exists and that there are clear winners and losers. The report goes on to state unequivocally that 'the inappropriate sexualization of children in Australia is of increasing concern' and that 'preventing premature sexualization of children is a significant cultural challenge' (2008, v). The report of the Committee is concerned about 'the sexualizing messages they [children] are receiving' (2008, 6) and assumes an exclusively negative influence by media. The British report is based around the assumption that 'sexualization is having a negative impact on young people's physical and mental health, and helping to normalize abusive behaviour towards women and children' (2010, 74). No evidence is provided in the report to support this assertion.

Second, the reports demonstrate a consistent concern with young women's sexuality to the exclusion of young men, and almost completely erase queer youth. While the APA acknowledges that sexualization can occur in anyone ('girls, boys, men, women'), they insist – as the title of the report suggests – that the primary concern must be girls because girls grow up to become women and the assumption is that adult women are sexualized beyond recovery (2007, 3). The report offers no justification for this assumption, nor does it address why it ignores boys altogether. Indeed, the phrase, 'sexualization of boys' does not appear once in the report, whereas 'sexualization of girls' appears 140 times. Similarly, although the Australian Senate report is ostensibly about all children, concern for girls appears at a much more frequent rate than boys. When sexualization of boys is discussed, the focus is on how boys contribute to the sexualization of girls by adopting the negative attitudes that they see in advertising and music videos (the two forms of mass media singled out in the report). The British report makes a clear distinction between the 'hyper-sexualizaton and objectification of girls on the one hand, and hyper-masculinization of boys on the other' (2010, 3).

Third – and we would argue, closely related to the second point – the reports all imply (although do not explicitly state) a heteronormative ideal of sexual development – the promotion of monogamous, romantic heterosexual sex as the best for young people. The Australian Senate report claims that schools, family, medical, and governmental regulation have important roles to play in realigning sexuality to 'reproductive health and relationships education' by forestalling sexual activity and promoting personal responsibility (2008, 77). In the report, 'normal' and 'healthy' sexuality is frequently touted, though poorly defined, as if it requires no explanation.

Included in definitions of abusive behaviour in the UK report is 'impersonal sex' wherein the hyper-masculinated young man exhibits 'a promiscuous, non-committal attitude towards sexual relations' (Papadopoulos 2010, 70). Casual sex – that is, sex between consenting individuals who do not have a prior intimate relational commitment – is defined as something young men do to objectify/violate young women and young women acquiesce to because they have internalized the processes of sexualization. In other words, young men do it *to* girls and young women do it *for* boys (2008, 60, 70). In taking such an approach these reports favour what Gayle Rubin called – as we noted in the Introduction – the 'charmed circle' of heterosexual, dyadic, intimate, relational, reproductive and vanilla sex (1984).

In one important way the British report makes an original contribution to debates about sexualization. The *Sexualisation of Young People Review* was part of a larger consultation process called *Together We Can End Violence Against Women and Girls*. Thus, it is concerned with 'the impact of the sexualization of young girls on violence against women' (2010, 3). This emphasis on a causal link between sexualization and violence takes the UK stance on sexualization one step further than its predecessors and repeats the foundational argument of anti-pornography activists. This theme of sexualization leading to sexual violence also appears in the Netherlands' 2008–11 emancipation policy, *More Opportunities for Women*. 'Gaining an understanding of the consequences of the sexualization of the role of girls and women in society' is listed under the objective of 'preventing and combating violence against women and girls' (2008, 49). As we demonstrated in Chapter 3, this linking of sexual explicitness with violence has a long history in the anti-pornography movement despite no convincing evidence to support such a link. When casual sex is understood as a form of violence we can see how this link underscores a heteronormative approach: the ideal culture is imagined as one where women successfully fend off the sexual demands of men and remain virginal until they are in committed, romantic, monogamous relationships. Casual sex is then understood as being violent because it 'ruins' girls for their inevitable role as wives and mothers.

As Amy Allen cautions in her analysis of the underlying theories of power within anti-pornography discourse, and as we repeatedly stress throughout this book, a dyadic and naturalized theory of gendered power (men are compelled by their biology to oppress naturally sexually passive women) not only imposes a heteronormative framework on sexual relations, but also makes exceedingly difficult any effort to consider specific relations of race, class, and other vectors of social oppression (Allen 2001, 516). We would also note that there is little space in these reports for female sexual agency – the possibility of women having sex on their own terms or in their own ways. They speak of a goal of 'empowerment' – but there is little sense in these reports as to what that might look like. All we are told by the authors of the reports is that it would certainly not involve women having casual sex, lesbian sex, exhibitionist sex, kinky sex, or any kind of sexual encounter other than traditionally feminine romantic heterosexual monogamy.

The concept of empowerment is a complex one. Some authors imagine complete agency, unrestricted in any way by the culture in which one has grown up or the social institutions within which one lives (see, for example, Corsianos 2007, 865). This, we insist, is a flat-out impossibility not only for sexual agency but for agency of any kind. The sexualization framework offers a poorly defined illusory goal of this kind of autonomy, whereby empowerment is an all-or-nothing high stakes gamble, and one sexual slip-up could devastate a young woman's chance for heteronormative happiness later in life. In fact, the APA clearly excludes sexual self-determination, defined by them as 'self-motivated sexual exploration . . . [or] age-appropriate exposure to information about sexuality' (2007, 1). Thus, the study begins from a position that so-called negative sexuality can be assessed in isolation from any considerations of what, exactly, self-determination, negotiation, and explanation of one's sexual identity vis-à-vis the media could look like. Instead, the APA provides a 'sexualization continuum' to measure only the negative impacts of the media on young women's sexuality without any critical introspection on how that negative sexuality has been defined. At best, a 'normal', 'healthy' sexuality is deemed one free of any social influences that may also include unhealthy or abnormal sexual cues that could potentially redirect a girl's sexuality into the dangerous territory occupied by too many women these days. The implication is that women, or more specifically young girls, are not actually capable of sexual self-determination, especially if they listen more to the media than they do to their governments, schools, and churches.

We are also concerned with the way that discussions of 'sexualization' have replaced 'sexism' in identifying and challenging inequitable gender relations. As an individualistic and normative term, sexualization diverts attention from the social systems of sexism, heterosexism, and misogyny. Social systems of inequity are understood as externalized impositions on an individual's self-awareness and identity formation that must be challenged and transformed. By contrast, sexualization is treated as an internalizing process that irrevocably alters an individual's identity. The focus of reparations in sexualization are not the systems of inequity but the individual who failed to adequately resist them.

Efforts to combat sexualization begin with the individual who is regarded as weak, susceptible, and irresponsible. Because of this, the emphasis on sexualization is able to make children the object of concern, and ignore feminist and queer concerns about social systems of (hetero)sexism and misogyny's overdetermination of sexual expression. It is, quite simply, easier to argue that children are weak and prone to making bad decisions when it comes to sexuality than it is to make this claim for adults. And, as McKee has argued elsewhere, such a move grants powerful social institutions like the APA or state-run commissions a controlling influence over the populace in ways that could never be accepted were it to be associated with adults (2010). Thus, the immediate and unproblematized connection between a passive, immature sexual identity and the apparently dangerous activity of non-relational sex offers an easy shorthand for moral panics that simultaneously sidestep any critical interrogation of sexism, misogyny, and queerphobia in all our social systems, not just the media, while indulging in melodramatic hand-wringing over silly, stupid, slutty girls.

The pornification framework

The sexualization thesis relies heavily upon an insistence that pornography has become more ubiquitous, easier to access, more explicit, more kinky, more violent, and more influential upon the generic and formal elements of other non-pornographic media – especially music videos and advertising. It is sometimes difficult to tease out the differences between sexualization and pornification, as the former quickly slides into the latter. Pornification is offered as self-evidently reliable proof that the media is more sexualized than ever before because of, well, porn. The UK's report places pornography at the centre of its connection of sexualization to violence, devoting a full chapter to it and naming 'the mainstreaming of pornography' as the lynchpin to the whole problem of sexualized media and its violent effects on women and girls (2010, 33). Australia's report notes that parents in particular express their concerns about media standards by connecting them to pornography. This unproblematized causal relationship between sexualization and pornography has resulted in an equally fervent concern over the 'pornification' of culture and its dire effects on otherwise 'normal' and 'healthy' sexual development in individuals, especially children.

Writers who decry a 'pornified' culture commonly take a heteronormative approach, bemoaning the loss of traditional gender roles in relation to sex. Pamela Paul was among the first to claim pornification was a dangerous trend 'fundamentally changing the lives of more Americans, in more ways, than ever before' (2005, 11). As with the writers on sexualization, of greatest concern to Paul is that porn may cause its viewers to become more 'sexually active and adventurous' outside the confines of matrimony (2005, 78). She sees sexuality as something to be curtailed, controlled, and redirected into other, more socially useful bodily activities like reproduction and dyadic love relationships. Porn is seen to obstruct that social good by its own inner logic that sex is something desirable and pleasurable in itself. The UK report's chapter on pornography similarly worries that pornography is 'increasingly normalizing aggressive sexual behaviour, blurring the lines between consent, pleasure and violence', but it is also 'normalizing what until very recently would have been seen as niche practices such as the removal of female pubic hair' (Papadopoulos 2010, 46). Here BDSM and genital grooming are linked as practices that are – the writer believes – self-evidently bad.

As with the concept of 'sexualization', 'pornification' is discussed by writers as though its definition is straightforward and agreed-upon. Clarissa Smith makes clear that this is not, in fact, the case as she offers an extensive catalogue of instances that have been claimed as examples of pornification in the media and popular culture:

> When pornographication links together Bratz dolls, pornstar t-shirts, playboy key rings, pole dancing, lads mags, push-up bras for teenagers, breast enlargement, breast reduction, vaginaplasty, Viagra, the sexual self-representation of sexblogs, sexting, Beautiful Agony and SuicideGirls, anime and hentai, burlesque, Cosmo, Miley Cyrus, Abu Ghraib, Max Hardcore, Girls Gone Wild, Sex and the City, etc. we should be ringing alarm bells at the conflation and supposed obviousness of the connections, not wringing our hands and looking to government for solutions. (2010, 106)

As with sexualization, writers on pornification rely on an essentialized sexual binary, where women are passive and must be protected from predatory male sexuality.

Nikunen et al. (2008) note that the APA's highly Americanized account of sexualization is by far the most popular definition used by regulatory and medical agencies around the world. Pornification derives out of this same context. Thus, both concepts rely on an ahistorical and immaterial context (Smith 2010, 104). Lack of attention to the historical and geographical specificity of pornography's interconnectedness with other cultural systems makes possible dangerously homogenous arguments that not only treat all sexual media as potentially pornographic but also all pornography as violent, objectifying, and oppressive. Again, as we insist here, such claims rest largely on the contradictory presumptions of the two most dominant groups within the anti-pornography movement: social conservatives and anti-porn feminists. In the case of the former, it is presumed that the natural or ideal form of sexuality takes place within a dyadic two-sexed relationship (one man and one woman). However, a cornerstone of the latter's politics is that pornography replicates a natural order of male domination over women. Since men are naturally prone to sexual violence against women, proponents of pornification assume that the only solution is to foreclose any possibilities of sexual experimentation and instead contain men in drab sexual relationships with sexually disinterested women where that instinct will never be ignited (Paul 2005, 154). The sexualization/pornification thesis largely ignores issues of racism, class oppression, sexism, heterosexism, or any other vector of power and inequity and its unique operations in a given society because that would undermine the overwhelming authority granted patriarchy and masculinity as universal and even biologically innate (Allen 2001, 515).

The neat effect of the sexualization/pornification thesis is that once men are exempted from consideration with the assumption that they are unable to help themselves, the onus is then placed not on men nor even on women but on girls to suitably modify their sexuality and be constantly vigilant that their behaviour does not lead to any triggering incidences. Anything other than a demure, marriage-minded sexuality is evidence of a weakness of character with attendant negative consequences that will not only last their lifetime, but will also result in the downfall of the men they ensnare. The relentless scrutiny of adolescent and prepubescent girls and the assumption that they are weak, insecure, and ignorant of the cultural forces seeking control over their sexuality brings with it, for us, a nagging discomfort. When girls are made the vessels of both purity and its contamination, they can simultaneously be denied any agency in determining their own modes of sexual self-expression while given full responsibility for all manner of behaviours and attitudes defined as sexually degenerate, including those behaviours directed at them. To put it bluntly, the cautionary words of the sexualization/pornification thesis are not intended to empower girls as sexual subjects but, rather, blame them for their power as sexual objects.

Sexualization, pornification – and sexism

We have explored the ways in which the concepts of sexualization and pornification have been used in government reports and
popular writing. It should be clear by now that although we are
deeply concerned about sexist, racist and heteronormative structures in our cultures and the role of media and other representations in supporting such structures, we are not convinced that the
concepts of 'sexualization' and 'pornification' are helpful replace-
ments for the idea of 'sexism' in understanding the production and
maintenance of gender inequity. Rather it seems to us that what is
actually at the heart of the sexualization and pornification theses
is a worry that a 'structure of feeling' – what Raymond Williams
defines as 'meanings and values as they are actively lived and felt,
and the relations between these and formal or systematic beliefs'
– is undergoing a cataclysmic realignment (1977, 132). In this
case, the structures of sexuality are seen as realigning themselves
in ways that not only transgress but also outright oppose their
naturalized containments within systems of personal restraint and
reproductive family values. As with any period of intense sociocul-
tural change, not everyone is happy about it – but that does not
mean that change is necessarily bad.

In his book, *Striptease Culture: Sex, Media and the
Democratization of Desire* (2002), Brian McNair's central thesis is
that, if anything, the ubiquity of pornography within an 'advanced
capitalist' society is an indicator of its attentiveness to women's
rights (2002, 56). His claims rest on the twofold argument that
access to sexually explicit images and discourse has expanded
significantly, and that therefore a 'more diverse and pluralistic
sexual culture' has also emerged. Furthermore, pornography is the
most significant catalyst for this sexual democratization, its higher
profile helping to spur a public debate about sexuality in which
pleasure and desire are foregrounded (2002, 12). McNair takes
special note of criticisms of pornography and their underlying class
biases. Such arguments, he points out, are grounded in fears that
audiences for pornography may come to understand and express

their sexuality in ways that no longer conform to heteronormative and bourgeois values of restraint and reproduction. Thus, fear over pornography is reflective of an imagined loss of a privileged class' rule over the hegemonic culture of sexuality, articulated as a concern to protect the ignorant and innocent (2002, 52).

In contrast to the dire warnings associated with pornification, McNair claims that the proliferation of pornography, and the increasing ease of both production and consumption, creates alternative 'structures of desire' that affect industry practices and audience demand alike (2002, 56). Other early contributors to the democratization of desire argument note that enhanced access through social media technologies blurs the boundaries between production and consumption, making it possible for individuals to perform both roles, and on very different terms than that determined by a mainstream heteromasculinist industry (Kibby and Costello 2001). As our chapters on technology and performance both demonstrate, the use of pornography as part of a larger toolkit to confront and challenge heterosexism, misogyny, and queerphobia – not to mention their investments in other forms of oppression such as racism and classism – is rapidly expanding. Pornification, in this context, is an affirmative stance that values sex and sexuality as legitimate spaces of self-making in what McNair calls 'the pornosphere': a reconfiguration of sexual space that collapses the boundaries between the already porous private and public spheres (2002, 37).

McNair's enthusiasm for pornification is infectious and his claims that the sexual rights of women and queer subjects are being advanced by this more explicit sexual culture are difficult to contest on many levels. This is not, of course, to suggest that all individual instances of pornography are positive. We have argued throughout this book for an understanding of the many different kinds of pornography, and the different technological, cultural and economic contexts that sustain them. As Allen notes, early feminist sex radical counter-claims to the anti-porn movement placed heavy emphasis on individual empowerment and resistance. Arguments that porn is, therefore, inherently transgressive and resistant to patriarchy were marshalled against anti-porn feminism – and were just as specious as claims that it was inherently oppressive (2001, 517). She cautions that when we 'conflate empowerment with resistance . . . we can appeal to what turns us on, as if this is automatically liberating and subversive, as if this is where the argument should stop' (2001, 521). We contend that this is where the argument should begin, by exploring the specific material conditions by which publicly mediated forms of sexual expression are produced, circulated, and consumed; with attention to how social structures of gender and sexual inequity inform these practices and are in turn influenced by them. Most importantly, such work proceeds without bias or assumption that all forms of publicly mediated sexual expression are inherently good or bad, healthy or unhealthy. That is not to say that no value judgements can be made, but rather that we must articulate how and why they are made and in whose interests.

Moving away from a homogenous vision of pornography also means moving away from a claim that society has been 'pornified', as though that is a single thing. Assuming pornification as a real social condition and not a convenient framing device from which to make proclamations about good or bad sexuality prevents close examination of specific situations whereby particular representations and practices are being combined in various media to articulate a complex matrix of sexual roles, relations, and values. We believe that the concept of sexism retains its explanatory power, and provides us with a more useful way to examine the media's role in promoting and sustaining gender inequity than does either 'sexualization' or 'pornification' (Gill 2012a 741). As Elizabeth Wilson warned decades ago, 'To have made pornography both the main cause of women's oppression and its main form of expression is to have wiped out almost the whole of the feminist agenda' (1992, 28).

What is most lacking in the sexualization/pornification thesis is a suitably sophisticated theory of power that treats publicly mediated sexuality in all its forms, not just pornography, as an ongoing process of negotiation, oppression, resistance, transgression, contradiction and confusion. Such a theory exists in the writings of feminists concerned with media sexism – and the place of sexuality in it. Rosalind Gill references a long list of feminist media scholars concerned with the 'technology of sexiness' who have revealed its centrality within neo-liberal logics of individual empowerment and personal responsibility (2012b, 493). Angela McRobbie expresses frustrations with the 'user-friendly' display of naked women in media addressed to heterosexual men alongside her satisfaction at seeing some women publicly subvert those displays into acts of defiance and discomfort. She argues for new vocabularies to be produced that will help speed the collapse of the 'heterosexual matrix' of sexuality (2008, 235). Linda Duits and Liesbet Van Zoonen insist that the sexualization debate is nothing more than a return of the porn wars only now focused on the bodies of girls instead of women. They contend that any claim of rampant sexualization in the media is only tenable if it ignores two key principles of media analysis: texts are polysemic and reception is active (2011, 492). These scholars share an insistence that sexism – defined here as systems of gender and sexual oppression that rigidly yet imperfectly enforce patriarchal and heteronormative controls over different practices of bodily expression – should remain at the core of any debates around sexually explicit media and its audiences.

Returning the debate to one of sexism rather than sexualization undermines heteronormativity and an essentialism of gender differences. Such a move also refuses the kind of individual psychopathology of media effects so preferred by these government reports, and rejects the belief that there can be easy solutions to complex issues resulting from shifting public and private modalities of sexuality. Importantly, thinking about sexism rather than sexualization insists on more localized, grounded analysis of the specific articulations of sexuality by different audiences under different historical and material circumstances. As Gill points out, sexualization posits 'the girl' as a unifying, universalizing category of feminine subjecthood that, in her unwavering quest towards sexual respectability, is coded as white, Americancentric, middleclass, and heterosexual (2012b, 493). In so doing, the sexualization thesis fails to notice how racism, classism, ageism, ableism, and heterosexism set boundaries so that only certain bodies are deemed worthy of sexual empowerment, often through the appro-priation and denigration of other sexual cultures (2012a, 741).

Whose pornographic gaze? Hip-hop and white prurience

If 'pornification' is the answer to every question about gender inequity, then racism, classism and other structural issues simply vanish. This tendency becomes especially noticeable in contempo-rary critiques of hip-hop and black urban musical cultures whereby conflations of racism, sexism and homophobia are explained away as the pernicious influence of pornography. In such critiques, if 'girls' are regarded as ignorant and innocent of the very practices of sexuality they embody, then women of colour are even more ignorant – but nowhere near as innocent since their bodies have long been marked as sexually irresponsible. We touched on the ways that neo-anti-pornography activists decry the racism they see in pornography in Chapter 3. As we stated, by treating the racism apparent in some pornography as akin to violence, pornography is blamed for the very existence of racism rather than exploring the specific structures of racism in different textual and production practices of pornography. In the pornification debates, this simpli-fied approach makes possible a media moral panic that entangles fear of racial difference with fear of sexual difference, treating black urban culture as a bottomless pit of uncivilized and debased sexual behaviour.

It is thus not surprising – even despite their decline in promi-nence – that music videos were the most commonly referenced media form cited in the reports on sexualization discussed above. Concerns ring out over the visual and aural economies of sex present in popular music, with particular emphasis on hip-hop and other genres associated with African American urban cultures, such as rap and R&B (APA 2007, 6; Papadopoulos 2010, 50). Framed strictly around the concept of sexualization, the reports do not seek to identify and clarify specifically sexist portrayals of women's sexuality. Indeed, the APA report makes no distinction between

117

'sexual behaviors [that] were sexual objectification' and 'women dancing sexually' (2007, 5). Australia's report recommends 'that broadcasters review their classification of music videos specifically with regard to sexualizing imagery' (Australian Senate 2008, 42) but offers little clarity other than 'there can be some debate as to whether certain styles of dancing can be classed as "visual depiction of sexual behavior"' (2008, 42). The UK report also forwards its concern that 'the portrayal of sexuality in popular music has become less subtle, [and] more explicit' (Papadopoulos 2010, 49; citing Arnett 2002). The UK report acknowledges specific issues arising for young black women as they contend with both their racial and gender identity, but only in the sense that they are being led astray by a 'pimp/ho chic' prevalent in the musical culture of their own communities (Papadopoulos 2010, 51).

It is not only the sexualization reports that use the concept of pornification to gloss over the structural factors that support racism. In their study, 'Women of color in hip-hop: the pornographic gaze', academic authors Margaret Hunter and Kathleen Soto decry a culture wherein 'sex work and pornographic culture (their economics and gender relations) have merged with rap in form and content' (2009, 172). Rather than untangling and materially situating 'the commingling of sex, race, objectification and violence in contemporary mainstream hip-hop', the authors simply contend that the genre is acutely vulnerable to pornification, without much explanation as to why. Thus Missy Elliott's anthemic 'Work It' is as bad as 50 Cent's 'P.I.M.P' because both make unapologetic, 'mundane' references to sex work (Hunter and Soto 2009, 177).

In their study of Chicana rap, Beauty Bragg and Pancho McFarland claim, 'Xicanistas struggle to reclaim their bodies from pornographic patriarchal definitions. They use the erotic to empower themselves socially, culturally, and politically' (2007, 5). However, the authors state, such efforts are persistently thwarted by the pornification of the music industry, which insists on a 'power over others. It is the power to destroy, degrade, and despise' (2007, 4). Thus, they claim, the problem is porn, not patriarchy.

Similarly, Albert Oikelome blames pornographic America for transforming a potentially uplifting project of nationalist Nigerian hip-hop into a sexist and misogynist genre that replicates the '"porno-visuals" like their Western counterparts' (2013, 88). He explicitly denies the specific problems of sexism in Nigeria, and is instead concerned with pornification as something foreign to all of Africa:

> It is totally 'un-African' to discuss the subject of sex in the graphic manners being portrayed in the hip-hop movies and songs. And just like their Western counterparts, Hip-hop singers are more likely to be sexist in that females are depicted as sex objects, yet in general, in African society, women are treated with respect and dignity, not as sex machines. (2013, 90)

The problematic assumption in the hip-hop pornification thesis (as a substrata of the sexualization/pornification thesis) is that black culture in particular cannot withstand the overwhelming and subsuming power of pornography. Moreover, and all too often, this critique claims that white suburban boys are the majority audience for hip-hop music (although empirical evidence for this fact is not typically provided) (Burgess 2012). Such claims seek to both discredit hip-hop as authentic black experience, and 'ignite national hand-wringing and hysteria among whites' (Sharpley-Whiting 2008, 19). The spectre of white men slavering over black women's bodies reiterates longstanding racist distrust of black women and hysterical fears that they could coopt and contaminate the white race with their wanton sexuality. This vision of dangerous black female sexuality is rooted in paternalistic and colonialist assumptions that it is not only risky and unruly, but also lacks the maturity and intellectual sophistication to be properly guided into healthy sexual fulfilment. In this sense, adult black woman are claimed to be as immature as young white girls alongside disturbing insinuations that they deserve their sexually oppressed status.

This hip-hop pornification thesis has two equally dangerous trends. One version is actually less concerned for black women's sexual autonomy than it is with safeguarding white women against any encroaching blackness to their sexuality. Another version is directed at black women but wants to contain them within a 'politics of respectability' in which they are exhorted to mimic white, middle-class heteronormativity. In neither case are the racial politics of media moral panics over hip-hop explicitly named as such, but are referenced obliquely in terms of fears of sexual promiscuity.

This elision of race and sexuality has a long and dishonourable history. Sander Gilman (1985) traces the history of Euro-American medical, governmental, psychological, and cultural discourses and how they converge to produce a pathology of the sexualized woman that irrevocably links non-heteronormative and undomesticated sexuality to a racialized character of Africanness – savage, primitive, excessive. As Richard Dyer explains in his classic text *White* (1997), popular discourses of heteronormativity bind race and gender together by positioning desire on a continuum from darkness (which is understood to be pleasure and passion-oriented) to whiteness (marital and reproductive duty-bound). Race thus becomes less about genetic or geographical heritage than it is about individual conduct and personal responsibility to uphold codes of heterosexuality, patriarchy and gender difference (Doane 1991, 246). Anybody who favours sexual pleasure rather than sexual duty risks behaving in a sexually 'black' manner, whatever their genetic inheritance. The persistence of this connection between race, gender, and sexuality within an individualized, psychological framework places the onus on white women to steel themselves against an invasive blackness, defined generically through specific genres of popular culture rather than in outright racist terms. Simultaneously, black women are exhorted to seek out the mollifying sexual respectability of white, middle-class heteronormativity and refuse the pleasures of their own cultures (Higginbotham 1993).

Mireille Miller-Young critiques the racist underpinnings of the hip-hop-pornification argument and claims instead that hip-hop and pornography use each other's tropes to mutually reinforce their desired status as subversive and counter-cultural to mainstream media, often through the reinvocation of racist and sexist stereotypes of black women's bodies (2007, 2010). While pornography has appropriated aspects of black culture since the late nineteenth century, Miller-Young notes that both industries began exploiting each other's generic tropes, conventions and stereotypes at an ever-accelerating rate beginning in the 1990s (2007, 262). Hip-hop genres such as 'Dirty South' and 'Bounce' heavily incorporate references to strip clubs and sexually suggestive dancing such as twerking, while musical stars such as Snoop Dogg have been featured as non-performing hosts in combination hardcore pornography/music video DVDs. In his exploration of Dirty South's rise from regional subculture to the mainstream of the hip-hop music industry, Matt Miller notes how the explicit sexuality on display in Dirty South was as much an effort to challenge and reclaim a long and brutal history of racist stereotypes of black sexuality as it was an inevitable cooptation by a white-dominated industry steeped in that same racism. Importantly, Miller does not criticize pornography or the sex work industry. Rather, he points to the wide matrix of decision makers and gatekeepers within the music industry – journalists, marketers, record labels, etc. – who ignore the complexity of the music's messages about race and sex and reducing them to insidious stereotypes about black people's sexual rapaciousness (Miller 2004, 206).

Miller performs an important analysis by keeping his focus on the particular investments and machinations of the music industry and holding it to account. Similarly, as Miller-Young suggests, pornography must be held to account for the way that women of colour are 'ghettoized' by framing them within the trappings of commercialized hip-hop culture (2010, 224). She notes that pornography can perpetuate racist stigmas against women of colour by treating their sexuality in fetishized and devalued ways. At the same time, she refuses a one-dimensional analysis that regards any representation of sexuality and sex work by women of colour as necessarily exploitative or evidence of either pornification or hiphopification. The sexualization/pornification thesis cannot imagine that for any black woman, sex work could be a rational or useful decision, because under this framework sexuality is defined in strictly negative, oppressive terms, and, as Gilman, Dyer, and others note, 'good sexuality' has historically been aligned to a presumed 'whiteness'.

Not surprisingly, women of colour are able to clearly articulate their investments in the pleasures that both pornography and hip-hop offer and their negotiations of the racism contained within them. Sinnamon Love, adult performer and fetish model, states that she is more concerned with making a statement about black women's sexuality than about gender because 'so many people fight the good fight on behalf of (white) women and so few are fighting for black women like me' (2013, 99). She notes that black women in pornography are too often relegated to one of two roles: 'assimilated to appear as close to white as possible' ('they are almost one of us') or completely ghettoized to reflect debased images of black culture (it doesn't matter because 'they are only one of them') (2013, 99). In this regard, she seems to be critiquing the influences of hip-hop ('Every curvaceous woman doesn't have to have booty shorts and bounce her ass as if she's in a music video' [2013, 104]) and white men's limited exposure to the variety of black culture in all its forms, for the systemic racism in much mainstream commercial pornography. Crucially, she offers a way out of this impasse by producing and performing in her own work: 'For me it is about agency. My black feminism is about helping women like me to be able to claim their sexuality in the face of decades of mis-education of African American women who were made to believe that they must choose between education, marriage, and family, or sexual freedom' (2013, 104).

Arguing on behalf of hip-hop, Theresa D. Sharpley-Whiting eschews the pornification thesis and insists instead that hip-hop demonstrates complex interconnections of racism and sexism. She further argues that it provides an important space for the exploration of women of colour's sexuality, beauty and labour against a moralizing panic that reduces their bodies to defiled otherness (2008, 156). Since the 1990s, highly successful hip-hop artists such as Missy Elliot, L'il Kim, and Rihanna have confronted such issues directly in their music. In the aforementioned song 'Work It', the apparently offending lyrics advise women that there 'ain't no shame' in any work they do to stay 'ahead of the game' – be it in an office or in a sex entertainment club. As bell hooks puts it:

> Ain't nothing wrong with sex work, 'cause a girl's gotta do what a girl's gotta do. And every girl I know who is working a sex tip has her reasons, but it ain't about sexual freedom. It's about getting paid. L'il Kim knows that. She's seen and done it all. She knows when it's fantasy and when it's real, when it's about getting paid or getting free. (1997)

Artists and critical scholars alike who refuse to name black sexuality as dangerous or damned foreground the specificity of the exploitative and discriminatory regimes that treat women of colour as less economically valuable and more sexually available than white women, both in and out of sex work (Agustin 2007; Brooks 2010; Chapkis 1997; Chang 2000). Calling women of colour sexualized or pornified fails to address the history of their exploitation and abuse under colonial and postcolonial rule, the current conditions wherein they still experience disproportionately higher levels of sexual and domestic violence, and ongoing systemic economic, political, and social discrimination that streams them into low-paying service labour, sexual or otherwise. Most importantly, such arguments fail to acknowledge women of colour's agency and ability to negotiate all these complexities in defining and expressing their own sexuality.

Our consideration of how women of colour are positioned in the sexualization/pornification thesis is to point out its homogenizing and essentializing approach to all gendered representation, based on a belief that all women experience the same sexual treatment from all men. As such, we are emphatic that this thesis is manifestly inadequate to understand the experiences of a wide range of women who do not comfortably fit the white, middle-class, heterosexual ideal that government reports on 'sexualization' hold up as a one-size-fits-all model. Thinking about 'sexism' – with its multiple articulations to racism, classicism, ableism and a range of other structural factors that discriminate against less powerful subjects – is, we argue, a more useful way to engage with these issues. We furthermore insist that sexism be understood as something that is felt, recognized, and negotiated. In that sense, the pleasure of media is not merely bait to entrap young women into regimes of objectification, exploitation, and violence – as sexualization contends. It can be that, but it can also be a way out of this trap: a way to confront rigid systems of sexuality that ignore self-determination and the political potential of pleasure to resist various structures of oppression, including but not limited to racism, classism, and heteronormativity.

Conclusion: The future of porn and the pleasurification of culture

Writers who claim that we are becoming too 'sexualized' or 'pornified' want young people to stick to conservative, monogamous, heterosexual, romantic, reproductive-oriented (i.e. heteronormative) sex. All other forms of sexual agency are deemed 'false empowerment' (Liss et al. 2010, 56) or 'false consciousness' (Allen 2001, 516). Such an approach treats relationships and reproduction, rather than pleasure, as the end-game of sex. It assumes that all women are the same, as are all men. It believes that men are biologically hardwired to dominate women, and regards sex as men's preferred weapon of oppression. It ignores differences in sexual subjectivities and the ways that other social identity systems, such as race, class, and ability, feed into our experiences of gender and sexuality. It assumes that everything that is pleasurable (the popular media) is bad, whereas all forms of duty (formal schooling, governmental allegiance) are good.

There's also a total lack of evidence in most of these reports about what the young women (and men) who are supposed to be at risk from sexualizing media actually do with the entertainment content they receive. Within the sexualization/pornification framework and with the limited questions at their disposal, the reports consistently fail to consider that perhaps the producers and consumers of sexual media are engaged in a thoughtful negotiation of their own self-expression and are seeking greater plurality than what is available to them through the more restrictive, state-sanctioned systems.

As feminist media scholars we are not happy with the current state of gender relations around the world. Too much gender inequity persists, even in those regions where McNair's ideal advanced sexual-capitalist democracies appear to thrive. Women still struggle with unequal pay, casual sexism, and restricted access to reproductive and sexual health services. There is much work to be done, but we don't believe that claiming the world is becoming 'sexualized' or 'pornified' helps improve things. At the same time, we don't believe that the best way forward to combat gender inequity is simply more pornography. Rather, we need to move away altogether from causal models of social-sexual contamination and recognize that any given society is imbricated with systems of hierarchical oppression and their potential refusal. Thus, changing the framework of debate and establishing different questions about the relations of gender and sexuality in the media can better illuminate these issues and all their complexities. The problem isn't that the media is teaching young people to have sex. In our opinion, the problem is that too much of the sex on offer isn't grounded in principles of respect, consent, diversity, equity, and open communication.

If anything, we think that the 'pornification' thesis is counterproductive in developing a world with greater gender equity. For 'pornification' writers, where pornography is present, sexual self-determination is impossible. The risk of such a position is that it cannot account for a person engaged in either the production or consumption of pornography as anything other than damaged, unhealthy, and abnormal. It therefore reinforces the stigmas and oppressions of individuals who fail to meet a very narrow litmus test of sexual normalcy. Furthermore, such an approach pathologizes pornography as a problem of individual weakness and privileges a sexual status quo with scant attention to the embedded hierarchies of power that maintain it. Eventually, as the keen government attention to sexualization around the globe suggests, such frameworks can lead the way towards increasingly restrictive governance schema that seek to curtail and even prevent a plurality of sexual expressiveness. What this means for sexual citizenship is explored in detail in the next chapter.

5

Pornography Governance and Sexual Citizenship

When governing pornography, whose interests should be fore-grounded? The answer influences the way that pornography is monitored and controlled in any given society. At the heart of por-nography restrictions, however determined, is a firm belief that the state has an abiding interest in the sexual practices and attitudes of its citizens. Thus proceeds the assumption that the state must provide some guiding principles that delineate acceptable forms of sexual expression. It is a rare nation that does not have some kind of regulatory, criminal, and/or juridical framework delineat-ing the extent of pornography's reach. The vast variety and com-plexity of these schemas make it impossible to provide a detailed overview of the global matrix of pornography governance. Thus, the goal of this chapter is to outline some of the key principles and frameworks that are used in the governance of pornography, and provide some examples of how those frameworks have been enforced in different countries. In so doing, we reflect carefully on the question posed above to determine the governmental subject of pornography.

Embedded within any governance framework for pornogra-phy is, of course, the question of censorship. However, it must be clearly noted that the issue for us is not about censorship in simplistic for or against terms. These arguments are about as pro-ductive as the pro/anti positions in relation to pornography itself. The suppression of certain forms of expression is present across all societies in different forms at different levels. Therefore, we recognize that censorship is an inevitable outcome of state over-sight and turn our attention to the underlying assumptions and values that determine those limits as they concern pornography.

It is necessary first to delineate three levels of governance as concerns sexual expression in general and pornography in particular. The first level of governance consists of regulatory frameworks – sets of rules laid out to enact governmental policies. They can govern content, dissemination, labour conditions, etc. The key to regulation is the assumption that the act or object itself is legal (or, more nebulously, decriminalized) and is therefore socially acceptable as long as it conforms to certain standards. This is the case, for example, in Canada, where in 2014 the regulatory body that governs national content in broadcasting sanctioned three Canadian-owned adult entertainment channels for failing to provide sufficient pornographic programming featuring Canadian production and performing personnel (Hopper 2014).

The second level of governance involves criminal legislation, which actively prohibits certain acts or objects from a society, with severe penalties often imposed on violators. Indonesia passed the draconian 'Bill Against Pornography and Pornoaction' in 2008 to prohibit not only pornographic media but also any kind of public behaviour that is deemed pornographic. This vague and broad-ranging law places a maximum twelve-year prison sentence for 'pictures, sketches, photos, writing, voice, sound, moving picture, animation, cartoons, conversation, gestures, or other communications shown in public with salacious content or sexual exploitation that violate the moral values of society' (Marks 2012). In 2012, the Religious Minister sought to use that law to impose a ban on skirts above the knee (Marks 2012).

Finally, there is the juridical level whereby regulatory and criminal controls are administered and assessed by the courts, taking into consideration constitutional and charter rights. In 1987, police in Manchester, UK, arrested sixteen men after a videotape of consensual BDSM acts was confiscated. Despite the fact that there was no complaint made and that all of the sixteen men arrested insisted that they had consented to the activity, the courts found the men guilty of 'unlawful and malicious wounding' and 'assault occasioning actual bodily harm' (R v. Brown [1994] 1 AC 212). The courts decided that consent was not sufficient justification for the state to allow such acts to occur. Four years later, in a case involving heterosexual BDSM, the defendants were exonerated on the grounds that consent had been obtained (Houlihan 2011).

Pornography governance is bound to highly contentious and unstable definitions of what constitutes acceptable sexual citizenship. This term refers to the ways that an individual's sexuality is valued according to a preconceived ideal of a national culture. Citizenship is here defined as the constitution of a subject with full rights, freedoms, and securities according to the laws of the nation to whom they have sworn allegiance (by birth or by naturalization). Sexual citizenship, therefore, refers to the ways that a subject's sexuality – their desiring, pleasuring, intimate and reproductive selves – determines their adherence and access to the rights, freedoms, and securities of citizenship more broadly.

Sexual citizenship can include issues such as the right to marry, to engage in particular sexual acts, to have access to birth control, and the right to be allowed to raise one's children, among a range of issues. In this it vacillates uncertainly between private sexual acts and the public expression of those acts. It therefore problematizes distinctions between public and private, which have been a crucial marker of citizenship more broadly. Historically, sex and sexuality have been deemed the most private aspect of a person's subjectivity and therefore the area where the state should have the least oversight – as long as it is contained with a heteronormative family unit (Giddens 1992; Richardson 1998; VanEvery 1996). Thus pornography, understood as a publicly mediated form of explicit sex for the purpose of inciting pleasure, crosses boundaries between both public and private and between sex-for-pleasure and sex-for-family that upset the social order. These facts invite questions about the definition and positioning of pornography in state regimes and how 'pornographic citizenship' might be constituted. Networks of sexual regulation, criminalization and jurisdiction appeal to a mode of sexuality that often runs counter to the open-ended pursuit of personal pleasure (Giddens 1992, 2). The repercussions of pleasure- and self-oriented sexuality upon patriarchal, heterosexual, and familial privilege cannot be exaggerated. They leave the state in the bewildering position of trying to freeze or fix an ideal image of sexual citizenship that is constantly challenged for being insufficient and outdated (Berlant 1995, 382).

This chapter explores the literature on sexual citizenship and how it takes into account debates about pornography's value to a society. It then examines some of the key frameworks of state oversight of pornography that have been operationalized by various countries and notes both commonalities and significant differences. The focus is predominantly on Western nations of Anglo-European descent (Australia, Canada, Great Britain, and the United States). Generally, most countries have some sort of legislation protecting minors from accessing sexually explicit materials. And, of course, the largest global network of pornography governance concerns the use of minors in sexually explicit media, with trafficking as the second highest priority. Few countries tolerate such abuses, at least formally. The child is a limited citizen, perhaps best understood as a fantasy of a future possible citizenship, and therefore increased surveillance and protection by the state is generally deemed warranted (Berlant 1995, 381). By contrast, when the focus of state oversight is on the production and circulation of sexually explicit media featuring consenting adults and targeted towards an audience of consenting adults, conflicts over the balance of rights and responsibilities to the state create contradictory and inequitable conditions of sexual citizenship. Thus, the focus for this chapter is on pornography for/by adults, although we do refer back to our review of child abuse materials from the chapter on industry, and of the way 'the child' is used to support state intervention into sexual media in the chapter on pornification.

Until the end of the twentieth century the dominant approach by Western governments to sanction pornography used the language of obscenity and community standards. In other words, pornography was subject to a determination of the limits of acceptability in accordance with an amorphous 'public'. In this chapter we explore the ways in which the anti-porn feminist movement of the 1970s and 1980s pushed for a new framework that moved sanctions from such a morality-based paradigm and towards governance based on the concept of harm, both personal and social. Thus, pornography became subject to a determination of its ability to negatively impact another person's citizenship rights either directly or obliquely. We then examine emerging debates about so-called extreme pornography and anxieties around the porn performer. It should be noted that the boundaries between the three forms of governance described above are highly porous. They bleed into one other in accordance with the political culture and the need to find a winning strategy to contain and control pornography so that it does not unduly compromise the state's ideal definition of sexual citizenship.

Sexual citizenship and pornography

'There is no place for the state in the bedrooms of the nation.' So spoke then Canadian Justice Minister (later Prime Minister) Pierre Elliot Trudeau in 1969 when he introduced sweeping legislation to decriminalize homosexuality, legalize birth control and abortion, and relax laws pertaining to 'gross indecency'. Canada was among many nations seeking to modernize its criminal code to reflect a more liberal attitude towards sexuality at this time. Yet, despite the lofty values asserted in this famous quote, the Canadian government continues to have a controlling interest in the bedrooms of the nation, as do most states. Regulations on the production and distribution of explicit sexual materials, criminal codes of obscenity and indecency, or harm and exploitation, and court decisions on such rules continue to play a major role in the maintenance of a national sexual culture and the definition of a good sexual citizen. Thus, it becomes apparent that any invocations to the bedroom as a 'zone of privacy' – the term used by the American courts when legalizing birth control in 1965 (Griswold v. Connecticut 381 US 479 (1965)) – is not an a priori right but, rather, is a privilege bestowed by the state onto certain citizens who willingly conform to an ideal sexuality.

Given the use of the trope of the bedroom – the most private space of the private home – it should come as no surprise that the ideal sexuality proposed by the state appears too often as a family ori- ented vanilla heterosexuality. We saw this in Chapter 3, where too often non-normative forms of sexuality are claimed as a kind of vio- lence, and Chapter 4, where pornography is seen to have some kind of sinister power to undermine educational, religious, and public health systems that insist on intimate relational sex as the only path to a healthy, happy life. Scholars including Berlant (1995), Donzelot (1979), Giddens (1992), Hubbard (2001), Richardson (1998), Rubin (1984), and Weeks (1995) have outlined the histori- cal conditions by which the heterosexual (or at least heteronorma- tive) reproductive family has been cast as the only valid path to full sexual citizenship. As such, Giddens notes, state controls over sexu- ality use the concept of privacy to prioritize the sexual pursuits of heterosexual men and their right to control those of women (1992, 2). Others note that alongside such patriarchal systems are deeply troubling compulsions to 'out' homosexuality or other 'dissident sexualities' in order to resuppress them as anathema to a national sexual culture (Bell 1995, Hubbard 2001). So-called 'scary hetero- sexualities' or 'outer limit' sex include, at the very least, fetishism, kink, BDSM, group sex, masturbation, sex toys and implements (Hubbard 2001, 57; Rubin 1984, 281). Pornography belongs in there because not only can it provide individuals with the depiction of such acts, but also, through its very form as publicly mediated sexual expression, it crosses the 'zone of privacy' and thrusts such acts into public space.

Thus, the delineation between public and private becomes a key mechanism in state strategies to control the limits of sexual citizenship. Diane Richardson argues that the very construction of dialectical public/private spheres is sexualized, founded upon the belief that only those forms of sexuality that are best at serving the state deserve privacy (1998, 90). These 'deserving' sexualities are so designated precisely on the grounds that not only do they take place out of sight, in the bedrooms of private homes, but also when in public they are invisible and unremarked upon in ways that normalize and stabilize their privilege. Phil Hubbard notes how present day responses to dissident sexualities visibly mark them as other and use that visibility to expel them from spaces of citizenship (2001, 60).

Governmental attempts to impose heteronormative forms of sexuality lead to new kinds of outlaw sexual citizens – the 'citizen-pervert', as David Bell names them. They live in the nebulous zones between private and public, seeking the right to visibility and thus acceptance – but that acceptance is awkwardly defined as a right to privacy. Meanwhile the state works counter to those desires. Bell writes:

> Indeed, law's eruptions into the private begin a process of reducing or even erasing the private as a site of pleasure, rendering pleasure a public – and by that a political – issue. For sexual dissidents there is an obvious tension between the desire for privacy and the need to be public, while law must draw things into the public only to thrust them back into a reduced private. (Bell 1995, 147)

The occasional moral panics over pornography, therefore, serve to justify state incursions into sexual practices. Pornography is regarded as not only a document of dissident sexualities in action, but also as a potential handbook on how otherwise good sexual citizens might practise deviancy.

Although this chapter is particularly concerned with how the state controls sexuality through its governance of pornography, exerting a 'power-over' citizens, we also note that those controls are resisted, subverted, transgressed and outright challenged by the citizen-pervert to keep systems of sexual governance in a state of flux. Pornography not only pushes sex into public space, but also in so doing, draws its constituents into ethical debates about community standards, harm, and bodily sovereignty grounded in the specific conditions of consent, respect, and communication among those citizens most deeply implicated (McKee 2013, 17). By contrast, governmental schema to limit pornography tends to downplay or outright diminish the rights of the citizen-pervert in favour of the upstanding heteronormative and wholly privatized sexual citizen. Yet, as the examination of obscenity and commu-nity standards in the evaluation of pornography that follows dem-onstrates, such attempts often fail to produce the desired results.

Whose community, whose standards?

Pornography tends to appear in state legislative codes both as itself and as material deemed obscene due to its excessive and distasteful sexuality. Obscenity is as difficult a term to define as pornography, but that has not prevented most countries from trying. In the United States, the law aligns it with the 'lewd, lascivious, or filthy . . . of indecent or immoral character' (18 US Code § 1465). It relies on a court ruling to determine obscenity:

> The basic guidelines for the trier of fact must be: (a) whether the average person, applying contemporary community standards would find that the work, taken as a whole, appeals to the prurient interest; (b) whether the work depicts or describes, in a patently offensive way, sexual conduct specifically defined by the applicable state law; and (c) whether the work, taken as a whole, lacks serious literary, artistic, political, or scientific value. (Miller v. California, 413 US 15, 24 (1972))

The UK's Obscene Publications Act does provide a brief list of specific sexual acts that constitute obscenity, including bestiality, urolagnia, and bondage, but applies the law unevenly according to whether 'the effect of any one of its items is, if taken as a whole, such as to tend to deprave and corrupt persons who are likely, having regard to all relevant circumstances, to read, see or hear the matter contained or embodied in it' (1959 c. 66 (Regnal. 7 and 8 Eliz 2), Section 1). Australia's obscenity laws are largely devolved to the states and territories, with a national Classification Board charged with refusing classification to materials that are '(a) indecent or obscene, or likely to be injurious to morality; or (b) likely to encourage public disorder or crime; or (c) undesirable in the public interest' (Parliament of Australia). Canada classifies obscenity under the section in the Criminal Code entitled 'Offences Tending to Corrupt Morals' (sec. 163). Bizarrely, the act defines two major instances where morals can be corrupted: obscene materials which depict 'the undue exploitation of sex, or of sex and any one of more of the following subjects, namely, crime, horror, cruelty and violence' (sec, 163.1(a), sec. 163.8); and crime comics (sec 163.1(b), sec. 163.7).

Thus, obscenity as it relates to pornography is somewhat obscurely defined as any depiction of sexuality that may compromise the moral character of the upstanding sexual citizen, the decision of which is tacitly left to the courts. Therefore, this ideal citizen is presumed more than defined, based largely on matters of middlebrow taste and what Lynda Nead has called the 'connoisseur'. In her study on *The Female Nude: Art, Obscenity and Sexuality*, Nead argues that definitional power over obscenity has been the privilege of the 'male, heterosexual connoisseur' (1999, 14). This imagined connoisseur has the ability to take what is otherwise the debased nakedness of pornography and clothe it in the transformative potential of art. Importantly, however, it is not the connoisseur whose sexual citizenship is at risk. Rather, he determines and bestows sexual citizenship on the bodies made available to him by authorizing the difference between the rarefied pleasure of respectable artistry and the pornographic pleasure of voyeurism (Nead 1999, 88). In other words, it is the body on sexual display that must earn its own citizenship from the connoisseur who is presumed to naturally possess it.

Thus, community standards become entwined with appeals to heightened privileges of taste and artistry as much as decency and morality, often with conflicting results. Three important cases that test these boundaries of pornographic abjection and artistic empowerment highlight the contentious configuration of sexual citizenship on the grounds of community standards. They are the Mapplethorpe Obscenity Trial against the Contemporary Arts Center in Cincinnati (1990); the trial against a series of paintings by Eli Langer on display at the Mercer Union Gallery in Toronto under newly passed child pornography laws (1994); and the seizure of photos by Bill Henson from the Roslyn Oxley9 Gallery in Sydney under threat of prosecution for 'publishing an indecent article' (2008). In each case, the works were initially denounced as obscene and pornographic. Significantly, in each case, the charges were either dropped or the defendants found not guilty.

A brief overview of the circumstances for each case is necessary.

A retrospective of works by photographer Robert Mapplethorpe, entitled 'The Perfect Moment', began touring the United States just months after his death in March 1989. Controversy dogged the show, reaching its peak once it opened at the Contemporary Arts Center in Cincinnati in the Spring of 1990. Police toured the exhibit and pressed charges of obscenity against the curator and the centre based on seven images: five of men including a self-portrait of Mapplethorpe with a bull whip inserted into his anus ('Self Portrait with Whip'), and two of children with their genitals exposed ('Rosie' and 'Jesse Mcbride'). Significantly, the demand for seizure and arrest came from anti-pornography groups. The National Coalition Against Pornography had its headquarters in Cincinnati. Judith Reisman, a conservative anti-porn activist who had previously called Mapplethorpe a Nazi and a child molester, was an expert witness for the prosecution (see Reisman 1989 F1, 4). On 6 October 1990, the jury acquitted the defendants on the basis that the images were obscene but may also have some artistic merit (Kidd 2003, 7).

Three years later, in Toronto Canada, police used a newly drafted law on child pornography to charge artist Eli Langer and the Mercer Union Gallery with obscenity. The Attorney General later dropped the charges against them but proceeded with charges against the actual works of art. This led to the absurd scenario of having to mount the artwork in the courtroom so that it could be present for its defence. Expert witnesses for the prosecution included the head of the police force's anti-pornography unit and the leader of the Citizens for Decency movement. The judge, who as a lawyer had a prior history of defending clients accused of obscenity and pornography offences, ruled in a similar and equally unsatisfying middle ground as the Mapplethorpe case. He declared that the works had sufficient artistic merit as to not be considered pornography but he also upheld the law that made it a crime to 'own, make, exhibit or sell anything that depicts a sexual act by anyone under 18' (Farnsworth 1995).

The final case under discussion here took place in Australia in 2008. When the head of Bravehearts, an anti-child porno-graphy group, saw an invitation for an upcoming exhibition by

Bill Henson that featured a highly stylized photograph of a nude prepubescent girl, she made a complaint to the police, who raided the Roslyn Oxley9 Gallery and seized the works. Henson and the gallery were charged under child pornography and indecency laws. The ensuing public controversy spurred politicians to make public statements supporting the police action. Perversely, as Brian Simpson notes, their statements that the images (all untitled and numbered) were 'offensive and disgusting', 'absolutely revolting', and just flat-out 'porn', had the effect of turning the subjects who had consented to the photos with the support of their parents into prurient spectacles of a sexual grotesque (2011, 292). Ultimately, a storm of protest from the art world in support of Henson led to charges being dropped and the artworks returned. The Australian Classification Board gave the images a PG rating, which meant that minors could attend the exhibition with parental guidance (The Age 2008).

What each of these failed cases has in common is that they included images of child sexuality produced by adult men, and they pit the community standards of anti-pornography crusaders against those of artistic and intellectual connoisseurs. Even more noteworthy is that in each case it was the upholders of values such as morality, decency, and child protection who lost their case against groups insisting on the values of freedom of expression and artistic merit. It draws attention to the fact that 'community stand- ards' are not merely inadequate to the task of defining obscenity but, moreover, the ideal standards of a familial and innocent sexu- ality imagined by the laws simply do not hold up against public scrutiny. The citizen-pervert, it would seem, prevails.

While many scholars tend to use these cases in order to explore the nebulous distinction between art and pornography, we suggest that such debates continue to uphold the idea of community stand- ards, only with a rather different community in mind. A response of 'not obscene' due to the consecrating envelope of an artistic and intellectual elite still leaves the legal concept of obscenity depend- ent upon a value judgement by an economically and culturally privileged community of art scholars and judges. Worth noting is that in the two cases that went to trial, the ruling struck a fragile middle ground that acknowledged the legitimacy of obscenity but granted determining authority to a community standard of freedom of expression and boundary pushing – as long as it was suitably 'artistic'. In the Henson case, it was the coordination of the art world that pressured authorities to withdraw charges.

By this point it was already obvious to anti-pornography activists from both the social conservative and feminist sides that in order to have success in prosecuting pornography, they needed to stop talking in terms of 'obscenity'. Clearly, using that terminology allows judges to make decisions based on the standards of the sexually liberal, artistically informed, connoisseur. During the height of the porn wars in the 1980s, a new framework was put forward that defined the problem with pornography not as obscene in the traditional moralistic sense, but rather as harmful to citizens (Plamondon and Weber 1996, 64). Anti-porn feminists in the United States and Canada initiated a number of legal challenges in the 1980s and 1990s to bring the concept of harm into the definition of obscenity as it pertains to pornography, and to insist that pornography was an infringement on women's rights as citizens whether or not they were directly engaged in pornographic production or consumption. Four municipal ordinances in the United States and one Supreme Court case in Canada tested the viability of harm in upholding charges of obscenity relating to pornographic materials. As we shall see, it has proven to be as much if not more elusive a legal status than community standards.

(H)arming the citizen against pornography

As the lead architects of the 'harm' argument on both sides of the border, Andrea Dworkin and Catharine MacKinnon stated emphatically:

> The act of introducing the antipornography civil rights ordinances into the legislative arena gave pornography's victims back some measure of the dignity and hope that the pornography, with its pervasive social and legal support, takes away. The ordinances, in formulating por-

nography's harms as human rights deprivations, captured a denigrated reality of women's experience in a legal form that affirmed that to be treated in these ways violates a human being; it does not simply reveal and define what a woman is. As ending these violations and holding their perpetrators accountable became imaginable for the first time, and women participated directly in making the rules that govern their lives, the disgrace of being socially female – fit only for sexual use, unfit for human life – was exposed as a pimp's invention. In these hearings, women were citizens. (1997, 5)

This form of legislative activism against pornography, therefore, is predicated on the assumption that pornography constitutes an infringement on women's rights as citizens as defined by a country's constitution. Such an approach can only succeed where the constitutional rights of the country involved are suitably limited. In the United States, it pits the civil rights of women against the First Amendment of the Bill of Rights that respects freedom of speech in broad terms. In Canada, the Supreme Court's decision on pornography and harm rested on the first section of the Charter of Rights and Freedoms, which insists on 'reasonable limits prescribed by law'. The difference is stark and reflects why harm failed repeatedly in the United States while becoming enshrined in Canadian law.

Working both together and separately, Dworkin and MacKinnon led initiatives in Minneapolis (1983, 1984), Indianapolis (1984), and Massachusetts (1992). MacKinnon also co-wrote the factum submitted by the Legal Education and Action Fund (LEAF), a feminist legal activist organization in Canada, to the Supreme Court of Canada when it was deciding on the legal status of harm. The differences between the approaches in two different countries include civil versus criminal law, the prioritizing of rights within constitutional law, and the status of gender equality in the respective Constitutions. The United States does not explicitly oppose gender or sex discrimination. Canada enshrines 'equality before and under law and equal protection and benefit of law' based on sex (but not gender) in section 15 of its Charter.

The first ordinance from Minneapolis stated that 'pornography is central in creating and maintaining the civil inequality of the sexes. Pornography is a systematic practice of exploitation and subordination based on sex which differentially harms women' (Dworkin and MacKinnon 1997, 427). Complainants would be able to bring a civil suit against producers and distributers of pornography in order 'to prevent and prohibit all discriminatory practices of sexual subordination or inequality through pornography' (1997, 428). The ordinance passed but was vetoed by the mayor twice. In between the two failed Minneapolis ordinances, a similar ordinance was drafted in Indianapolis with the assistance of MacKinnon that narrowed its definition of pornography to 'the graphic sexually explicit subordination of women'. That definition included at least one of six qualifiers including scenes of pain and humiliation, pleasure in rape, bondage or dismemberment, penetration by objects or animals, scenarios of degradation or hurt, or postures of servility or submission (1997, 444). It was easily passed by a socially conservative council, but in 1986 it was declared unconstitutional by the Seventh Circuit Court of Appeals as a violation of the first amendment (Bronstein 2011, 326).

In the meantime, social conservative activists jumped on the anti-pornography ordinance bandwagon. Phyllis Schlafly, who led opposition to the failed Equal Rights Amendment that would have enshrined equal rights for women into the American constitution, endorsed the Minneapolis and Indianapolis ordinances. In 1985, three other jurisdictions failed to pass ordinances. Suffolk County, NY, voted down an ordinance introduced by a socially conservative legislator who claimed pornography led to sodomy and 'the destruction of the family unit'. The Los Angeles County Board of Supervisors failed to pass its ordinance. Voters in Cambridge, MA, rejected a referendum on an anti-pornography ordinance (Bronstein 2011, 328).

Success finally came in 1992 but in a whole other country. Donald Butler, the owner of a pornographic video store in Winnipeg, Canada, was arrested in 1987 and found guilty on multiple obscenity charges. However, LEAF, dissatisfied with his sentence, appealed and in 1991 Butler was found even more guilty. He then appealed to the Supreme Court of Canada, which unanimously upheld the guilty verdict and recommended that obscenity laws be interpreted according to the principle of harm. LEAF hailed the ruling not only as a victory against pornography but, crucially, one that changed the narrative from a moral-conservative appeal to decency in favour of one that emphasized the danger pornography posed to women's rights as citizens (Gotell 1997, 49). The ruling states unequivocally:

> There has been a growing recognition in recent cases that material which may be said to exploit sex in a 'degrading or dehumanizing' manner will necessarily fail the community standards test, not because it offends against morals but because it is perceived by public opinion to be harmful to society, particularly women. . . . [Furthermore] the appearance of consent is not necessarily determinative. (R. *v.* Butler, [1992] 1 SCR 452)

Harm was defined as that which 'predisposes persons to act in an anti-social manner, in other words, a manner which society formally recognizes as incompatible with its proper functioning. The stronger the inference of a risk of harm, the lesser the likelihood of tolerance.' Thus portrayal of sex with violence or 'explicit sex which is degrading or dehumanizing', or explicit sex that is otherwise 'generally tolerated' but employs children constitutes a social harm (R. *v.* Butler, [1992] 1 SCR 452).

The imagined subject of this ruling was clearly the woman-child. They are the two subjects singled out in the court's decision as most susceptible to the impingement of harm via pornography, and are repeatedly defined as lacking any power over their sexuality (Cossman 1997, 124; Gotell 1997, 50). Indeed, the ruling linked 'women and children' together as most likely to experience 'abject and servile victimization' (R. *v.* Butler, [1992] 1 SCR 452). Thus, as far as pornography is concerned, the law considers women as more akin to children than to adult men. As Berlant notes, such reasoning enshrines 'an image of the citizen as a minor, female, youthful victim who requires civil protection by the state whose adult citizens, especially adult men, seem mobilized by a sexual- and capital-driven compulsion to foul their own national culture' (1995, 390). How that harm would manifest was left loosely defined in the court decision:

There is a sufficiently rational link between the criminal sanction, which demonstrates our community's disapproval of the dissemination of materials which potentially victimize women and restricts the negative influence which such materials have on changes in attitudes and behaviour, and the objective. While a direct link between obscenity and harm to society may be difficult to establish, it is reasonable to presume that exposure to images bears a causal relationship to changes in attitudes and beliefs. (R. *v.* Butler, [1992] 1 SCR 452)

Brenda Cossman (1997) argues that the harm implied in the ruling uses the idealized woman-child to reinforce a moral argument on behalf of the heterosexual family as the pre-eminent sexual citizen. She notes that the Butler decision not only negates consent but also defines pornography as that which 'appeals only to the most base aspect of individual fulfilment' and therefore 'does not stand on an equal footing with other kinds of expression which directly engage the "core" of the freedom of expression values' (R. *v.* Butler, [1992] 1 SCR 452). By erasing consent, invoking a naturalized victimized status for the woman-child, and treating pornography as a debased right, the framework of harm manages to diminish full citizenship for the adult woman by infantilizing her. Simultaneously, it makes an appeal to 'good sex' practices as the only way for this diminished woman-child to access citizenship in the future. Indeed, as the lengthy quote from Dworkin and MacKinnon that we provided earlier in this chapter claims, it is only by foreswearing pornography and agreeing that it is harmful that women can be citizens. With this appeal to the child citizen-in-waiting, adults must voluntarily give up their citizen rights to individual fulfilment through sexual expression. Thus, the subject lurking in the background of the harms framework is the sexual dissident who refuses to sublimate their sexuality in the name of national heterosexuality. It comes as no surprise, therefore, that the key targets of the newly revamped obscenity laws in Canada were members of the LGBTQ community (Bell et al. 1997).

After two queer-positive bookstores, Glad Day in Toronto and Little Sisters in Vancouver, were targeted for obscenity charges, and both lost their cases in court, the very constitutionality of the Butler decision was heavily contested by LGBTQ and feminist activist groups, including by LEAF, which had been a major intervenor in the Little Sisters case (Busby 2004). Dworkin and MacKinnon published an open statement dissociating themselves from Butler (1994). LEAF frankly declared that 'the broad principles articulated in *Butler*, especially the "degrading and dehumanizing" test, have at times been used to justify thinly disguised attacks on gay and lesbian materials' (Busby 2004, 136). By 2005, in a transformed landscape of queer rights, the Supreme Court backtracked on its previous confidence in recognizing causal harm and ruled instead:

> Vague generalizations that the sexual conduct at issue will lead to attitudinal changes and hence anti-social behaviour will not suffice. The causal link between images of sexuality and anti-social behaviour cannot be assumed. Attitudes in themselves are not crimes, however deviant they may be or disgusting they may appear. What is required is proof of links, first between the sexual conduct at issue and the formation of negative attitudes, and second between those attitudes and real risk of anti-social behavior. (R. *v.* Labaye, [2005] 3 SCR 728, 2005 SCC 80)

As Alan Young (2008) notes, the legacy of harms legislation and its ultimate inadequacies raises questions about who, exactly, the state seeks to protect from pornography. He points out that Canada has all but given up on criminal prosecution of pornography (except, quite rightly, child abuse materials) and turned its attention to prostitution instead. In the United States, where community standards still prevail, a smattering of expensive and high profile cases have gone to court with widely varying results (Breslin 2012). The United Kingdom, and Australia have attempted a different framework that targets 'extreme pornography'. How that is defined, and who is determined to require protection from it, raises old questions in seemingly new yet distressingly familiar frameworks.

Extreme pornography and mute/ant bodies

With the onset of Internet pornography and the admitted difficulties in regulating online content in the same way as film, publishing, or broadcasting material, there is a concomitant sense, as we discussed in our chapter on technology, that what's 'out there' is far worse than can be imagined. As the chapter on violence explores, a foreboding suspicion that pornography has become uglier, meaner, and altogether more extreme – despite lack of evidence proving that this material is what consumers actually look at – has pushed some regions into drastic prohibitions. In particular, we have seen a recent spate of laws attempting to control what is named as 'extreme pornography'. This category usually includes not just child abuse materials and bestiality – where there is in most developed countries a consensus that such representations are non-consensual and should be criminalized – but also consensual BDSM between adults. This last example of 'extreme pornography' raises the most difficult and interesting questions about the governance of sexually explicit materials. Consensual BDSM involves only adults who have consented to – and can indeed be taking sexual pleasure from – physical acts that would be violent in other contexts (including whipping, closed fist play or restraint). How does the state prove that such 'extreme pornography' causes harm if the actors involved in its production, and the consumers who view the material, have both consented to the representation of the practices being shown?

While some argue that a feminist framework of harms is perpetually undermined by either a moral-conservative framework of community standards or a liberal-progressive framework of anti-censorship and individual rights (Busby 2004; McGlynn 2010), we question the efficacy of the concept of harm itself. It is based on fundamental assumptions within anti-porn feminism that women lack any real power to define their sexuality because, these activists claim, a patriarchal society always places men in a position of power over them. Furthermore, such an approach assumes that the representation of sexual violence and sexual degradation, loosely defined within the laws, can only be indicative of these oppressive power relations (Carline 2011, 315) – as with the anti-BDSM strand of early radical feminism discussed in Chapter 3. With such assumptions in place, efforts to define a pornography that is beyond the pale of human tolerance pay scant attention to the rights and security of the individuals performing these 'extreme' sex acts. They are deemed exploited persons, 'who may be the victim of crime' while 'society, particularly children', stand at greatest risk (Home Office 2005, 2, cited in Carline 2011, 316). Thus, the incompetent adult and the innocent child are confusingly conflated and presented as proof that individuals cannot be trusted with their own sexuality.

England's 'extreme pornography' law came into effect at the beginning of 2009, and Scotland implemented its own in 2011. Although not named as such, Australia had previously revised its classification guidelines and online regulations to also prohibit similar forms of pornography that feature violence or fetish. What makes these laws unique is that they target consumers rather than producers and distributers (Carline 2011, 313). In all instances, the production, circulation and consumption of child abuse materials are set out separately as a particularly heinous crime requiring special attention. We agree with that status and therefore focus here on those laws covering pornography made by and for adults. England's rules have a three-part test whereby the material must be '(a) pornographic (b) explicit (c) real or appears to be real act (these would be objective tests for the jury). It would cover: (i) serious violence (ii) intercourse or oral sex with an animal (iii) sexual interference with a human corpse' (Woodhouse 2014, 5). The pornographic is defined as being 'of such a nature that it must reasonably be assumed to have been produced solely or principally for the purpose of sexual arousal' (Criminal Justice and Immigration Act 2008 c. 4, part 5, 63(3)).

In Australia, the Federal Register (2008) lists material that is Refused Classification (and is thus illegal to consume in the country). It includes 'violence, sexual violence, sexualized violence or coercion' as well as 'sexually assaultive language'. Additionally, 'Nor does it allow consensual depictions which purposefully demean anyone involved in that activity for the enjoyment of viewers. Fetishes such as body piercing, application of substances such as candle wax, "golden showers", bondage, spanking or fisting are not permitted'. Bestiality is also 'Refused Classification'. In Australia, it is illegal for an ISP to host a website that contains either X18+ or RC material, including a broadly stated ban on any 'real depictions of actual sexual activity' (ACMA 2011) (although generally this law is neither observed nor policed).

The fierce public debate over extreme pornography laws often triangulates the moral-conservative, liberal-progressive, and feminist-harms frameworks. McGlynn laments the opportunities lost in England by the initial assertion of feminist anti-pornography arguments that were then quickly sublimated by the more politically expedient concerns of community standards vis-à-vis individual rights (2010, 190). By contrast, Paul Johnson argues that the foregrounding of 'moral disgust' provides a much better control mechanism than the vague and highly contested concept of harm precisely because it makes that moral bias explicit and transparent, thus limiting its scope of application (2010, 148). Harm, he argues, is an ineffectual legal concept since it conflates three very distinct levels of harm: that to the individual performer, that to an individual in contact with a viewer of extreme pornography, and that to the status of a group living in a society where extreme pornography is tolerated. The ability to judge whether harm has occurred is not merely different for each but also, he argues, categorically impossible (2010, 154).

By emphasizing harm-by-proxy to consumers, and aligning women with children, the harms paradigm cannot imagine a performer possessing sufficient self-determination to consent. It simply assumes that no woman would ever consent to engage in any activity relating to extreme pornography except as a coerced or exploited victim. The evidence of women who do, therefore, requires their erasure either through legal efforts to reform or rescue them or by simply not acknowledging their performance as labour (Carline 2011, 320). Thus, such laws reassert heteronormativity and passive feminine sexuality as ideal forms of national sexual citizenship (319). Furthermore, we argue via Bell (1995), they treat the porn performer as a reduced or diminished citizen-pervert. Such an approach makes it possible for the state to ignore sex work as labour deserving the same kinds of autonomy, safety, health, and collective bargaining representation granted most other work that incorporates high levels of bodily risk.

It becomes starkly evident that pornography laws are drafted to prioritize the rights of the unwilling consumer while treating the performer as a diminished citizen. It is rare to see a country legislate on pornography in ways that acknowledge it is happening on their sovereign territory, and therefore to be concerned for the safety and wellbeing of the consensual worker. It is not always possible to prove beyond a doubt that coercion, abuse, or exploitation occurred while producing pornographic materials. However, it should also be recognized that in laws governing 'extreme pornography' there are no references to extant labour laws or the possibility of strengthening those laws to protect pornographic sex workers. Ironically, this may actually be for the best, given the way that California, which is home to the largest legal pornographic industry in the world, has attempted to intervene in workplace health and safety.

Unlike many nations, which rely on plausible deniability (or perhaps wilful ignorance) that pornography is being produced within its jurisdiction, California can make no such claims. As Chapter 1 notes, behemoths like Vivid, Hustler, Playboy and Kink all reside in California and therefore pornography is a major employer for cultural workers both above and below the line. The industry enjoys protection as 'free speech' according to the Supreme Court ruling California v. Freeman (488 US 1311 (1989). Therefore, the United States recognizes pornography as a legal industry subject to all regulations relating to film and media production, plus a few extra in deference to its unique labour practices. The most pertinent regulation specifically targeting pornography is 18 US Code § 2257, drafted to reduce the possibility of using children or legal minor performers. It requires 'individually identifiable records pertaining to every performer' that verify they are of legal age. Documents to be obtained include official records that provide the performer's legal name, date of birth, and any former, professional or alias names.

Both the state and the legal pornography industry implement regulations overseeing health and safety, particularly concerning STI risk. Until it declared bankruptcy in 2011, the Adult Industry Medical Health Care Foundation ran a voluntary STI screening programme to which many of the major production companies subscribed, and the California Occupational Safety and Health Administration maintains a website (https://www.dir. ca.gov/dosh/adultfilmindustry.html) 'to inform AFI [adult film industry] workers of their rights and employers of their responsibilities, including having an exposure control plan, an injury and illness prevention plan, providing worker training and any required medical monitoring or vaccination' (Rodriguez-Hart et al. 2012, 1).

In 2012 Los Angeles County, which has been estimated to house as much as eighty per cent of global adult film production, passed 'Measure B' with strong support from its Department of Public Health and from the federal agency, The Center for Disease Control and Prevention. It requires 'that performers are protected from sexually transmitted infections by condoms', and that the costs of enforcing that regulation will be borne exclusively by the production companies through the purchase of an 'adult film production public health permit' (County of Los Angeles 2012). In 2013, the state of California introduced Assembly Bill 1576, that adopted the principles of Measure B, making its violation a criminal offence and further requiring that performers' STI test results (which are voluntary and not state-mandated) be disclosed to the Department of Industrial Relations (AB 1576). In the face of concerted political pressure by major porn companies, which threatened to move their operations out of state, the Senate Appropriations Committee suspended debate on that bill in August 2014, essentially defeating it before it even came up for a vote.

Maintaining the health and safety of performers is absolutely paramount but, as the ensuing controversy over both Measure B and AB 1576 suggests, how to regulate for best outcomes remains fraught. It must be stated that the debate was not simply one of the porn industry against anti-porn activists. Heated public discussion ensued between and among performers who insist on high ethical standards and safe working conditions. The debate included the usual claims to freedom of expression and civil rights. These present problematically as it is more often the industry leaders making such proclamations, and they too often fail to take into account the differential power relations between employers and employees, and between employees of varying levels of status, experience, and reputation. As Chauntelle Tibbals notes, 'performers, themselves, very rarely weigh in on these discussions' (2012, 237). More interestingly, some performers expressed concerns about the danger of imposing the same precautionary measures for 'private sex' on paid performance sex, while others countered that informal practices of coercion do occur far too frequently on set and need to be addressed more forthrightly.

Lorelei Lee claims that by not mandating testing, and prioritizing condom use over all other forms of STI protection, Measure B imposes a normative framework of sexual health based on private sexual acts (Lee 2012). She further notes that the legislation could result in deepened stigma for sex workers and even less ability to self-determine the conditions of their performance:

'When our jobs are illegal, they not only become more dangerous, they also become more stigmatized', she says. 'In a time when porn performers already face the abrupt closing of our bank accounts, discrimination in hiring and in housing applications, and a risk of firing from other non-sex-work jobs we might obtain, the question of our livelihood moving underground becomes one of survival.' (Clark-Flory 2014)

Other performers, such as Nina Hartley, Stoya, and Dana DeArmond all raised concerns that latex allergies and 'friction burn' can actually heighten risk of STI, and that the state initiatives did nothing to restore testing facilities (Hess 2012). Most importantly, there was no consultation with working porn performers prior to drafting either Measure B or AB 1576. Instead, government officials privileged public health agencies, AIDS organizations, former porn workers, and porn abolition agencies like the Pink Cross Foundation.

To be clear, there are porn performers in favour of mandatory condom usage. Both Satine Phoenix and Aurora Snow were
candid about indirect and informal pressure on performers to
forego condoms or risk losing job opportunities (Hess 2012).
Arguments that such coercion is a reasonable risk associated with
the profession are unacceptable. Major companies like Wicked
Productions have a mandatory condom rule, as do certain directors contracted to condom-optional companies. Feminist porn
producer Tristan Taormino has a condom-mandatory policy,
while her colleague Courtney Trouble does not. Thus, debating
whether the rule should be mandatory or optional, and framing
it around individual choice, is ultimately a distraction that does
not acknowledge the unique discriminatory practices in labour
regulations, especially around health and safety risk, for porn performers. Health and safety regulations are a part of every workplace, and where there are recognized higher risks of bodily harm
– such as in construction, food preparation, heavy industry, etc. –
workers and their representatives are usually consulted during the
process of drafting governmental policies. The exception seems to
be sex work. Tibbals argues, 'The condom debate is all too clear
an indicator of the disconnect existing between the adult industry
producers and performers, regulators, and the wider social world'
(2012, 251). When regulations are put into place that do not
prioritize the issues and concerns of the workers most at risk, it
reinforces stigma and erasure at the highest levels of governance.

Conclusion: The future of pornographic citizenship

The citizen of porn is defined negatively, and the connection with
pornography cancels out citizenship in a variety of ways. The
consumer who seeks out pornography is deemed disgusting or
harmful. The person exposed to pornography against his or her
will is deemed infantile, susceptible, victimized, or harmed. The
adult engaged in pornography performance is deemed to be both/
either disgusting and harmful and/or infantile, susceptible, victimized and harmed. The only exception to this value system, it would

appear, is Nead's connoisseur (1999), protected by the privileged and elite space of good taste, artistry, and bourgeois masculinity (see also Kendrick 1996; McNair 2002). Pornography is largely governed according to the presumption that any publicly mediated form of sexual expression that puts forward pleasure as its primary or exclusive intention threatens the stability of heternormativity upon which most nations build their sexual culture.

Thus, at all levels of pornography governance, it seems as if the last person to be considered is the actively working porn performer. Pornography legislation tends to treat production as if it does not happen within territorial boundaries and prioritizes the rights and freedoms of a nebulous citizenry that desires minimal exposure. In one of the rare regions offering specialized regulation on pornography as a legal industry and not some ad-hoc concatenation of underground, offshore, black market, and subcultural practices, the voices of workers are explicitly overlooked. By prioritizing public health advocates, porn performers are treated problematically not as workers but as public nuisances and/or outright dangers. As this overview of existing governance frameworks reveals, Bell's theory of a 'reduced private' (1995, 146) for the citizen-pervert seems especially applicable when it comes to those engaged in pornography production.

Yet, despite all government efforts to minimize or outright abolish pornography, it persists and even flourishes. Furthermore, as Giddens (1992) and others note, sexuality itself is rapidly expanding in definition and purpose. The stigma associated with pornography consumption is collapsing in on itself (Attwood 2009; McNair 2002; Smith 2007). However, the same cannot be said for pornography production and performance. Banks like JPMorgan Chase and City National Bank, and e-commerce sites like PayPal have shut down the accounts of porn performers (Morris 2013). Performers also comment frequently on differential treatment by health and police services and feel that they don't have 'the same protections as a woman not in [pornography]' (Hayoun 2014). The fact that performers' sense of vulnerability is not based on the work itself but is due to a state apparatus that does not take seriously its obligations to them is deeply disturbing.

Thus, it is imperative to begin to imagine the subject of pornography governance as a self-determining worker in full compliance with the rights and responsibilities of citizenship as laid out by the state. Where coercion, exploitation, and abuse occur, the laws that are already in place to prevent them can be strengthened and vigorously applied. As Paul Johnson notes, there do exist acts (pornographic and otherwise) that are considered immoral and reprehensible, and are restricted accordingly. The very existence of a state presumes the right and responsibility to limit the actions of its citizens (2010, 158). Explicit sexual materials that use children is one such restricted practice, as is bestiality. Both these practices lack consent and autonomy, and recognize the need for the state to intervene on behalf of someone (or something) who cannot adequately protect themselves. Yet, while child abuse materials are usually governed separately, bestiality tends to be lumped in with numerous other sexual acts that involve only adult humans, as if those acts render them animalistic and therefore less worthy of citizenship. Until and unless porn performers are made the central and abiding interests of the systems that govern their work, not in an imagined frame of harmed/harmful subjects but as capable sexual and labouring subjects, then governments will continue to deny them full citizenship. Yet, more and more, performers are speaking up and demanding respect and recognition for their work, drafting new frameworks to explain pornography as an ethical, political practice. We close this book with an examination of their important contributions.

6

Performing Pornography, Practising Sexual Politics

Why are the experiences of pornography performers so marginalized in scholarly, governmental, and activist debates that seek to abolish or diminish pornography's influence? What do these performers say about their work and how would they like to improve pornography as an industry, sexual politics, and creative practice? The goal of this chapter is to place the pornography performer at the centre of analysis and to appreciate how they draw meaning and value from their labour. We revisit the production of pornography as discussed in Chapter 1 but this time from the perspective of the on-camera performers. In so doing, we also revisit all other facets of pornography explored in this book to take seriously our own criticisms of existing frameworks and point the way towards what we see as more nuanced and ethical modes of scholarship. At stake in the exploration of pornography as performance is a de-emphasis on pornography consumption with its attendant concerns of a sadistic, controlling gaze over unwilling and unwitting victims. In its place, we offer a way to recognize and appreciate the performers' centrality to the work of pornography, their ability to direct attention to their body, their skill in manipulating it, and the different ways that this work is offered within various regimes of commercialization.

This chapter locates analysis along three key nodes: fully exploitative, fully self-determining, and somewhere in the middle. These categories derive from research and policy directives developed by sex worker coalitions and harm reduction agencies. They identify what has been called a 'Continuum of Sexual Politics' embedded in the production and consumption of publicly mediated forms of sexual expression and the provision of sexual services, both commercialized and privatized (Davis 2008, 6). Historically, pornography debates have tended to rage at either extreme end of the continuum, but increasingly there is awareness that such positionings neglect the way power and constraint are negotiated within all sexual exchanges – commercial or otherwise. Therein lies the significance of studying pornography from the perspective of the performer. In the first place, it assumes at least the potential for agency and self-determination unless proven otherwise. This upsets the standard model of power in anti-pornography discourses that present women as passive and victimized, and can only recognize reluctant or repentant women workers while ignoring or vilifying men who perform in or consume pornography. Trans or genderqueer performers are simply ignored by anti-pornography activists. Thus, second, and related, examining the specific conditions of porn performance in ways that draw upon the performer's self-explanation provides compelling insights into how sexual expression and gender identity can be articulated and valued by non-normative and marginalized gender and sexual subjects. Anti-pornography discourses, whether they come from feminist, public health, moralistic, or governmental standpoints, tend to emphasize traditional gender norms of masculine/feminine with the former in a position of power over the latter. They consider explicit sexual performance as the reiteration of this power dynamic and a denigration of the feminine, even when the performers are not man/woman (see for example Kendall 2006).

Scholarly and activist attention to sexual and gender performance in pornography begins from the position that some pornography confronts, articulates, and transgresses dominant social structures of gender, and maintains its focus on these practices. This is a far cry from the violence or sexualization/pornification frameworks that view commercialized sexual exchange as necessarily exploitative and a perpetuation of heteropatriarchal oppressions of women by men. Proponents of these frameworks often seek support in the testimonial evidence of former sex workers who experienced deep forms of coercion and abuse, usually at the hands of men. A performance framework, by contrast, seeks to be informed by a community of non-normative and marginal-ized gender identities, expressions, and sexual orientations. This is sometimes referred to as the 'quiltbag': queer/questioning/ undecided/intersex/lesbian/trans/bisexual/asexual/ally/gay/gender-queer. Members of this community are producing and performing in sexually explicit media as part of larger artistic, activist, and educational practices to test the boundaries of gender fluidity and sexual expression. In between these two frameworks sit neo-liberal models of individualism and choice that problematically normal-ize gender inequity and sexual coercion as simply part of the busi-ness while offering limited opportunities for self-determination, self-authorship, and pride in skill. This position, most popular within sensationalist reporting in mainstream media, demon-strates exactly why it is so necessary to dig behind any claim that doing sex work is inherently either exploitative or empowering, and to closely analyse the experiences of the performer. To begin such analysis requires first examining the most pervasive trope in defining pornography performance both within the industry and mainstream media's speculations on the lives of performers: that of the porn 'star'.

'Porn stars':
porn performance and sexual authenticity

In Chapter 1 we noted that 'stars' in the pornography industry – as in all film and television production – represent a vanishingly small minority of performers. But in terms of their representation in the wider media, this is not the case. Porn 'stars' are increasingly visible as the face of pornography performance. As early as 1979, Richard Dyer laid out a framework for studying the discourses and industrial practices of stardom in the film industry, noting its gendered frameworks of desire that marginalize the work of women actors in particular to cultivate highly glamorous, seduc-tive personas both on screen and through extra-cinematic texts such as fan magazines, studio portraits, and other systems of publicity. As he points out, stars are simultaneously signifying images and social facts: real, labouring bodies presenting themselves as desirable objects (1979, 9).

Key to creating a successful star persona is authenticity, an ability to persuade the audience that the performances both on and off-screen are indicative of the performer's real life and true sense of self. Identification is arguably the other most important marker to achieve stardom. As Jackie Stacey notes, identification is central to the relationship between performers and their audiences as both cinematic and extra-cinematic presentation seeks to reproduce a persona that is just 'like us' only better (Stacey 1994, 126). Within a cinematic performance, authenticity is a marker of the actor's ability to embody the role and create a 'pure presence of character unadulterated by any sense of the performer's separate identity' (Maltby 2003, 395). Ironically and rather contradictorily, those performances distinguished for their authenticity are not the unknown character actors who provide invaluable support to a star role, but the top-billed star whose authentic performance only serves to reinforce their extra-cinematic personal: think James Dean, Robert De Niro, or any of the revered Method actors of the mid-to-late-twentieth century. Thus, authenticity ultimately depends on identification, an extra-cinematic sense that the actor is opening up their soul to the audience, revealing the same kind of affectual and desiring needs as their devoted fans, only that much more intense.

How do identification and authenticity operate within pornography to produce the porn star out of the sex worker? Unlike in popular cinema where the audience knows the actor is playing a role that is not them (but is imagined to be like them), a pornographic performance can blur that line beyond distinction. In Chapter 1 we considered the conditions of production of pornography; but the construction of a porn star persona relies on erasing this work, denying the labour of performance, and presenting the star as someone just doing what they would be doing anyway. Thus the pornography star system reinforces a gender dynamic that denies the star – again, still most often a cisgender woman – self-determination over their sexuality.

A scene from the first season of the Canadian docuporn series *Webdreams* (2005) illustrates how the discourses of porn stardom can over-determine the worker as a commodified spectacle. Malezia, an aspiring self-declared porn star, is rushing about her hotel room trying to get ready for an audition at Vivid Studios while her mentor/manager Dugmor stands by impatiently. This classic scene of a man waiting for a woman to primp herself into acceptable beauty standards seems taken right out of a Blondie cartoon. Dugmor rolls his eyes knowingly at the camera, sharing a moment of understanding with the audience about 'women'. Apparently even porn stars occasionally misplace a shoe and have trouble deciding what to wear. However, unlike everyday life, this woman showers while wearing caked-on glam make-up and searches desperately for her shoe fully naked with her back arched cat-like and rubbing her genitals on the carpeted floor with legs splayed for maximum visibility. It is a full-on pornographic performance masquerading as a social performance of both women's eroticized incompetence and unceasing sexual availability, narrated by Dugmor's asides about Malezia's unprofessionalism and general stupidity. Thus, in this scene and throughout the series the implication remains that Malezia is entering pornography not because she sees it as a lucrative career in which she has some valuable skills, but as an oversexed yet otherwise unaccomplished individual who just wants it all the time. Such has become the definition of 'porn star' far too often.

These concerns raised about the unproblematized use of the term porn star are not meant to deny or dismiss the work of stardom. If anything, it is to argue that stardom needs to be better recognized as a complex labour process of self-cultivation and presentation. Certainly the term is used frequently among independent contractors, entrepreneurs, and self-defined feminist and/ or queer pornographers. Two of the most internationally well-known members of the feminist/queer porn community, Courtney Trouble and Zahra Stardust, both use the term 'porn star' in their online self-descriptions, while also clearly noting their political, professional, creative, and intellectual endeavours. In *C'lick Me: The NetPorn Reader*, the term porn star is used throughout to recognize the way that independent porn workers turn to the Internet to self-author a persona and self-manage that persona as a marketable commodity. In one particularly noteworthy example, Mireille Miller-Young notes that for African American performers, operating independently and calling themselves porn stars grants them the ability to move beyond the racist and misogynist 'cyberghetto' porn networks. By refusing that historical entwinement of black women with fetishized and illicit acts of sexual and physical violence perpetrated by white men, independent black porn star websites place emphasis on self-determining labour and expert self-construction (Miller-Young 2005, 208). Thus, the term porn star can be appropriated to signify the thoughtful, labouring body of the porn performer. Attention to how this term is used strategically in porn performance offers insights into where the work itself fits along the continuum of sex exchange.

Coerced performance and porn recovery

Among the harms that have concerned anti-pornography activists are those experienced by women involved in the production of pornography. Andrea Dworkin's revised 1989 introduction to *Men Possessing Women* recounts testimony from numerous former porn workers before the Public Hearings on Ordinances to Add Pornography as Discrimination Against Women held by the Minneapolis City Council in 1983. She uses their testimony not as speech-acts against the misdirections of anti-censorship but in order to place the real, labouring body at the centre of public debate. 'They write – in blood, their own', to proclaim that 'They are real . . . even though this society will do nothing for them' (Dworkin 1981, xvii–xviii). The testimonies collected by Dworkin and other anti-porn feminists offered the first sustained glimpse into the mechanisms of the industry and its labour practices, but they did so from a position of 'reform' or 'rescue' and insisted that experiences of complete and total coercion were the only available narratives. The story of Linda Boreman, aka Linda Lovelace, the star of the legendary porno-chic film *Deep Throat*, makes clear that the experiences of pornography performance are more complicated than this.

In 1980, with support from Andrea Dworkin, Gloria Steinem, and members of Women Against Pornography (WAP), Linda Boreman published her first post-pornography autobiography, *Ordeal*. In 1983 and again in 1986, she presented testimony about her experiences working in the industry first to the Minneapolis City Council and then the Attorney General's Commission on Pornography. A second autobiography, *Out of Bondage*, was published in 1986. These two books counter her star autobiographies, *Inside Linda Lovelace* (1973) and *The Intimate Diary of Linda Lovelace* (1974), written as part of the promotional machine for *Deep Throat*, in which she presents her work as just who she is: a compulsive sex fiend whose sole concern is the pleasure of her male partners. By the 1980s, broke and battered by the porno-chic craze that treated her as a cultural joke, Boreman speaks compellingly of the physical and sexual abuse she endured at the hands of her husband and manager, Chuck Traynor. What follows is an account of Boreman's experiences, much of which is extremely disturbing and may cause distress to the reader.

The major turning point in Boreman's terrorized relationship was Traynor's decision to force her into prostitution and pornography for his financial gain. Her first film was a bestiality short in which she is used and humiliated by her sex partner and then abandoned to sexually fulfil herself by having oral sex with a German Shepherd. Boreman recounts that Traynor forced her to the studio and then, when she refused, the director, assistant, and Traynor all threatened her with a gun. 'This is direct disobedience to a fucking order. You know the only choice you've got? You make this movie or you're going to die. That's your big choice', Traynor said to her (Lovelace 1980, 147). In *The Other Hollywood*, an oral history of the pornography industry, *Deep Throat*'s director, Gerard Damiano, and co-star Harry Reems both say that they witnessed Traynor beat Boreman severely and harass her on the set to the point where they would create diversions to send him away long enough to finish a scene. Traynor himself candidly asserts that he would 'beat her ass or something if she didn't do so-and-so', but claims the abuse was simply part of the business of creating 'a superstar': 'And you don't create a superstar by namby-pambyin', kiss-assin' around, and givin' her roses – it just don't work, you know?' (McNeil et al. 2005, 61–3).

Boreman as Lovelace was most certainly a superstar of the 'porno-chic' or 'Golden Age of Pornography' era of the early 1970s. *Deep Throat* was a huge success and reviews of her performance were uniformly positive – perhaps in part because she was ordered to perform oral sex on interviewers and porn magazine publishers like Al Goldstein (*Screw*) to secure their support. Goldstein recalls his encounter with her as hostile and alienated, leaving him numb and barely able to orgasm. 'It was like working. I felt like a hooker faking it with a john' (McNeil et al. 2005, 72), he says with an amazing lack of self-awareness. Lovelace's performance in *Deep Throat* was noted for a naturalness and innocence reminiscent of Marilyn Monroe, but as even Goldstein had to admit, it lacked any kind of authenticity or self-determination. She is barely able to look at the camera, her face is often tightly drawn and her body restless, with bruises clearly visible from Traynor's beatings. Her breathy voice signals less a feminine eroticism and more general confusion and a desire for escape. What makes her performance stand out is her uncanny ability to swallow the entirety of a man's penis and perform fellatio on camera in ways that hadn't been seen before. Such a talent was presented in her promotional autobiography as a patriotic duty: 'If American men insist on getting blown, and I'm in America, then it must be important to learn how to do it, and do it well' (Lovelace 1974, 69).

Despite the efforts of many within the pornography industry to discredit Boreman as either a 'masochist', 'a fucking idiot', or a woman 'who never took responsibility for her own shitty choices' (McNeil et al. 2005, 73, 207), it must be acknowledged that her experiences in pornography occurred within a closed system of abuse and terror, tacitly accepted by those around her who seem to also blame her. It is, therefore, completely unacceptable to gloss over that history with nostalgia for 'a golden age'. However, the question of agency brings complexity to any understanding of Boreman's traumatic experiences. She states that if it weren't for *Deep Throat* and her newfound fame as Linda Lovelace, she might never have escaped from Traynor. Once her fame grew, and entertainment moguls from both within and outside pornography sought to cash in on her name recognition, Boreman was able to assert herself more and more and gain allies who wanted to distance themselves from Traynor and others who gave the business such a bad name. As Boreman herself reflects, 'In time, I came to dislike the name [Lovelace] because of what it stood for. But the truth is this: Linda Boreman and Linda Traynor never managed to get away from Chuck. It took a Linda Lovelace to escape' (McNeil et al. 2005, 66).

After years touring alongside anti-porn feminists, Boreman posed for the now-defunct fetish magazine *Leg Show*, clad in a gold bustier and stockings. It is an attractive image of a woman now in her fifties, although Boreman readily admitted she did the pin-up strictly for the money as her speaking engagement career had dried up and medical bills were mounting. In the accompanying interview with the magazine, she publicly excoriates her one-time supporters for financially and morally exploiting her: 'I guess I'm more disappointed in the Women's Movement than anything.' She also defends her decision to be featured in the magazine by arguing, 'there's nothing wrong with looking sexy as long as it's done with taste' (2001, 79). Her apparent flip-flopping caused many on both sides of the porn debate to dismiss her as an erratic, neurotic, and unstable individual not to be trusted. However, that assessment only suffices within a framework that can only consider two subject positions: fully exploited or fully empowered. As Judith Butler argues in *Excitable Speech*, assertions of personal agency and responsibility are never so pure and do not represent an escape from systems of constraint as much as they do a negotiation within them (1997, 28). How constraints are defined and situated thus become key to the practices of self-determination in pornography work. Nowhere is this question being more interrogated than in feminist/queer porn performance and scholarship.

Feminist/queer porn and the performance of consent

Anti-pornography activist Susan Cole argued in 1992:

> I do think that creating alternative erotica has the potential to be an empowering strategy. The problem is, how? . . . Much of the so-called feminist materials spewed out over the past five years reproduces the conventions and subordinating practices of pornography. (137)

Over two decades ago, her assessment of 'feminist erotica' was certainly tenable. Available women-centred pornography tended to be over-invested in the same kind of naked women imagery on offer at any adult video store, only instead draped in gauze and gold filters. Today, the discussion has evolved considerably and has been heavily influenced by advances in queer scholarship and activism. Queer theory and activism recognize that sexual desire and pleasure are central to identity formation and that, further, societal efforts to direct sexuality into heteronormative, monogamous, intimate, and reproductive relationships are nothing less than human rights injustices against non-normative sexual subjects. Such restrictive sexual systems maintain only two genders, men and women, and further insist that women's sexuality is 'feminine' – pliant, passive, submissive, emotional – and men's is 'masculine' – aggressive, overbearing, dominating, and emotionally detached. Thus, feminist/queer pornography is part of a larger political strategy aimed at dismantling these dominant systems of gender and sexual identity through the explicit performance of differing and transgressive desires.

A growing community of feminist/queer porn performers, directors, and producers incorporate educational and activist work into their practice. Through online blogs and other social media outlets, they provide frank discussions about what it means to do feminist/queer pornography and how to make those politics transparent on screen. Academic scholarship has been playing catch-up with the work and writings of feminist/queer pornographers. That has led to a situation whereby scholars and activist-performers

have broken down barriers between their work and their professional practices to inform each other and continue to interrogate
the potential, as well as some of the pitfalls, of producing feminist/
queer pornography. The Feminist Porn Awards and the Feminist
Porn Conference are held concurrently every year in Toronto,
Canada, to maximize cross-relationships across these two sectors.
This section of the chapter pays most attention to the analyses of
individuals working in pornography and the way they negotiate
their commercial porn enterprises with their feminist and/or queer
politics. Many of these self-defined 'porn stars' use that moniker
deliberately to connote their active engagement with their bodies
as sites of desire and pleasure. Their bodies are the primary tool
of their craft of offering public expression to different gender and
sexual identities. This is a very different kind of stardom from the
one granted Linda Lovelace. It celebrates a knowing, skilled body
invested in and deriving satisfaction – erotic, professional, creative, skilled, and/or financial – from performing for an audience.

Dylan Ryan, a self-described 'feminist porn star . . . and self-
professed gender and sexuality geek', states, 'My engagement with
porn was not one challenged by shame. I respected the women
who I saw in the films and had little to no preconceived judgements
about them, but I would find myself critiquing them as performers and considering what I would do differently and better' (Ryan
2013, 122). Performer Lorelei Lee insists that 'I found strength in
the part of my identity that developed out of my experiences as a
sex worker. I found a manifesto of my own ethics, and I found that,
to my surprise, I believe deeply in the positive power of sexually
explicit imagery' (2013, 200). The evolution of Lee's feminist porn
ethos did not come easily or simply, and required careful consideration of both her sexual desires and her financial and social needs.
From her first nude photo shoot at the age of nineteen through to
her current work in 'extreme' porn, Lee confronts complex issues
of consent, empowerment, bodily manipulation, financial compensation, audience expectation, and personal relationships in defining
her career. Tristan Taormino outlines some of her practices in producing 'sex-positive, non-exploitative, revolutionary porn'. Some
of her on-set practices include a Yes List of what performers enjoy

doing and with whom, extensive pre-filming consultation with performers, and filmed interviews that are intercut with the sex scenes (2013, 258). She outlines her process:

> First, the production must be a fair and ethical process and a posi-tive working environment for everyone. Performers set their own pay rates and know up front what I am hiring them to do; there is absolute, explicit consent and no coercion of any kind. They choose their sexual partners for the scene. There is mutual respect between performers and production crew. The work space is clean and safe. Performers must comply with the industry's self-mandated testing policy: testing for STIs every thirty days or less. They may request that their scene partners have a more recent test (some people, for example, have a personal policy of fifteen days). In addition, I offer everyone the options to use safer sex barriers, including condoms, gloves, and dental dams, and have those items on set [Taormino has recently switched to condom-only production]. (2013, 260)

Ryan, Lee, and Taormino's interest in forwarding consent and respect among performers raises other issues about how to make those conditions visible and readable by the audience in the final product. Ms Naughty's film *That's What I Like* provides some insight into feminist porn production practices to visualize consent. It is a straight vanilla film of a woman and man, Mia and Andy, having sex with a minimum of kink, guided by Mia's desires first and foremost. Winner of the 2009 Petra Joy award for first-time women porn filmmakers, *That's What I Like* is avail-able on the subscription site brightdesire.com. The rest of the site provides the consumer with a context within which to make sense of its feminist practices. On Ms Naughty's site, every film is envel-oped in a hyperlinked space that provides insights into the actions and intent of everyone involved. The tone underscores a sense of respect and appreciation for the performers and other workers on set and behind the scenes. Hyperbolic rhetoric of 'hot and horny honeys' is replaced with thoughtful explanations of the perform-er's choices throughout the shoot, technical problems with low/no-budget productions, and directorial intention. Also included on the site are full interviews with both Mia and Andy, a post-scene shower sequence, and the trailer.

The site explains that Naughty had numerous phone calls with both performers to determine how best to plot the scene. A few days before the shoot, on their own initiative, Mia and Andy met and had a 'practice fuck'. There are two versions available on the site. The narrated version opens with Mia explaining her reasons for doing the film while she applies her make-up. She is a bit giggly as she talks about what she likes, but her voice and body are relaxed and natural as she explains why she wants to do porn performance at this point in her life and how she finds it both enjoyable and financially worthwhile. She matter-of-factly explains the various stages of sex that most appeal to her, as the camera switches back and forth between her explaining what she likes and showing her and Andy performing it. Importantly, the film focuses as much on Andy's enjoyment as on Mia's. His face is featured even in close-ups of performing oral sex on her, as they hold hands and she strokes his hair. The sex does not climax with Andy's ejaculation but returns to him performing oral sex while she orgasms, and then a final shot of them relaxing in each other's arms after both are fully satisfied. Mia's voice closes the film as she explains that she performs sex for money because she enjoys it, and if she didn't it wouldn't matter how much it paid. It is a critical distinction to acknowledge that both financial compensation and a respectful, consensual environment are necessary components for Mia to ply her craft.

Ms Naughty's site is representative of feminist porn filmmakers who increasingly ensure that their material is closely controlled and kept off non-subscription or hub sites. This is itself an evolution of ethical porn practices, which has wrestled with the commercial/capitalist aspect of porn filmmaking. Katrien Jacobs discusses how activist pornographers have developed a business model that operates according to smaller-scale general or gift economies in which lines are blurred between consumer and producer (2004, 76). The subscriber becomes a part of a networked community that integrates the voyeuristic pleasures of pornography with documentary evidence of its production practices and performer intentions, reflective essays on the experience of making and watching the porn produced, links to other online sites that share in their ethical codes, and opportunities for consumer feed-back and dialogue. Thus, added to the practices of consent is an aesthetic commitment to the depiction of authentic pleasure by the performers. However, performers are acknowledging that authenticity can be a smoke screen that denies their skill at authoring a performance that is intended more for the pleasure of the audience – and for the continued employability of the performer – than it is at deriving sexual satisfaction for themselves.

The authenticity of performance

The performance of consent is integral to feminist pornography but often aligns itself with another key element that is currently under greater scrutiny: that of authenticity. In a study of porn consumers, McKee notes that many of his interviewees emphasize recognizing 'real enjoyment', and 'genuine interest' coming from the actors as criteria of 'quality' pornography (2007, 526). How to determine that authenticity requires a more active and discerning engagement from the viewer than is often assumed and speaks to the unique dynamic between performers and viewers in pornography. Of course, not every consumer is concerned with authenticity and genuine pleasure from pornography, but to discount this as insignificant or marginal to porn viewing and production practices is to disregard a vast set of socio-sexual relationships that reproduce differing power dynamics invested in pornography.

Consumers may desire authenticity in their pornographic performances, but what does that term mean for performers? In 2014, Arabelle Raphael, a feminist/queer performer, announced on her Twitter feed that 'the emphasis on authenticity in feminist porn can be problematic. It erases the fact that performing is labour.' Melinda Chateauvert, the author of *Sex Workers Unite*, tweeted back that it further reduces performance – a self-aware, constructed, and skilful act – to performativity, the unconscious iteration of gender and sexual norms (see Butler 1990). More and more porn performers are rejecting a definition of authenticity that corresponds to natural or genuine pleasure. They argue that it inadvertently reasserts a 'respectability hierarchy' within sex work that treats porn performers whose primary motivation is financial or needs-based as subordinate to more 'empowered' (read: privileged) performers. Authenticity, suggests performer Siouxie Q, is turning into a fetish category up there with MILF. As she notes, 'Performing in porn is a job and I certainly don't need every scene to be the hottest event of my life in order to deliver an engaging performance that can read as "authentic". When I am paid well and respected for my work, I always do a good job' (Q 2014).

It is not hard to see the links between authenticity and tropes of stardom that erase labour by foregrounding an actor's natural charisma and effortless adoption of a persona. To illustrate, the Feminist Porn Awards insist that films must depict 'genuine pleasure, agency, and desire'. While on the surface that seems an important and laudatory goal, it does also run the risk of sidelining labour, craft, and skill. Without a clear recognition that the performance is work, there exists the risk that critics could dismiss a porn performer's motivations as nothing more than their own consumerist, narcissistic need to be turned into spectacle. Certainly, as Chapter 3 outlined, anti-pornography activists have claimed that women who claim pleasure or empowerment by working in porn are engaged in a wilful self-deceit and harming other women.

Feminist/queer pornographers are exploring the concepts of authenticity and empowerment in pornography performance in ways that draw attention to their inequitable application within the industry. They seek to redefine authenticity as a labour practice – not a natural disposition – that can potentially transform gender and sexual norms. In their keynote to the Feminist Porn Conference in 2014, feminist/queer pornography producer and performer Courtney Trouble argues for a politics of empowerment that places the most marginalized at the centre of pornography activism. Such a position recognizes differential privilege among porn performers and the need to build safer, inclusive, respectful environments where the work of pornography is regarded without scepticism, revulsion, pity, or contempt. In this sense, authenticity is not grounded in any assertions of innate naturalness or personal empowerment, but in the way that the self-determining performer crafts their performance through the skilful manipulation of their body. Zahra Stardust notes that porn requires performers to construct their image and display their bodies according to specific audiences, genres, and aesthetics, and that the ability to do so convincingly constitutes a form of authenticity of labour, not disposition (Stardust 2012).

The process of self-discovery through an awareness of the expectations for different performances suggests a definition of authenticity based on reflexivity, difference, and boundary transgression rather than on an arbitrary category of what constitutes real or innate pleasure. In this mode, Trouble suggests that pornography performance led them on a journey of self-reflection towards identification as genderqueer. 'While I knew I was queer before I made porn, producing and performing in porn helped me find my gender' (Trouble 2014b, 197). Trouble acknowledges that key to their porn politics is to perform pleasure authentically as a 'fully embodied performer' (198). Through various performances in which they played with the possibility of having 'psychic dick' and contrasted it with more conventionally defined 'butch' performances, Trouble was able to arrive at a self-awareness that they were more than 'gender variant'. Thus, authenticity becomes not only about sexual pleasure but also about connectedness in performance and the possibility for performers to 'expand and affirm their own identities and desires' (Trouble 2014b, 197). This understanding of authenticity does not deny the labour of performance – rather it is constructed through it. Putting work at the centre of porn performance challenges hierarchical and socially privileged claims of empowerment and authenticity, and makes possible deeper scrutiny into the mainstream commercial porn industry where politics take a back seat to profits.

Re-assessing the 'harms' of mainstream porn performance

In one of the most legendarily controversial documentaries on pornography, the National Film Board of Canada's *Not a Love Story*

(1981), a young woman explains her decision to make a living by performing sex shows with her husband. Identified by her legal name, Patrice Lucas shows obvious pride in her craft as she complains about the club's advertising that calls her show 'raunchy', and reflects on the autonomy given her by the management to choreograph the show according to her own vision. Her confident and articulate explanation of her work lies in stark contrast to her surroundings. She is working in one of the seediest porn supermarkets in Times Square during the squalid 1980s, and she casually notes that her mother was a prostitute and that she, as she puts it, 'lost her virginity' at the age of nine. The interview can leave a deeply uncomfortable impression that this woman is nothing more than an exploited victim of pornography who doesn't even know it herself. Certainly in 1981, when the film was first released, there really wasn't any other framework available to understand someone like Lucas. Decades later, that self-serving pity directed at her can be redirected as a challenge to audiences about how pornographic performers remain stigmatized. The example of Linda Lovelace discussed earlier offered insight into the worst excesses of sexual, domestic and labour abuse. The work of feminist/queer performers like Courtney Trouble and Lorelei Lee offers great possibility for self-determining performance. Yet it must be acknowledged that the vast majority of pornography production occurs somewhere in the middle. How to account for workers like Patrice Lucas is an urgent question for pornography studies.

Just as in most forms of physical work, porn performers must negotiate the demands of the industry according to their own bodily and psychical limits. Unlike the feminist/queer porn community, the mainstream pornography industry tends to still be run mostly by men (although that is changing), places financial profit as the central motivation of its business practices, and caters primarily to a cisgender and heterosexual audience of men. As such, it relies heavily on a roster of young, able-bodied, conventionally attractive women. In exploring the mid ranges of the continuum of sexual politics, between coercion and self-determination, we examine here star performers working for Vivid Entertainment. As mentioned in Chapter 1, Vivid is the most mainstream of mainstream pornography production – mass entertainment reaching large global audiences with conventional aesthetics, making huge profits for the producers in the company but not so much for performers. While we focused on the experiences of mid-range performers in Chapter 1, here we explore the experiences of some of the top female performers at the heart of this brand in order to make clear the interactions between institutions and individuals, structure and agency, in the performance of being a porn star.

In 1985, Steven Hirsch, the founder of Vivid, plotted a new pornographic business model designed around the wholesome attractiveness of performer Ginger Lynn. He focused on new distribution models such as home video and, later, the Internet to tap into the undeveloped audience of couples and women-friendly pornography. Key to his plan was to maintain a stable of contract performers similar to the old studio-model of Hollywood, and to promote his films around their star persona. Vivid is now one of the biggest adult entertainment conglomerates in the world – although Lynn now lives in poverty – and, as the example of Malezia shows, the Vivid Girl is a hallmark of mainstream success for performers. With the proliferation of subscription-based websites dedicated to one actor, as well as spin-off potential in sex toys, and live appearances or strip performances, on-screen porn workers now must navigate a complex web of creative and financial control over their work, cultivating a persona that will distinguish them from a crowded market, lead to more lucrative and less onerous work schedules, and extend their careers, and therefore their financial security.

The Vivid Girl adapted the promotional model of stardom initiated in the 1970s with performers like Lovelace and Marilyn Chambers, and made it a cornerstone of legitimate porn business practices. Beginning in 1985, Vivid recruited women to their company with clearly worded contracts that detailed exactly what kinds of performances the employee would do, the number of films in which they would appear on a yearly basis, exemptions for independent contract work in strip clubs and other live appearances, name billing, and marketing campaigns devoted exclusively to the performer. As the company proudly proclaims:

Steven [Hirsch] changed the perception of the adult industry forever with the box cover for his first VHS, *Ginger*, by making it look like a glamorous and sexy magazine cover rather than the typical gritty and low-end porno cover. . . . He invested heavily in marketing and promotion to build their names and establish a fan base for the Vivid Girls. (Vivid Entertainment 2009)

Until Hirsch, the porn home video market was largely low budget with shoddy, tacky packaging. Under his direction, production values increased and marketing was centralized around the star performer. Often referred to by first name only (Ginger, Savannah, Jenna, etc.) to maximize their appeal as a kind of pornographic Everywoman, Vivid Girls are part of a publicity machine that prominently features their names, faces, and discreetly clothed bodies as the face of a new porn respectability.

Key to these star personas are the well-publicized details of their porn specialties on screen, which make claim to representing new levels of consent and self-determination. For example, Sunny Leone (one of the few Vivid Girls who is not white and the first of Indian descent) rose to the top of the Vivid Girl ranks in the mid 2000s on the basis of exclusively doing girl/girl scenes. She has subsequently included sex with men in her films since 2007, and her star popularity certainly rose along with that decision. The company also actively sought crossover appeal in non-pornographic media, displaying their marquee stars on expensive billboards in prime locations like Times Square and Sunset Boulevard, and securing media spots for Vivid Girls in tabloid television and satellite radio. A few, like Sunny, have also appeared in mainstream erotic films.

While the more transparent performer-based practices of Vivid are certainly a welcome change to the industry, there is no denying that the company owns the product – just as MGM owned Judy Garland once upon a time. Except for those at the very top of the stardom pyramid, the financial benefits and personal control over their careers has been declining precipitously for Vivid Girls. A 2002 article in the *Los Angeles Times* about the rise of Vivid notes, 'Hirsch's system, however, imposes controls that would have other workplaces in revolt. After Hirsch handpicks each actress, the company dictates the cut of their clothing and the size of their breasts and negotiates the frequency and types of sex acts they perform' (Frammolino and Huffstutter 2002). It all starts to sound like Vivid exploits its workers. But once again, agency interacts with structure: in the 2000s, their most popular contract performers negotiated lucrative deals with Vivid after already attaining considerable success elsewhere. The cases of Sasha Grey and Jenna Jameson represent two examples of women making their own careers under highly restrictive and even subordinating conditions but succeeding with unprecedented levels of professional and personal control nonetheless.

Grey is a controversial figure not only for her extreme and oftentimes violent sex acts but also because of her killer intellect in disarming her outraged critics. During her career in pornography she worked for Vivid on occasion but represents herself as an independent contractor. She has now retired from pornography, and continues to seek out work in non-pornographic performance, with limited success. From the outset of her career, she connected herself with a network of alternative artists operating in Los Angeles, and regards her career in pornography as just one stage of her evolving creative practice to explore sexuality within environments in which she feels safe and in control. Speaking about her 2011 book of photography, *Neu Sex*, Grey explains her self-portraits working on porn sets as highly constructed forms of self-examination and self-presentation of a persona created expressly for pornography (Vice 2010). Her critical and thoughtful engagement with a pornographic self refuses the normal porn star trope of blurred identities and clearly establishes that not only her porn scenes but also her porn persona was a crafted performance. Nonetheless, Grey's success in securing work in mainstream cultural industries has been limited and she remains typecast as a sex worker in many roles.

Jenna Jameson, arguably the most famous porn star in recent memory, entered into a lucrative contract with Vivid to launch her own online enterprise, Club Jenna, after she catapulted to fame with Vivid's rival company, Wicked. She too has now retired from pornography and, like Grey, continues to seek out non-pornographic performance work, also with limited success. In contrast to Grey's highly intellectualized and artistic explorations of pornography, Jenna Jameson has fully embodied the persona of porn star – including its least empowering characteristics. In the 1990s, her conventional girl-next-door looks, glamorized to fit a rock-and-roll aesthetic, became the gold standard of the industry. Jameson's autobiography, *How to Make Love Like a Porn Star* (2004), is far less a sex education manual than a wild tale of sex, drugs, broken relationships, and criminal fringe activity. In other words, it draws on almost every trope of pornography stardom to loosely weave together a fantasy of illicit desires that ends in a fairytale romance of monogamous family oriented love. Jameson presents herself as a broken doll searching for love and accept-ance in a hostile world filled with rapists, drug-dealing biker boyfriends, on-the-lam absentee fathers, suitcase pimps, and con-niving women trying to steal away her hard-earned stardom.

In between the melodrama and souped-up sex scenes are candid depictions of her shrewd business skills and control over her own image. A section in the middle of the book provides an example of a standard contract for a new porn performer with notes detailing how it is set up to benefit the producer and leave the performer with nothing. She carefully reviews how she was able to rise to unprecedented levels of fame even while limiting her actual sexual performances to predominantly girl/girl or vanilla straight. In her assessment of Jameson's autobiography, Boyle rightly criticizes the glossed over depictions of physical, sexual, and psychological violence Jameson experienced. She calls it a discourse of legiti-mated exploitation that reiterates a problematic attitude within neo-liberal discourses of pornography that sex workers somehow invite, deserve or even tacitly consent to their abuse just because it's porn (Boyle 2011, 596). Yet, the emphasis could be just as much on Jameson's deft manipulation of these tired pornographic clichés, her knowing wink to the artifice of porn stardom by dress-ing as Marilyn Monroe for the garishly over-the-top cover, and her self-determination to be the most successful porn performer in history. As tabloid stories surface that Jameson continues to strug-gle with drug addiction and personal family estrangements (http://

popdust.com/2013/10/22/jenna-jameson-drug-addiction-oxycon tin-rehab/), she can all too easily be claimed by anti-pornography activists as yet another cautionary tale. However, that suggests that it was her work in pornography that caused all her troubles (or even exacerbated them), and requires disregarding Jameson's own frequently stated pride in becoming the best in the business.

Comparing the cases of Grey and Jameson provides useful insights into the relationship between coercion and self-determination in the performance of being a porn star. The similarities are clear: neither of them had complete control over their pornographic careers, and neither made as much money from their performances as did the producers they worked for. And neither of them regrets their pornographic career, nor sees themselves as having been a victim of it. But the differences between them are also notable, and speak to the relationship between structure and agency in this industry – as in all others. Grey presents herself as an artist for whom her pornographic performance was part of her develop-ing practice of creative and sexual self-expression. For Jameson, pornography was a wild and exciting ride that she now wants to leave behind in an embrace of heteronormativity. The differences between them and their experiences in the mainstream commercial industry, working for the same company, challenge the claim that a monolithic industry produces identical, malleable subjects. Like Patrice Lucas in *Not a Love Story*, the stories they tell reveal their attempts to navigate their work lives in ways that allow them to be fairly compensated for their work while also achieving personal success in their everyday lives.

Conclusion: the future of porn performance politics

None of us is completely free in the choices that we make. Institutional and structural constraints limit all of us in our choice of careers, and many of us experience our work lives as involving some degree of alienation or exploitation. For example, academ-ics – arguably among the most autonomous and unalienated professionals – report high levels of tension, anxiety and stress in their jobs (Olivier 2005). Examining pornography from the standpoint of performance allows us to think about it from the perspective of the labourer, offering greater nuance and empirical foundations for our analyses. Such analyses need not shy away from deplorable labour conditions, exploitative and criminal practices, and the bodily risks involved in sex work but, as part of their critiques, they foreground the agency and self-determination of individuals who decide to become porn performers for a variety of reasons, not all of them fully unconstrained.

Drawing on the explanations and self-perceptions of their work by some of the most well-known performers in pornography explicates the wide range of possibilities for engaging in this work and attempting to command respect on the set – and from society at large. This is not 'porn apologia' as some critics contend. There are no apologies accepted from those who abuse, exploit, or coerce others into sexual acts regardless of whether it is for financial or personal gain. Nor can we any longer tolerate prurient acts of condemnation from those outside pornography against performers – especially since it comes from many who have enjoyed pornographic media. Practices of self-determination including respect, consent, authenticity, persona construction, and empowerment through skilled labour are as important to the porn star as they are to any actor or media personality. When they are absent, they must be challenged and refused. When they appear present, they must be questioned, scrutinized, refined, and redirected towards even higher levels of self-determination. What this book has argued for is a recognition of pornography as a critical part of our media and cultural practices, understood as a vast matrix incorporating industrial, labour, activist, representational, governmental, and creative performance practices. The future of pornography – and of pornography studies – must move in a direction that critically yet affirmatively reveals and questions the diversity of publicly mediated forms of sexual expression. They have much to teach us.

Conclusion

The Future of Pornography Studies

Pornography is changing. As we have shown in this book, the production of sexually explicit materials in developed countries has seen increasing acceptance. Thus, while stigma towards sex workers persists, there is also greater attention to their workplace health and safety. However, in an increasingly globalized world, the trade in sexually explicit images raises the same questions of supply chain ethics that all companies now face. Are the workers in developing countries granted the same level of consideration as those in Western hubs like Los Angeles? Where sexual freedoms are highly constrained and gender roles remain rigid, what is the political potential of pornography? Technological changes are making pornography more varied and more interactive than ever before. There is no doubt that it is creating the potential for greater global exploitation, but it is also making possible enhanced global community building. The Internet has lowered the barriers to entry and new players have entered the game, including queer and feminist practitioners. 'Legacy' pornography survives, and even, in some cases, flourishes, continuing the tradition of unrealistic bodies and fantasy scenarios that are not clearly indicated as such. Nonetheless, it sits alongside new forms of representation that allow a variety of body types and sexual practices to be represented, and clearly articulate ethical labour practices and the difference between consent and coercion in explicit sexual media.

Public debates about pornography have been focused on violence and harm, with governments showing an increasing willingness to claim protection of women as the engine behind their censorious desires, while worries about the 'pornification' of culture have allowed conservative arguments opposing women's sexual agency to be reintroduced under the guise of concern over the exploitation of children. Against these institutional structures, the performers in pornography are exploring forms that a new kind of pleasure-positive sexual politics might take. They refuse simple binaries of exploitation versus authenticity in order to interrogate and challenge the practices of labour involved in making sexually explicit material. In doing so, queer and feminist pornographies offer us new ways of thinking about how sexual agency can be practised. It is no longer a question of either/or, but more like both/and. Pornography has offered up some of the most exploitative images of gender and sexual identity, and also some of the most inspiring. It can reinforce structures of oppression, but it can also reveal new ways of organizing bodies, desires, pleasures, and politics.

We have tended to emphasize the political potential of pornography throughout this book not because we discount its problematic associations with very real gender and sexual oppressions. Still, we feel that calling for the eradication or abolition of pornography is unrealistic and even dangerous. Such calls often mask attitudes about gender and sexuality that mimic the very oppressions they claim exist in pornography: passive feminine sexuality subject to paternalistic masculine control; heteronormative pleasure as the only right path to a 'healthy' sexual life; and privileged sexual citizenship for those who conform to essentialized gender and sexual roles. In order to make such claims, the work of pornography performers is ignored, especially how they articulate that work in the context of their creative, professional, and personal lives. Our claim isn't that pornography is 'good', but that we must strive to make it better. To do that, we need to listen to those whose lives are most at stake.

This book details how the story of pornography has been told, but with a double focus. We have explored both the object itself, and the academic approaches that have been brought to bear upon it. We noted that before 1970 it is difficult to find academic writing about pornography *per se*. After that time we see two dominant strands of work emerging. The first is quantitative social science research – particularly experimental psychology – which has sought to prove, through hundreds (if not thousands) of experiments that consumption of pornography is damaging to healthy sexual development. Although forty years of work have still not yet found this link, the experiments continue, and the journalistic coverage continues to report each new finding with the energetic hope that this finding, finally, will be the one that provides unquestionable proof that pornography is bad. Alongside that tradition, the work of radical and neo-anti-porn feminists has rejected empirical evidence in favour of 'listening to harm' in order to argue – from quite different axioms – that pornography is bad.

But apart from these traditions – which are certainly the most visible in public debates about pornography – other academic approaches have developed. Within a range of disciplines, particularly film studies, media studies, and cultural studies, researchers have examined pornography from multiple perspectives: the history of pornography, its aesthetics, and the functions it has served for different sexual communities, including all of those within the 'quiltbag'. In the Introduction, we outlined this new field of porn studies and its insistence on 'radical contextualism'. Such an approach deeply informs our own analysis throughout this book, and further enriches our ongoing inquiry into pornography, sex work, and the discourses of sex valuing. Concluding this book, we offer our own contribution to discussions about the development of pornography studies, with some suggestions for ways in which future research can usefully contextualize studies of pornography.

Our first suggestion is that we would like to see more work that compares and contrasts pornography with the industrial and labour practices of other cultural forms. As we noted in Chapter 1, the inequities of porn production are in many ways the inequities of the creative industries more widely. There are differences around stigma and the particularities of bodily risks that Occupational Health and Safety regulations must face. However, the facts that producers make the money, the vast majority of performers are powerless and badly paid, the nomadic nature of employment – all of these are issues in the creative industries more generally, rather than being specific to pornography. And yet much writing on pornography takes an exceptionalist approach, where writers describe inequities in the production of pornography, and claim that this is a problem unique to pornography and therefore proof that pornography as an industry is inherently exploitative and should be eradicated.

Second, and related, we see that the most productive venues of pornography scholarship are those that treat it as a distinct but nonetheless integrated cultural form. As we noted in Chapter 3, early radical feminist positions on pornography claimed that pornography was somehow different from the rest of culture. As far as sexism goes, they insisted that pornography is worse than any other media form and may even be the cause of media sexism in general. The fact that this argument gained such traction is curious given that the earliest work of feminist media activists recognized problems across the media: in advertising, newsreading, and art films as much as in pornography. No evidence has been provided to back up the claim that pornography is more sexist, or differently sexist, from other forms of culture. Nor can it be proven that the fault of sexist media is pornography, that it exerts an insidious influence on all other media forms that would otherwise be more equitable in its gender and sexual representations if it weren't for pornography.

Deciding, a priori, that pornography is a special case, such approaches don't feel the need to compare their claims about pornography with other forms of culture to see what might be common problems in a sexist society and how they are mutually reinforced. We feel that such approaches can no longer bear scrutiny. If we are concerned about whether exposure to pornography might cause negative attitudes towards subordinated groups, surely we should be asking how those negative attitudes relate to similar affectual relationships in fashion magazines – or the Bible, or Shakespeare. The fact that we don't do this kind of comparative work raises issues of the racist, classist, colonialist, and heterosexist underpinnings of anti-pornography research.

When considering the history of modern Western entertainment as a form, it becomes clear that a remarkably consistent and stable aesthetic system has held sway for at least the past two hundred years. Entertainment is vulgar, and that is key to its enjoyment. It has a story. There is a continuity and familiarity in plot and characters. It offers happy endings, or at least tidy, satisfactory conclusions. It is interactive, fast, loud and spectacular. It provokes an emotional response in the consumer. And it is fun (McGrath 1982, 54–9; McKee 2012). For entertainment these are positive qualities. Analysing pornography through this lens makes clear that the term 'adult entertainment' is not simply a euphemism. Rather, it is an accurate description of pornography's raison d'être: to provide entertainment for a sexually mature audience. Our third recommendation therefore is that we need to study pornography as part of the media entertainment matrix and ask questions about what it does for its audience, why it persists, why people want to work in it, and what kinds of meanings and values can be derived from consuming it.

Entertainment's vulgarity operates in two ways. First, it conforms to the definition of vulgar as meaning 'of or pertaining to the common people'. It is also true in the sense that it is 'rude' (which also means 'lacking in knowledge or book learning') and sexually graphic. Vulgar performances of sexual ribaldry, double entendres, and carnivalesque antics exist in the earliest recorded forms of entertainment from classical theatre and storytelling. By the nineteenth century, middle-class moral guardians became increasingly suspect of vulgarity and turned a censorious gaze over the music halls and other venues where non-white and lower class audiences thronged (Bailey 1998, 136). These 'moral panics' continue today, and pornography, as we discussed in the book, is often a target. Thus, more exploration into how moral panics arise, and what common traits their targets share can draw attention to the unequal and hierarchical valuing of sexually explicit entertainment.

Similarly, story is a central characteristic of entertainment – a series of events, in a cause and effect order, driven by characters who demonstrate plausible psychologies. Regardless of how poorly constructed or even outright laughable it may be, story is often central to even the most traditional male-oriented pornography. If you abandon the story and just have random images of body parts edited together then you no longer have pornography. You end up with art. In the same way, happy endings have been a central part of entertainment throughout its history (Leavis, 1968 [1932], 193; Nasaw, 1993, 167). Often this is literally happy – the lovers end up together forever, the villains are vanquished, etc. And even when entertainment endings are sad they always take place in a world where positive values exist – hope, friendship, joy, love. And so it is with pornography. This is a world untroubled by the messy realities of long-term relationships. At its best, pornography is about joyous encounters with sexual pleasure as its goal. And when the encounters appear as decidedly unjoyous for some, we must draw attention to the archetypal and generic qualities that make possible such narratives and challenge them in whatever form they may take, pornographic or otherwise.

Good entertainment is fast and loud. These are key entertainment virtues and have been since the emergence of this cultural form. Pornography fits well into this tradition. While art films may seem to take an interminable amount of time to establish the basis of a relationship and the psychology of the characters, in no time at all pornography has gone through a dizzying number of sexual relationships from start to finish. Quaint terms for women who enjoy sex are 'fast' and 'loose'. Pornography plays fast and loose with our sexuality, and the results can be exhilarating and cathartic. Pornography is also loud – not only the music for which it is infamous but in the noises of sex, dubbed in after the fact because of their importance to signify as clearly as possible that sex is taking place and pleasure is being had. Even the visual pleasure is loud, signalling noisily the amazing or unusual. Such spectacular loudness is at the heart of entertainment's aesthetic system.

As part of the entertainment spectacle, attractive young men and women show their bodies for visual pleasure (Neale 1983). The entertainment consumer wants to see things that they have never seen before, places they have never been, tricks they would have thought impossible, things blowing up that they would never have thought could have blown up. Pornography is a spectacular medium that offers noisy, intense pleasure. Often it adds to this a sense of the amazing and unusual. Sometimes the sheer beauty of the performers, so far removed from the everyday, amazes us. Othertimes it could be the non-normativeness that appeals, the amazement of different bodies engaged in similar kinds of pleasure. And of course there exists a whole genre of pornography which visualizes the most extreme body-work – fisting and double penetration, stretching orifices and pushing boundaries. This pornography is based around the fascination of watching people explore what bodies are capable of, amazing us by letting us see things that we would have otherwise sworn were quite impossible.

While work on the entertainment potential of pornography is a hallmark of the 'visual pleasure' model, we urge that it go further and consider the specificity of entertainment: its industrial organization, technological transformations, the unique configurations of audience and performer dynamics, and the public concern that some entertainment lacks sufficient edifying qualities that preserve the privileges of a heteronormative status quo. By contextualizing pornography – comparing it with other cultural forms, with other histories and situations – we can see what is, in fact, unique about our object of study, and what it shares with other social structures of gender and sexuality.

For example, we noted in Chapter 3 that anti-porn feminists have long claimed that working in pornography is damaging to women. If one looks only at pornography and ignores all comparisons, one can find examples – as we discussed in the book – of terrible treatment of women. But how does that compare to the experiences of women in other jobs? When Griffith et al. compared surveys of 177 porn actresses with 177 non-sex worker women matched on age, ethnicity and marital status they found that: 'porn actresses had higher levels of self-esteem, positive feelings, social support, sexual satisfaction, and spirituality compared to the matched group' (Griffith, Mitchell, Hart, Adams, and Gu 2013, 621). Furthermore, and demonstrated throughout the book, more and more porn performers are speaking out about their experiences and their reasons for staying with the job. They are neither wholly critical nor exuberantly positive, but carefully delineate their negotiations of the good and the bad, that which must not continue and possible directions for future advancement of their goals. They also compare and contrast their experiences in pornography with other working conditions. Exceptionalist approaches think that everything about pornography is unique – mostly uniquely bad – but that is only because they are looking so closely that they miss the world around the pornography, in which many characteristics are common.

One final way forward for studies of pornography suggested here, and another useful contextualizing practice, would be to move away from studies of how pornography causes harm to sexual development, and instead to study the wider question – what is healthy sexual development? Who gets to define it, and what criteria do they use? And what role do all social structures – families, churches, schools, the news, pornography – play in its formation? We noted in Chapter 3 the strange alliance that has emerged between anti-porn feminists and conservative Christians. The alliance is a strange one in the sense that while these two groups can agree about what is bad – sex for fun, commodified sex, non-committal sex – if they ever risked asking each other what defines healthy sexuality, they would find nothing to agree on. For some radical feminists, traditional marriage and even het-erosexuality itself are part of the problem. Some have insisted that a healthy sexual development would place political duty above pleasure, perhaps promoting political lesbianism, and sometimes rejecting any form of intercourse as a form of patriarchal invasion. By contrast, conservative Christians embrace traditional marriage and gender roles – for them, healthy sexual development would mean the unquestioning acceptance of patriarchal domesticity. That contemporary neo-anti-porn feminism has rejected much of the radical separatist politics and adopted language that equates violence and harm with kink, commercialized, or transient sexual encounters is acutely worrying. Their decision has seemed to be to adapt or outright betray their politics in order to ally with groups that are otherwise anathema to feminism.

The danger of discussing 'healthy' sexual development is that it always runs the risk of falling into normativity. Our focus in the book has been mostly on heteronormativity, but we have noted that it often takes on characteristics that privilege certain racial and class positions, as well as other forms of normativity welcomed in the 'charmed circle' of sex. As the long history of sexual oppression demonstrates, it is dangerous to be prescriptive in saying that people must engage in certain behaviours, or have certain feelings, in order to be judged healthy. Yet, exploring the contours of healthy sexuality, as a discursive concept itself, is a challenge that is worth embracing, rather than calling it too hard and giving up. McKee et al. (2008) proffer a non-heteronormative account of healthy sexual development that builds on the idea of informed consent, and avoids prescription into particular forms of sexuality. They suggest that healthy sexual development involves fifteen 'domains': freedom from unwanted activity; an understanding of consent; education about biological aspects; an understanding of safety; assertiveness skills; the development of sexual agency; an acceptance of lifelong learning; resilience; being raised with open communication about sex; that sexual development should not be 'coercive or joyless' (which are commonly signs of child sexual abuse); self-acceptance of one's own identity and body; an acceptance that sex can be pleasurable; an understanding of parental and societal values; awareness of public/private boundaries; and competence in deciphering and negotiating publicly mediated forms of sexual expression.

Interestingly, feminist/queer pornography activists are on the front lines of such work in redefining healthy sexuality along non-normative lines. Yet, as Courtney Trouble rightly complains:

Porn stars are not allowed to talk to queer youth or volunteer at schools. We can't teach sex ed, or become mentors. We can't become teachers or psychologists. We are not encouraged to take roles of authority in our own fields of activism. We are not welcome to run for office, propose initiatives, or lobby the government.

I see academics, administrators, journalists, the companies we work with, online resources, and even fans censoring and exploiting us simply because of how our society views sex workers. They misquote us, they use our private names, they list our class schedules, they post our home addresses, they steal our money, they steal our content, they flag and report our social media accounts. They do everything but tie us to a stake and burn us like Witches. (2014a)

Recognizing that we need to have better conversations about what constitutes healthy sexual development allows us to bring some greater context to studies of pornography users and protesters. One study based in Australia found that being religious, or voting for a right-wing political party, was more strongly correlated with having negative attitudes towards women than was consumption of sexually explicit material (McKee, 2007). The chapter on technology noted a similar study based in the United States, which found that those regions most opposed to pornography on religious-moral grounds were also the ones with the highest consumption rates (Edelman 2009). Once again, rejecting an exceptionalist approach allows us to study pornography and its influence on gender and sexual relations in the contexts in which it is produced, distributed and consumed. We champion a form of pornography studies that begins by questioning how healthy sexuality is defined and actually practised by different stakeholder groups, so that we can come to better terms with what can be good about pornography.

Throughout this book we have returned to questions about agency, the multi-faceted relationships between structures and individuals. There is no such thing as a completely free choice, for any of us, in any context. We build our identities from the resources that are made available to us at any given time, using the language that others have developed for us, and sometimes contributing our own. There exist power dynamics between people, and between people and things. But this does not mean that agency vanishes when inequity is experienced. We call for a better understanding of self-determination as meaning neither the goal of free choice or unfettered empowerment nor the defeated position of domination and oppression. Rather, through the concept of self-determination, we call for ethical engagement in both the production of pornography and in the study of pornography. Ethical engagement is a call for listening to those who are most directly and immediately affected by our work. We call for respect of differences. We call for continued dialogue on what, precisely, active consent requires. And we insist that the voices of those most implicated in pornography be heard first and loudest. The practices of ethical queer and feminist pornographers are at the cutting edge of thinking through all these issues, and these performers are putting their bodies on the line to help us achieve better ways of doing pornography. We hope that this book has contributed to a future where researchers take on the responsibility of ethical engagement and develop collaborative, intersectional frameworks for the study of pornography in all its forms and contexts.

References

Abbott, S. (2010) Motivations for pursuing a career in pornography. In Weitzer, R. (ed.) *Sex for Sale: Prostitution, Pornography and the Sex Industry*. Routledge, New York, 47–66.

Abelove, H., Abraham, J., Alderfer, H., et al. (1983) Notes and letters: 'The Barnard Conference'. *Feminist Studies* 9: 1, 177–80.

Ackerman, S. and Ball, J. (2014) Optic Nerve: millions of Yahoo webcam images intercepted by GCHQ. *Guardian* [Online] 28 February. http://www.theguardian.com/world/2014/feb/27/gchq-nsa-webcam-images-internet-yahoo

Agustin, L. M. (2005) New research directions: the cultural study of commercial sex. *Sexualities* 8: 5, 618–31.

Agustin, L. M. (2007) *Sex at the Margins: Migration, Labor Markets and the Rescue Industry*. Zed Books, London.

Akdeniz, Y. (2008) *International Child Pornography and the Law: National and International Responses*. Ashgate Publishing Ltd, Aldershot.

Alexa (2012) xhamster.com [Online] http://www.alexa.com/siteinfo/xhamster.com

Allen, A. (2001) Pornography and power. *Journal of Social Philosophy* 32: 4, 512–31.

Allen, M., Emmers, T., Gebhardt, L., and Giery, M. A. (1995) Exposure to pornography and acceptance of rape myths. *Journal of Communication* 45: 1, 5–26.

Alptraum, L. (2014) If the government cares about the safety of porn performers, why doesn't it ever listen to them? Nerve [Online] 26 June. http://www.nerve.com/culture/if-the-government-cares-about-the-safety-of-porn-performers-why-doesnt-it-ever-listen-to-them

Amazon Amanda (undated) Amazon Amanda. [Online] https://twitter.com/AmazonAmanda

American Psychological Association [APA] (2007) *Report of the APA Task*

References

Force on the Sexualization of Girls. American Psychological Association, Washington.

Ang, I. and Hermes, J. (1991) Gender and/in media consumption. In Curran, J. and Gurevitch, M. (eds.) *Mass Media and Society*. Edward Arnold, London, 325–47.

Association of Sites Advocating Child Protection (2010) The ASACP [Online] http://www.asacp.org/whitepaper/ASACP-whitepaper-9–10–2010.pdf

Attwood, F. (2002) Reading porn: the paradigm shift in pornography research. *Sexualities* 5: 1, 91–105.

Attwood, F. (2009) *Mainstreaming Sex*. I. B. Taurus and Co., London.

Attwood, F. and Smith, C. (2014) Porn studies: an introduction. *Porn Studies* 1: 1, 1–6.

Auerbach, D. (2014) Vampire porn. Slate [Online] 23 October. http://www.slate.com/articles/technology/technology/2014/10/mindgeek_porn_monopoly_its_dominance_is_a_cautionary_tale_for_other_industries.single.html

Australian Communication and Media Authority (2011) Online regulation. [Online] http://www.acma.gov.au/Industry/Internet/Licensing--I-want-to-be-an-ISP/ISP--ICH-responsibilities/online-regulation

Australian Senate Standing Committee on Environment, Communications and the Arts (2008) Sexualisation of Children in the Contemporary Media. [Online] http://www.parliament.qld.gov.au/Documents/TableOffice/Tabled Papers/2014/5414T4838.pdf

Bailey, P. (1998) *Popular Culture and Performance in the Victorian City*. Cambridge University Press, Cambridge.

Baldwin, M. A. (1989) Pornography and the traffic in women. *Yale Journal of Law and Feminism* 1: 1, 111–55.

Baron, R. A. and Richardson, D. R. (1994) *Human Aggression*, 2nd edn. Plenum Press, New York and London.

Basiliere, J. (2009) Political is Personal: Scholarly Manifestations of the Feminist Sex Wars. *Michigan Feminist Studies* 22: 1, 1–25.

Beaty, B. (2005) *Fredric Wertham and the Critique of Mass Culture*. University Press of Mississippi, Jackson.

Begum, S., Hocking, J. S., Groves, J., Fairley, C. K., and Keogh, L. A. (2013) Sex workers talk about sex work: six contradictory characteristics of legalised sex work in Melbourne, *Australia. Culture, Health and Sexuality* 15: 1, 85–100.

Bell, D. (1995) Pleasure and danger: the paradoxical spaces of sexual citizenship. *Political Geography* 14: 2, 139–53.

Bell, L. (1987) *Good Girls, Bad Girls: Sex Trade Workers and Feminists Face to Face*. Women's Press, St Paul.

Bell, S., Cossman, B., and Gotell, L. (eds.) (1997) *Bad Attitude/s on Trial: Pornography, Feminism, and the Butler Decision*. University of Toronto Press, Toronto.

Berlant, L. (1995) Live sex acts. *Feminist Studies* 21: 2, 379–404.

References

Blumenthal, R. (1973) 'Porno chic'. *New York Times*. 21 January.

Boeringer, S. B. (1994) Pornography and sexual aggression: associations of violent and nonviolent depictions of rape and rape proclivity. *Deviant Behavior* 15: 3, 289–304.

Boyle, K. (2000) The pornography debates: beyond cause and effect. *Women's Studies International Forum* 23: 2, 187–95.

Boyle, K. (2008) Courting consumers and legitimating exploitation. *Feminist Media Studies* 8: 1, 35–50.

Boyle, K. (2011) Producing abuse: selling the harms of pornography. *Women's Studies International Forum* 34: 6, 593–602.

Bragg, B. and McFarland, P. (2007) The erotic and the pornographic in Chicana rap: JV vs. Ms. Sancha. *Meridians: feminism, race, transnationalism* 7: 2, 1–21.

Braun-Courville, D. and Rojas, M. (2009) Exposure to sexually explicit websites and adolescent sexual attitudes and behaviors. *Journal of Adolescent Health* 45: 2, 156–62.

Breslin, S. (2012) The obscenity police are coming. Forbes. [Online] 13 September. http://www.forbes.com/sites/susannahbreslin/2012/09/13/mitt-romney-porn/

Brickell, C. (2009) Sexuality and the dimensions of power. *Sexuality and Culture* 13, 57–74.

Bridges, A. J., Wosnitzer, R., Scharrer, E., Sun, S., and Liberman, R. (2010) Aggression and sexual behavior in best-selling pornography videos: a content analysis update. *Violence Against Women* 16: 10, 1065–85.

Broderick, R. (2014) According to Pornhub, the South watches more gay porn than any other part of the US. Buzzfeed. [Online] http://www.buzzfeed.com/ryanhatesthis/according-to-pornhub-the-south-watches-more-gay-porn-than-an

Bronstein, C. (2011) *Battling Pornography: The American Feminist Anti-Pornography Movement, 1976–1986*. Cambridge University Press, New York.

Brooks, S. (2010) Hypersexualization and the dark body: race and inequality among Black and Latina women in the exotic dance industry. *Sex Research and Social Policy* 7, 70–80.

Brown, J. D. and L'Engle, K. L. (2009) X-Rated: sexual attitudes and behaviors associated with early adolescents' exposure to sexually explicit media. *Communication Research* 36: 1, 129–51.

Brown, M. (2010) *Make Adult Videos for Fun and Profit! The Secrets Anybody Can Use to Make Money in the Adult Video Business*. CreateSpace Independent Publishing Platform.

Brownmiller, S. (1993 [1975]) *Against our Will: Men, Women and Rape*. Fawcette Columbine, New York.

Burgess, O. (2012) True colors: race, and the misnomer of hip hop as 'Black music'. Hip Hop DX. [Online] 5 September. http://www.hiphopdx.com/index/editorials/id.1947/title.true-colors-race-and-the-misnomer-of-hip-hop-as-black-music

References

Burke, J. (2013) Bangladesh garment workers set for 77% pay rise. *Guardian* [Online] 14 November. http://www.theguardian.com/world/2013/nov/14/bangladesh-garment-workers-pay-rise

Busby LLM, K. (2004) The queer sensitive interveners in the Little Sisters case. *Journal of Homosexuality* 47: 3, 129–50.

Bussel, R. K. (2008) Beyond yes or no: consent as sexual process. In Friedman, J. and Valenti, J. (eds) *Yes means Yes: Visions of Female Sexual Power and a World Without Rape*. Seal Press, New York, 43–52.

Bussel, R. K. (2013) Organic, fair-trade porn: on the hunt for ethical smut. *The Daily Beast*. [Online] 13 April. http://www.thedailybeast.com/arti cles/2013/04/13/free-trade-organic-porn-on-the-hunt-for-ethical-smut.html

Butler, J. (1990) *Gender Trouble*. Routledge, New York.

Butler, J. (1997) *Excitable Speech*. Routledge, New York.

Cade, L. (2014) Why I went to war. The Official Lily Cade.com [Online] 17 June. http://www.lilycade.com/2014/06/why-i-went-to-war/

Cadwalladr, D. (2013) Porn wars: the debate that's dividing academia. *Guardian Observer* [Online] 16 June. http://www.theguardian.com/culture/2013/jun/16/internet-violent-porn-crime-studies

Caldwell, J. (2008) *Production Culture: Industrial Reflexivity and Critical Practice in Film and Television*. Duke University Press, Durham.

Campbell, A. (2014) Can custom porn save a flaccid industry? *Huffington Post* [Online] 25 January. http://www.huffingtonpost.com/2014/01/17/porn-indus try-piracy-pay_n_4613642.html?ncid=edlinkusaolp00000003

Carline, A. (2011) Criminal justice, extreme pornography and prostitution: protecting women or promoting morality? *Sexualities* 14: 3, 312–33.

CCSO Cybercrime Working Group (2013) Report to the federal/provincial/territorial ministers responsible for justice and public safety: cyberbullying and the non-consensual distribution of intimate images. [Online] http://www.justice.gc.ca/eng/rp-pr/other-autre/cndii-cdncii/pdf/cndii-cdncii-eng.pdf

Champagne, J. (1997) Stop reading films! *Cinema Journal* 36: 4, 76–97.

Chang, G. (2000) *Disposable Domestics: Immigrant Women Workers in The Global Economy*. South End Press, Boston.

Chapkis, W. (1997) *Live Sex Acts: Women Performing Erotic Labor*. Routledge, New York.

Christakis, E. (2012) A modest proposal: the case for fair trade porn. *Huffington Post* [Online] 3 February. http://www.huffingtonpost.com/erika-christakis/fair-trade-porn_b_1252494.html

Clark-Flory, T. (2010) http://www.salon.com/2010/07/20/lorelei_lee_stagliano_trial/

Clark-Flory, T. (2014) 'Performative sex is utterly different from private sex': A porn star takes on the California State Capitol. Salon [Online] 24 April. http://www.salon.com/2014/06/24/performative_sex_is_utterly_different_from_private_sex_a_porn_star_takes_on_the_california_state_capitol

References

Coalition for a feminist sexuality and against sadomasochism (1983) Leaflet distributed at Barnard Conference. *Feminist Studies* 9: 1, 180–2.

Cole, S. G. (1992) *Pornography and the Sex Crisis.* Second Story Press, Toronto.

Collins, P. C. (2000) Pornography and black women's bodies. In O'Toole, L. L., Schiffman, J. R., and Kiter Edwards, M. L. (eds.) *Gender Violence: Interdisciplinary Perspectives,* 2nd edn. New York University Press, New York, 389–94.

Collis, C., McKee, A., and Hamley, B. (2010) Entertainment industries at university: designing a curriculum. *Continuum: Journal of Media and Cultural Studies* 24: 6, 921–32.

Comella, L. (2010) Remaking the sex industry: the adult expo as a microcosm. In Weitzer, R. J. (ed.) *Sex for Sale: Prostitution, Pornography, and the Sex Industry.* Routledge, New York, 285–306.

Coopersmith, J. (1998) Pornography, technology and progress. *Icon* 4, 94–125.

Corsianos, M. (2007) Mainstream pornography and 'women': questioning sexual agency. *Critical Sociology* 33, 863–85.

Cossman, B. (1997) Feminist fashion or morality in drag?: the sexual subtext of the *Butler* decision. In Bell, S., Cossman, B., and Gotell, L. (eds.) *Bad Attitude/s on Trial: Pornography, Feminism, and the Butler Decision.* University of Toronto Press, Toronto, 147–51.

County of Los Angeles (2012) Text of the proposed measure county of Los Angeles safer sex in the adult film industry act [Online] http://www.lavote.net/voter/PDFS/ELECTION_RELATED/11062012_LACOUNTY_WIDE_MEASURE_B.pdf

Cribb, R. (2013) Toronto man charged in huge worldwide child-porn bust. *The Star* [Online] 14 November. http://www.thestar.com/news/world/2013/11/14/toronto_man_charged_in_international_childporn_network_bust.html

Crofts, T. and Lee, M. (2013) 'Sexting', children and child pornography. *Sydney Law Review* 35, 85–106.

Davies, K. A. (1997) Voluntary exposure to pornography and men's attitudes toward feminism and rape. *Journal of Sex Research* 34: 2, 131–7.

Davis, S. (2008) Leading the way: strategic planning toward sex worker cooperative development. BC Coalition of Experiential Communities. [Online] http://bccec.files.wordpress.com/2008/03/leading_the_way.pdf

Dejanikus, T. (1982) Charges of exclusion and McCarthyism at Barnard conference. *Off Our Backs* 12: 6, 5.

Dickson, E. J. (2013) Growing backlash against Duke porn star in adult film industry. Salon. [Online] 29 March. http://www.salon.com/2014/03/30/growing_backlash_against_duke_porn_star_in_adult_film_industry_partner/

Dines, G. (1998a) Dirty business: *Playboy* magazine and the mainstreaming of pornography. In Dines, G., Jensen, R., and Russo, A. (eds.) *Pornography: The Production and Consumption of Inequality.* Routledge, New York and London, 37–63.

References

Dines, G. (1998b) Living in two worlds: an activist in the academy. In Dines, G., Jensen, R., and Russo, A. (eds.) *Pornography: The Production and Consumption of Inequality*. Routledge, New York and London, 163–6.

Dines, G. (2009) Pornography and race. Gail Dines. [Online] 10 September. http://gaildines.com/2009/09/pornography-and-race/

Dines, G. (2010) New York Post. Gail Dines. [Online] 11 July. http://gaildines.com/2010/07/new-york-post/

Dines, G. (2011) *Pornland: How Porn Has Hijacked Our Sexuality*. Beacon Press, New York.

DiNucci, D. (1999) Fragmented future. *Print* 53: 4, 32.

Doane, M. A. (1991) *Femme Fatales*. Routledge, New York.

Doherty, B. (2012) Ball back-down as Sherrin ends child labour. *The Sydney Morning Herald* [Online] 26 September. http://www.smh.com.au/national/ball-backdown-as-sherrin-ends-child-labour-20120925–26jjh.html

Donenfeld, J. (2008) The war is over, Blu-ray wins! Jeffrey Donenfeld. [Online] 28 January. http://jeffreydonenfeld.com/blog/2008/01/the-war-is-over-blu-ray-wins/

Donnerstein, E. and Berkowitz, L. (1981) Victim reactions in aggressive erotic films as a factor in violence against women. *Journal of Personality and Social Psychology* 41: 4, 710–24.

Donzelot, J. (1979) *The Policing of Families*. Johns Hopkins Paperbacks, Baltimore.

Dreier, Hannah. (2014) Porn production moves to Vegas after condom law. Associated Press [Online] 17 Jan. http://bigstory.ap.org/article/porn-production-moves-vegas-after-condom-law

Duits, L. and Van Zoonen, L. (2011) Coming to terms with sexualisation. *European Journal of Cultural Studies* 14: 5, 491–506.

Dworkin, A. (1980) Beaver and male power in pornography. *New Political Science* 1: 4, 37–41.

Dworkin, A. (1981) *Pornography: Men Possessing Women*. The Women's Press, London.

Dworkin, A. and MacKinnon, C. (1994) Statement by Catharine A. Mackinnon and Andrea Dworkin regarding Canadian customs and legal approaches to pornography [Online] 26 August. http://www.nostatusquo.com/ACLU/dworkin/OrdinanceCanada.html

Dworkin, A. and MacKinnon, C. (eds.) (1997) *In Harm's Way*. Harvard University Press, Cambridge.

Dyer, R. (1979) *Stars*. British Film Institute, London.

Dyer, R. (1997) *White*. Routledge, New York.

Economist (1999) Branded flesh. *Economist* [Online] 12 August. http://www.economist.com/node/232069

Economist (2011) At a XXX-roads: the changing adult business. *Economist* [Online] 1 October. http://www.economist.com/node/21530956

References

Edelmen, B. (2009) Red light states. *Journal of Economic Perspectives* 23: 1, 209–20.

Eisenstein, E. L. (1979) *The Printing Press as an Agent of Change*. Cambridge University Press, Cambridge.

Endrass, J., Urbaniok, F., Hammermeister, L. C., Benz, C., Elbert, T., Laubacher, A., and Rossegger, A. (2009) The consumption of Internet child pornography and violent and sex offending. *BMC Psychiatry* 9: 43 [Online] http://www.biomedcentral.com/1471-244X/9/43

Farnsworth, C. H. (1995) Artist regains works in Toronto obscenity case. *New York Times* [Online] 23 April. http://www.nytimes.com/1995/04/23/world/artist-regains-works-in-toronto-obscenity-case.html

Fisher, W. A., and Barak, A. (1991) Pornography, erotica, and behavior: more questions than answers. *International Journal of Law and Psychiatry* 14: 1, 65–83.

Forna, A. (2001 [1992]) Pornography and racism: sexualizing oppression and inciting hatred. In Itzin, C. (ed.) *Pornography: Women, Violence and Civil Liberties*. Oxford University Press, New York, 102–12.

Foster, M. (2010) *Getting Into Porn – The Handbook: A Simple Guide to the Porn Industry*. CreateSpace Independent Publishing Platform.

Frammolino, R. and Huffstutter, P. J. (2002) The actress, the producer, and their porn revolution. *Los Angeles Times* [Online] 6 January. http://articles.latimes.com/2002/jan/06/magazine/tm-20634/6

Frizell, S. (2014) Israel bans 'revenge porn'. Time. [Online] 07 January. http://world.time.com/2014/01/07/israel-bans-revenge-porn/

Funk, R. E. (2004) What does pornography say about me(n)? How I became an anti-pornography activist. In Stark, C. and Whisnant, R. (eds.) *Not For Sale: Feminists Resisting Prostitution and Pornography*. Spinifex Press, Melbourne, 331–51.

Gall, G. (2007) Sex worker unionisation: an exploratory study of emerging collective organization. *Industrial Relations Journal* 38: 1, 70–88.

Garcia, L. T. (1986) Exposure to pornography and attitudes about women and rape: a correlational study. *Journal of Sex Research* 22: 3, 378–85.

Gerhard, J. (2001) *Desiring Revolution: Second-Wave Feminism and the Rewriting of American Sexual Thought, 1920 to 1982*. Columbia University Press, New York.

Giddens, A. (1992) *Transformation of Intimacy: Sexuality, Love, and Eroticism in Modern Societies*. Polity, Cambridge.

Gill, R. (2012a) Media, empowerment and sexualisation of culture. *Sex Roles* 66, 736–45.

Gill, R. (2012b). Sexualisation of culture? *Social and Personality Psychology Compass* 6: 7, 483–98.

Gillis, S. (2004) Cybersex. In Gibson, P. C. (ed.). *More Dirty Looks: Gender, Pornography and Power*. BFI Publishing, London, 92–101.

References

Gilman, S. R. (1985) *Difference and Pathology: Stereotypes of Race and Madness*. Cornell University Press, Ithaca, NY.

Global Network for Sex Work Projects. (undated) Global Network of Sex Work Projects [Online] http://www.nswp.org/

Goldberg, M. (2014) What is a woman? *The New Yorker* [Online] 4 August. http://www.newyorker.com/magazine/2014/08/04/woman-2

Gotell, L. (1997) Shaping *Butler*: the new politics of anti-pornography. In Bell, S., Cossman, B., Gotell, L. (eds.) *Bad Attitude/s on Trial: Pornography, Feminism, and the Butler Decision*. University of Toronto Press, Toronto, 48–106.

Griffin, S. (1971) Rape: the all-American crime. *Ramparts Magazine*. September 1971 26–35.

Griffin, S. (1981) *Pornography and Silence: Culture's Revenge Against Nature*. Harper and Row Publishers, New York.

Griffith, J. D., Mitchell, S., Hart, C. L., Adams, L. T., and Gu, L. L. (2013) Pornography actresses: an assessment of the damaged goods hypothesis. *Journal of Sex Research* 50: 7, 621–32.

Gross, D. (2013) Under pressure, Facebook targets sexist hate speech. CNN. [Online] 30 May. http://www.cnn.com/2013/05/29/tech/social-media/facebook-hate-speech-women/

Groves, J., Newton, D. C., Chen, M. Y., Hocking, J., Bradshaw, C. S., and Fairley, C. K. (2008) Sex workers working within a legalised industry: their side of the story. *Sexually Transmitted Infections* 84: 5, 393–4.

Gupta, P. (2014) Duke porn star Belle Knox has lost her financial aid. Salon [Online] 17 June. www.salon.com/2014/06/17/duke_porn_star_belle_knox_has_lost_her_financial_aid/

Hayoun, M. (2014) Porn stars battle stigma with sex awareness amid bank account closures [Online] 29 April. http://america.aljazeera.com/articles/2014/4/29/porn-star-battlesstigmawithsexawarenessamidbankaccountclosures.html

Herdt, G. (2009) Introduction: moral panics, sexual politics, and cultural anger. In Herdt, G. (ed.) *Moral Panics, Sex Panics: Fear and the Fight Over Sexual Rights*. New York University Press, New York, 1–46.

Hern, A. (2014) Adult stars launch #payforyourporn campaign against porn piracy. *Guardian* [Online] 8 May. http://www.theguardian.com/technology/2014/may/08/adult-stars-launch-payforyourporn-campaign-against-porn-piracy

Hern, A. (2013) Facebook's changing standards: from beheading to breastfeeding images. *Guardian* [Online] 22 October. http://www.theguardian.com/technology/2013/oct/22/facebook-standards-beheading-breastfeeding-social-networking

Hess, A. (2012) Porn stars may soon have to wear condoms. Will you still watch? Slate [Online] 25 October. http://www.slate.com/blogs/xx_factor/2012/10/25/california_s_measure_b_what_s_so_bad_about_condoms_in_porn.html

Hester, H. (2014) *Beyond Explicit: Pornography and the Displacement of Sex*. SUNY Press, New York.

References

Heywood, L. (2000) Athletic versus pornographic eroticism: how muscle maga-zines compromise female athletes and delegitimize the sport of body-building in the public eye. Meso Morphosis Interactive 1: 1 [Online] 19 January. https:// thinksteroids.com/articles/athletic-pornographic-eroticism-muscle-magazines-female/

Higginbotham, E. B. (1993) *Righteous Discontent: The Women's Movement in the Black Baptist Church*. Harvard University Press, Cambridge.

Hill, K. (2014) How revenge porn king Hunter Moore was taken down. Forbes. [Online] 24 January. http://www.forbes.com/sites/kashmirhill/2014/01/24/how-revenge-porn-king-hunter-moore-was-taken-down/

Hodgson, Nichi (undated) Ethical Porn Partnership [Online] ethicalporn.org.

hooks, b. (1997) Hardcore honey: bell hooks goes on the down low with Lil Kim. Paper [Online] 11 July. http://www.papermag.com/2014/07/lil_kim_bel_hooks.php

Hopper, T. (2014) Your porn is not Canadian enough, CRTC warns erotica channels. *National Post* [Online] 5 March. http://news.nationalpost.com/2014/03/05/your-porn-is-not-canadian-enough-crtc-warns-erotica-channels/

Houlihan, A. (2011) When 'no' means 'yes' and 'yes' means harm: HIV risk, consent and sadomasochism case law. *Law and Sexuality: A Review of Lesbian, Gay, Bisexual, and Transgender Legal Issues* 20, 31–59.

Hubbard, P. (2001) Sex zones: intimacy, citizenship and public space. *Sexualities* 4:1, 51–71.

Hudson, H. E., Cusack, D. D., Dietz, P. E., Dobson, J., Ritter, B., Schauer, F., Tilton-Durfee, D., Becker, J., and Levine, J. (1986) Attorney General's com-mission on pornography final report. US Department of Justice [Online] http:// obu-investigators.com/xuk/porn/meese/index.htm

Hughes, D. M. (2004) The use of new communications and information tech-nologies for sexual exploitation of women and children. In Waskul, D. D. (ed.) *Net.sexxx: Readings on Sex, Pornography and the Internet*. Peter Lang, New York, 109–30.

Hunter, M. and Soto, K. (2009) Women of color in hip-hop: the pornographic gaze. *Race, Gender and Class* 16: 1–2, 170–91.

Illouz, E. (2008) *Saving the Modern Soul: Therapy, Emotion, and the Culture of Self-Help*. University of California Press, Berkeley.

International Labour Organization (2014) Profits and Poverty: The Economics of Forced Labour [Online] http://www.ilo.org/global/topics/forced-labour/publi-cations/profits-of-forced-labour-2014/lang--en/index.htm

Jacobs, K. (2004) Pornography in small spaces and other places. *Cultural Studies* 18: 1, 67–83.

Jacobs, K. (2007) *Netporn: DIY Web Culture and Sexual Politics*. Rowman and Littlefield Publishers, Inc., New York.

Jameson, J. and Strauss, N. (2010) *How to Make Love Like a Porn Star: A Cautionary Tale*. Daystreet Books, New York.

References

Jeffreys, S. (1990) *Anticlimax: A Feminist Perspective on the Sexual Revolution.* The Women's Press, London.

Jeffreys, S. (2009) *The Industrial Vagina: The Political Economy of the Global Sex Trade.* Routledge, New York.

Jeffreys, S. (2014) *Gender Hurts: A Feminist Analysis of the Politics of Transgenderism.* Routledge, New York.

Jensen, R. (1998) Using pornography. In Dines, G., Jensen, R., and Russo, A. (eds.) *Pornography: The Production and Consumption of Inequality.* Routledge, New York, 101–46.

Jensen, R. (2004) Blow bangs and cluster bombs: the cruelty of men and Americans. In Stark, C. and Whisnant, R. (eds.) *Not For Sale: Feminists Resisting Prostitution and Pornography.* Spinifex Press, Melbourne, 28–37.

Jensen, R. (2006) The relevance of radical feminism for gay men. In Kendall, C. and Martino, W. (eds.) *Gendered Outcasts and Sexual Outlaws: Sexual Oppression and Gender Hierarchies in Queer Men's Lives.* Harrington Park Press, Binghamton, 19–25.

Jensen, R. (2007) *Getting Off: Pornography and the End of Masculinity.* South End Press, Boston.

Jensen, R. and Dines, G. (1998) The content of mass-marketed pornography. In Dines, G. Jensen, R., and Russo, A. (eds.) *Pornography: The Production and Consumption of Inequality.* Routledge, New York. 65–100.

Johnson, J. (2010) To catch a curious clicker: a social network analysis of the online pornography industry. In Boyle, K. (ed.) *Everyday Pornography.* Routledge, New York, 134–46.

Johnson, P. (1996) Pornography drives technology: why not to censor the Internet. *Federal Communications Law Journal* 49: 1, 217–26.

Johnson, P. (2010) Law, morality and disgust: the regulation of extreme pornography in England and Wales. *Social and Legal Studies* 19: 2, 147–63.

Johnson, R. (2009) Life as a film extra: Hollywood's least powerful. *Telegraph.* London [Online] 9 September. http://www.telegraph.co.uk/culture/film/star sandstories/6152039/Life-as-a-film-extra-Hollywoods-least-powerful.html

Jowett, G., Jarvie, I. C. and Fuller, J. (1996*) Children and the Movies: Media Influence and the Payne Fund Controversy.* Cambridge University Press, New York.

Kappeler, S. (1986) *The Pornography of Representation.* University of Minnesota Press, Minneapolis.

Keating, C. (1965) *Perversion for Profit.* [Film] Citizens for Decent Literature Inc. and Quality Information Publishers Inc.

Kendall, C. (2006) Pornography, hypermasculinity and gay male identity: implications for male rape and gay male domestic violence. In Kendall, C. and Martino W. (eds.) *Gendered Outcasts and Sexual Outlaws: Sexual Oppression and Gender Hierarchies in Queer Men's Lives.* Harrington Park Press, Binghamton, 105–30.

References

Kendrick, W. (1996) *The Secret Museum: Pornography in Modern Culture*. University of California Press, Berkeley.

Kibby, M. and Costello, B. (2001) Between the image and the act: interactive sex entertainment on the Internet. *Sexualities* 4: 3, 353–69.

Kidd, D. (2003). Mapplethorpe and the new obscenity. *Afterimage* 30: 5, 6–7.

King, J (2009) *Get Into Porn: An Industry Insider's Guide to Becoming a Porn Star*. Joy King Marketing (GIP Productions).

Kipnis, L. (1996) *Bound and Gagged: Pornography and the Politics of Fantasy in America*. Duke University Press, Durham.

Klein, B. (1981) *Not a Love Story*. [Film] National Film Board of Canada, Montreal.

Knox, B. (2014) I'm Belle Knox and tonight's 'Law and Order SVU' is ripped from my headline. Xojane [Online] 22 Oct. http://www.xojane.com/it-hap pened-to-me/belle-knox-evie-barnes-law-and-order-svu

Lahey, K. A. (1991) Pornography and harm: learning to listen to women. *International Journal of Law and Psychiatry* 14: 1–2, 117–31.

Lane III, F. S. (2001) *Obscene Profits: The Entrepreneurs of Pornography in the Cyber Age*. Routledge, New York.

Langman, L. (2004) Grotesque degradation: globalization, carnivalization, and cyberporn. In Waskul, D. D. (ed.) *Net.sexxx: Readings on Sex, Pornography and the Internet*. Peter Lang, New York. 193–216.

Latapy, M., Margnien, C. and Fournier, R. (2013) Quantifying paedophile activity in a large P2P system. *Information Processing and Management* 49: 1, 248–63.

Leavis, Q. D. (1968 [1932]) *Fiction and the Reading Public*. Chatto and Windus, London.

Lee, J. (2014) Tricks of the Trade: Porn's 'best practices' for content trades and shares. PinkLabel-TV [Online] undated. http://www.pinklabel.tv/ on-demand/tricks-of-the-trade-porns-best-practices-for-content-trades-and-shares/?CA=934717–0000&PA=1689358

Lee, J. (2011) Five ways you can fight porn piracy. JizLee.com [Online] 13 June. http://jizlee.com/fight-porn-piracy/

Lee, L. (2012) Porn performer: why I'm against government mandated condom use in porn. AlterNet [Online] 18 January. http://www.alternet.org/ story/153810/porn_performer%3A_why_i%27m_against_government_man dated_condom_use_in_porn?paging=off&current_page=1#bookmark

Lee, L. (2013) Cum guzzling anal nurse whore: a feminist porn star manifesta. In Taormino, T., Parreñas Shimizu, C., Penley, C., Miller-Young, M. (eds.) *The Feminist Porn Book: The Politics of Producing Pleasure*. The Feminist Press, New York, 200–14.

Lee, T. (2004) In and out: a survivor's memoir of stripping. In Stark, C. and Whisnant, R. (eds.) *Not For Sale: Feminists Resisting Prostitution and Pornography*. Spinifex Press, Melbourne, 56–63.

References

Lehman, P. ed. (2006) *Pornography: Film and Culture*. Rutgers University Press, New Brunswick.

Levy, A. (2010) *Female Chauvinist Pigs: Women and the Rise of Raunch Culture*. Black Inc., Collingwood.

Lewis, J. (2008) Presumed effects of erotica: some notes on the report of the commission on obscenity and pornography. *Film International* 6: 36, 7–16.

Ley, D., Prause, N., and Finn, P. (2014) The emperor has no clothes: a review of the 'pornography addiction' model. *Current Sexual Health Reports* 6: 2, 94–105.

Liptak. A. (2014) Justices rule child pornography restitution is too high. *New York Times* [Online] 23 April. http://www.nytimes.com/2014/04/24/us/poli tics/justices-void-3-4–million-award-to-child-pornography-victim.html?_r=0

Liss, M., Erchull M., and Ramsey L. (2010) Empowering or oppressing? Development and exploration of the enjoyment of sexualization scale. *Personality and Social Psychology Bulletin* 37: 1, 55–68.

Lockhart, W. B. (1970). *The Report of the Commission on Obscenity and Pornography*. Superintendent of Documents, US Government Printing Office, Washington, DC.

Los Angeles Times (2010). About (late) last night: Natalie Portman, injured on set, is healthy for Oscar season. Los Angeles Times Show Tracker [Online] 23 November. http://latimesblogs.latimes.com/showtracker/2010/11/about-late-last-night-natalie-portman-injured-on-set-is-healthy-for-oscar-season.html

Love, S. (2013) A question of feminism. In Taormino, T., Parreñas Shimizu, C., Penley, C., Miller-Young, M. (eds.) *The Feminist Porn Book: The Politics of Producing Pleasure*. The Feminist Press, New York, 97–104.

Lovelace, L. (1973) *Inside Linda Lovelace*. Heinrich Hannau Publications Ltd, London.

Lovelace, L. (1974) http://www.amazon.com/The-intimate-diary-Linda-Lovelace/dp/0523003943

Lovelace, L. (2001) Linda Lovelace: the ordeal is over. *Leg Show* January, 79–81.

Lovelace, L. M. and McGrady, M. (1980) *Ordeal*. Citadel, New York.

MacKinnon, C. A. (1989) *Toward a Feminist Theory of the State*. Harvard University Press, Cambridge.

Malamuth, N. M. (1981) Rape fantasies as a function of exposure to violent sexual stimuli. *Archives of Sexual Behavior* 10: 1, 33–47.

Maltby, R. (2003) *Hollywood Cinema*. Wiley-Blackwell, London.

Marks, K. (2012) Minister's bid to ban miniskirts using anti-pornography law angers Indonesian women. The National (Abu Dhabi) [Online] 23 April. http://www.thenational.ae/news/world/asia-pacific/ministers-bid-to-ban-mini skirts-using-anti-pornography-law-angers-indonesian-women

Marsh, T. (2004) My year in smut: inside Danni's hard drive. In Waskul, D. D. (ed.) *Net.sexxx: Readings on Sex, Pornography and the Internet*. New York: Peter Lang, 237–58.

References

Mason-Grant, J. (2004) *Pornography Embodied: From Speech to Sexual Practice*. Rowman and Littlefield, Oxford.

Matyszczyk, C. (2012) Is anyone actually going to *.xxx domains? C Net [Online] 2 May. http://www.cnet.com/news/is-anyone-actually-going-to-xxx-domains/

Mayer, V. (2008) Guys gone wild? Soft-core video professionalism and new realities in television production. *Cinema Journal* 47: 2, 97–116.

Mayhem, M. (2013) Tales of Kink.com. Maggie Mayhem [Online] 2 December. http://missmaggiemayhem.com/2013/02/12/tales-of-kink-com/

Mazières, A., Trachman, M., Cointet, J. P., Coulmont, B., and Prieur, C. (2014) Deep tags: toward a quantitative analysis of online pornography. *Porn Studies* 1: 1–2, 80–95.

McGlynn, C. (2010). Marginalizing feminism: debating extreme pornography laws in public and policy discourse. In Boyle, K. (ed.) *Everyday Pornography*. Routledge, London, 190–202.

McGrath, J. (1982) *A Good Night Out: Popular Theatre: Audiences, Class and Form*. Methuen, London.

McKay, J. and Johnson, H. (2008) Pornographic eroticism and sexual grotesquerie in representations of African American sportswomen. *Social Identities* 14: 4, 491–504.

McKee, A. (2001) A cultural policy argument for government subsidies of gay porn production in Australia. In Atkinson, K. J. and Finnerty J. J. (eds.) *Queer in the Twenty-First Century: The Body – Queer and Politic*. GLWA Inc., Brisbane, 118–37.

McKee, A. (2007) The relationship between attitudes towards women, consumption of pornography, and other demographic variables in a survey of 1,023 consumers of pornography. *International Journal of Sexual Health* 19: 1, 31–45.

McKee, A. (2012) The aesthetics of entertainment. In McKee, A., Collis, C., and Hamley, B. (eds.) *Entertainment Industries: Entertainment as Cultural System*. Routledge, New York.

McKee, A. (2013). How did children become the most important audience for pornography in Australia? In Moran, A. and Aveyard, K. (eds.) *Watching Films: New Perspectives on Movie-Going, Exhibition and Reception*. Intellect Books, Bristol, 89–100.

McKee, A., Albury, K., and Lumby, C. (2008) *The Porn Report*. Melbourne University Press, Melbourne.

McNair, B. (2002) *Striptease Culture: Sex, Media and the Democratisation of Desire*. Routledge, Abingdon.

McNeil, L., Osborne, J., and Pavia, P. (2005) *The Other Hollywood: The Uncensored Oral History of The Porn Film Industry*. Regan Books, New York.

McNeill, T. (2013) Sex education and the promotion of heteronormativity. *Sexualities* 16: 7, 826–46.

References

McRobbie, A. (2008) Pornographic permutations. *The Communication Review* 11, 225–36.

Mearian, L. (2006) Porn industry may be decider in Blu-ray, HD-DVD battle. MacWorld [Online] 2 May. http://www.macworld.com/article/1050627/pornhd.html

Mehta, D. (2013) Project Spade, massive international child porn bust centred on Toronto, net 348 arrests in horrific sexual act. *National Post* [Online] 13 November. http://news.nationalpost.com/2013/11/14/at-least-386-victims-rescued-after-project-spade-a-massive-child-porn-bust-that-started-in-toronto/

Miller-Young, M. (2005) Sexy and smart: Black women and the politics of self-authorship in netporn. In Jacobs, K., Janssen, M., and Pasquinelli, M. (eds.) *C'Lick Me: A Netporn Studies Reader*. Institute of Network Cultures Amsterdam, 205–17.

Miller-Young, M. (2007) Hip-Hop honeys and da hustlaz: black sexualities in the new hip-hop pornography. *Meridians: Feminism, Race, Transnationalism* 8: 1, 261–92.

Miller-Young, M. (2010) Putting hypersexuality to work: black women and illicit eroticism in pornography. *Sexualities* 13: 2, 219–35.

Miller, C. (2009) *Automated Adult Income: Making Cash While You Sleep with Adult Videos Online*. Chris Miller Standard Copyright Licence.

Miller, M. (2004) Rap's dirty south: from subculture to pop culture. *Journal of Popular Music Studies* 16: 2, 175–212.

Mondin, A. (2014) Fair-trade porn + niche markets + feminist audience. *Porn Studies* 1: 1–2, 189–92.

Moraga, C. (1982) Barnard Sexuality Conference: played between white hands. *Off Our Backs* 12: 7, 23–6.

Morgan, R. (1993 [1974]) Theory and practice: rape and pornography. In Morgan, R. (ed.) *The Word of a Woman: Selected prose 1968–1992*. Virago Press, London, 78–89.

Morley, David (1995) Theories of Consumption in Media Studies. In Daniel Miller (ed.) *Acknowledging Consumption: A Review of New Studies*, pp. 296–328. Routledge, London and New York.

Morris, C. (2013) Porn and banks: drawing a line on loans. CNBC [Online] 17 May. http://www.cnbc.com/id/100746445

Mulvey, L. (1975) Visual pleasure and narrative cinema. *Screen* 16: 3, 6–18.

Murphy, J. (2008) Montreal: one of the world's capitals in pornography production. Life Site [Online] 25 August. http://www.lifesitenews.com/news/montreal-one-of-the-worlds-capitals-in-pornography-production

Musil, S. (2014) Revenge porn site operator arrested on hacking charges. C Net [Online] 23 January. http://www.cnet.com/news/revenge-porn-site-operator-arrested-on-hacking-charges/

Nakamura, L. (2002) *Cybertypes: Race, Ethnicity, Identity on the Internet*. Routledge, New York.

References

Nasaw, D. (1993) *Going Out: The Rise and Fall of Public Amusements.* Harvard University Press, Cambridge.

Nead, L. (1999) *The Female Nude: Art Obscenity and Sexuality.* Routledge, New York.

Neale, S. (1983) Masculinity as spectacle. *Screen* 24: 6, 2–17.

Nikunen, K., Paasonen, S., and Saarenmaa, L. (2008) *Pornification: Sex and Sexuality in Media Culture.* Berg Publishers, London.

Nixon, R. (1970) Statement about the Report of the Commission on Obscenity and Pornography. The American Presidency Project [Online] 24 October. http://www.presidency.ucsb.edu/ws/?pid=2759

O'Connor, T. and DeJohn, I. (2014) Duke porn star Belle Knox will return to school despite death threats. *New York Daily News* [Online] 19 March. http://www.nydailynews.com/news/national/belle-knox-duke-university-porn-star-returning-campus-due-death-threats-article-1.1726730

Obendorf, S. (2006) Reading racial gaze: Western gay society and pornographic depictions of Asian men. In Kendall, C. and Martino, W. (eds.) *Gendered Outcasts and Sexual Outlaws: Sexual Oppression and Gender Hierarchies in Queer Men's Lives.* Harrington Park Press, Binghamton, 153–75.

Ogas, O. and Gaddam, S. (2011) *A Billion Wicked Thoughts: What the World's Largest Experiment Reveals About Human Desire.* Dutton/Penguin, New York.

Oikelome, A. (2013) 'Are real women just bad porn?': women in Nigerian hip-hop culture. *Journal of Pan-African Studies* 5: 9, 83–98.

Olivier, M. A. J. (2005) How do academics handle job related stress? *South African Journal of Higher Education* 19: 2, 345–58.

Padgett, Vernon, R., Brislin-Slutz, J., and Neal, J. A. (1989) Pornography, erotica, and attitudes toward women: the effects of repeated exposure. *Journal of Sex Research* 26: 4, 479–91.

Papadopoulos, L. (2010) *Sexualisation of Young People.* Home Office, London.

Parliament of Australia (undated) Legislation relating to pornography in Australia. http://parlinfo.aph.gov.au/parlInfo/search/display/display.w3p;query=Id%3A%22library%2Fprspub%2FG1610%22

Paul, P. (2005) *Pornified: How Pornography is Damaging Our Lives, Our Relationships, and Our Families.* St Martin's Griffin, New York.

Penley, C. (2004) Crackers and whackers: The white trashing of porn. In Williams, L. (ed.). *Porn Studies: A Reader.* Routledge, New York, 309–333.

Perdue, L. (2004) EroticaBiz: how sex shaped the Internet. In Waskul, D. D. (ed.) *Net.sexxx: Readings on Sex, Pornography and the Internet.* Peter Lang, New York, 259–93.

Perraudin, F. (2014) Social porn: why people are sharing their sex lives online. *Guardian* [Online] 19 March. http://www.theguardian.com/lifeandstyle/2014/mar/18/social-porn-sharing-sex-lives-online-porntube-pinsex-pornostagram-pornography?CMP=twt_gu

References

Peter, J. and Valkenburg, P. M. (2007) Adolescents' exposure to a sexualized media environment and their notions of women as sex objects. *Sex Roles 56*, 381–95.

Plamondon, A. and Weber, C. (1996) As nasty as they want to be: a challenge for popular culture in multicultural societies. *Communications and the Law*, 57–83.

Porn MD (2014) Global Top Searches. Porn MD [Online] http://www.pornmd.com/sex-search

Q, S. (2014) Authentically yours: feminist porn gets political. SF Weekly [Online] 16 April. http://www.sfweekly.com/sanfrancisco/authentically-yours-feminist-porn-gets-political/Content?oid=2949245

Randolph, B. M. and Ross-Valliere, C. (1979) Consciousness Raising Groups. *American Journal of Nursing 79*: 5, 922–4.

Ray, L. (2011) *Violence and Society*. Sage, Thousand Oaks.

Ray, R. (2010) Content Marketing 101: Content is NOT King. Content distribution is King. Small biz technology [Online] 19 August. http://smallbiztechnology.com/archive/2010/08/content-marketing-101–content.html/

Reeve, B. 2010. 'Distribution is king'. Brock Reeve [Online] 21 June. http://brockreeve.com/post/2010/08/21/Distribution-is-King.aspx

Reisman, J. (1989) Promoting child abuse as art. *The Washington Times* 7 July, F1, 4.

Reuters (2006) Porn stars strut their stuff at awards. [Online] 9 January. http://tvnz.co.nz/content/646884/3362663.xhtml

Richardson, D. (1998) Sexuality and citizenship. *Sociology 32*, 83–100.

Rodriguez-Hart, C. et al. (2012) Sexually transmitted infection testing of adult film performers: is disease being missed? *American Sexually Transmitted Diseases*, 1–6.

Rosen, D. (2013) Is success killing the porn industry? AlterNet [Online] 27 May. http://www.alternet.org/sex-amp-relationships/success-killing-porn-industry

Rubin, G. (1984) Thinking sex: notes for a radical theory of the politics of sexuality. In Vance, C. S. (ed.). *Pleasure and Danger: Exploring Female Sexuality*. Pandora, London, 267–93.

Rubin, G. (1984) Thinking sex. In Vance, C. (ed.) *Pleasure and Danger*. Routledge, New York, 267–319.

Rush, E. and La Nauze, A. (2006). *Corporate Paedophilia: Sexualisation of children in Australia*. The Australia Institute, Canberra.

Russo, A. (1998) Feminists confront pornography's subordinating practices: policies and strategies for change. In Dines, G. Jensen, R., and Russo, A. (eds.) *Pornography: The Production and Consumption of Inequality*. Routledge, New York, 9–35.

Rutter, J. (2009) Vivid's 25th Anniversary: how Steven Hirsch's company thrust porn into mainstream America. AVN (Adult Video News) [Online] 30 September. http://business.avn.com/articles/video/Vivid-s-25th-Anniversary-How-Steven-Hirsch-s-Company-Thrust-Porn-Into-Mainstream-America-359979.html

References

Ryan, D. (2013) Fucking feminism. In Taormino, T., Parreñas Shimizu, C., Penley, C., and Miller-Young, M. (eds.) *The Feminist Porn Book: The Politics of Producing Pleasure*. The Feminist Press, New York, 121–9.

Same, S. (2014) Private porn footage is popping up on webcam sites. Same Same [Online] 24 April. http://www.samesame.com.au/news/10839/Private-webcam-footage-is-popping-up-on-porn-sites

Sarikakis, K. and Shaukat, Z. (2008) The global structures and cultures of pornography: the global brothel. In Sarikakis, K. and Regan Shade, L. (eds.) *Feminist Interventions in International Communication: Minding The Gap*. Rowman and Littlefield Publishing Inc., Lanham, 106–26.

Sere, A. (2004) Sex and feminism: who is being silenced? In Stark, C. and Whisnant, R. (eds.) *Not For Sale: Feminists Resisting Prostitution and Pornography*. Spinifex Press, Melbourne, 269–74.

Sharlot, L. 2003. *How to be an Internet Pornographer*. Booksurge, North Charleston.

Sharpley-Whiting, T. D. (2008) *Pimps Up, Ho's Down: Hip-Hop's Hold On Young Black Women*. New York University Press, New York.

Simonton, A. and Smith, C. (2004) Who are women in pornography? In Stark, C. and Whisnant, R. (eds.) *Not For Sale: Feminists Resisting Prostitution and Pornography*. Spinifex Press, Melbourne, 352–61.

Simpson, B. (2011) Challenging childhood, challenging children: children's rights and sexting. *Sexualities* 16:5/6, 690–709.

Smith, C. (2007) *One for the Girls: The Pleasures and Practices of Reading Women's Porn*. Intellect Books, Bristol.

Smith, C. (2010) Pornographication: a discourse for all seasons. *International Journal of Media and Cultural Politics* 6: 1, 103–8.

Snow, A. (2014) My 'Kink' nightmare: James Franco's BDSM documentary 'Kink' only tells part of the story. *The Daily Beast* [Online] 30 August. http://www.thedailybeast.com/articles/2014/08/30/my-kink-nightmare-james-franco-s-bdsm-porn-documentary-kink-only-tells-part-of-the-story.html

Spark Tech Talk (2012) Content curation and distribution is king. *Spark Tech Talk* [Online] accessed 25 June. http://soundcloud.com/sparktechtalk/content-curation-and-distribution-king.

Spriggs, J. (2008) *Make Money with Adult Websites: a guide to the adult Internet business and how to profit from Internet sites*. Venture Books.

Sprinkle, A. (1998) *Post-Porn Modernist*. Cleis Press Inc., San Francisco.

Stacey, J. (1994) *Star-gazing: Hollywood Cinema and Female Spectatorship*. Routledge, New York.

Stanko, E. (2001) Violence. In McLaughlin, E. and Muncie, J. (eds.) *The Sage Dictionary of Criminology*. Sage, London, 315–18.

Stardust, Z. (2012) What is 'fake' and 'real' in the sex industry? *The Scavenger* [Online]. 13 August. http://www.thescavenger.net/feminism/body-politics/858 –what-is-fake-and-real-in-the-sex-industry.html

References

Stark, C. (2004) Girls to boyz: sex radical women promoting pornography and prostitution. In Stark, C. and Whisnant, R. (eds.) *Not For Sale: Feminists Resisting Prostitution and Pornography.* Spinifex Press, Melbourne, 278–91.

Strub, W. (2006) Perversion for profit: Citizens for decent literature and the arousal of an anti-porn public in the 1960s. *Journal of the History of Sexuality* 15: 2, 258–91.

Szalai, G. (2010) Vivid: a new business model for porn. *The Hollywood Reporter* [Online] 02 September. http://www.hollywoodreporter.com/news/vivid-new-business-model-porn-27414

Tankard Reist, M. and Bray, A. (eds.) (2011) *Big Porn Inc: Exposing the Harms of the Global Pornography Industry.* Spinifex Press, Melbourne.

Taormino, T. (2013) Calling the shots: feminist porn in theory and practice. In Taormino, T., Parreñas Shimizu, C., Penley, C., and Miller-Young, M. (eds.) *The Feminist Porn Book: The Politics of Producing Pleasure.* The Feminist Press, New York, 255–65.

Tedeschi, B. (2012) Safeguarding a child's mobile device from pornography. *New York Times* [Online] 11 January. http://www.nytimes.com/2012/01/12/technology/personaltech/guarding-a-childs-mobile-device-from-pornography.html?_r=0

The Age. (2008) No charges for Henson. [Online] 6 June. http://www.theage.com.au/national/no-charges-for-henson-20080606–2mnv.html

Theroux, L. (2012) How the internet killed porn. *Guardian* [Online] 5 June. http://www.theguardian.com/culture/2012/jun/05/how-internet-killed-porn?newsfeed=true

Tibbals, C. (2012) '(A)nything that forces itself into my vagina is by definition raping me . . .' – adult film performers and occupational safety and health. *Stanford Law and Policy Review* 23: 1, 231–51.

Trouble, C. (2014a) Porn's new keywords. Feminist Porn Conference Keynote [Online] courtneytrouble.com

Trouble, C. (2014b) Finding gender through porn performance. *Porn Studies* 1:1–2, 197–200.

Trueman, P. A. (2014) Porn creates demand for sex trafficking. *Miami Herald* [Online] 2 July. http://www.miamiherald.com/2014/07/23/4251372/porn-creates-demand-for-sex-trafficking.html

Ulanoff, L. (2011) Opinion: XXX domains an obvious failure [Online] 12 December. http://www.cnn.com/2011/12/12/tech/web/xxx-domains-failure-mashable/

Urban Dictionary. (2006) Rule 34. Urban Dictionary. [Online] http://www.urbandictionary.com/define.php?term=Rule+34

US Department of Justice (2010) The National Strategy for Child Exploitation Prevention and Interdiction: US Department of Justice [Online] August. http://www.justice.gov/sites/default/files/psc/docs/natstrategyreport.pdf

References

Vance, C. S., Harvey, B., Willis, E., Califia, P., Rubin, G., and Allison, D. (1983) Notes and letters. *Feminist Studies* 9: 3, 589–615.

VanEvery, J. (1996) Heterosexuality and domestic life. In Richardson, D. (ed.) *Theorising Heterosexuality*. Open University Press, London, 39–54.

Vice (2010) Neu Sex – part 1 [Online] vimeo.com/20058544

Virtual Global Taskforce (2012) Virtual Global Taskforce [Online] http://www.virtualglobaltaskforce.com/

Vivid Entertainment (2009) All-American porn. 25 years of erotic photography from Vivid Entertainment group [Online] http://www.25yearsofvivid.com/

Voon, V., Mole T. B., Banca P., et al. (2014) Neural correlates of sexual cue reactivity in individuals with and without compulsive sexual behaviours. *PLoS ONE* 9:7, 1–10.

Waskul, D. D. (2004a) The naked self: body and self in televideo cybersex. In Waskul, D. D. (ed.) *Net.sexxx: Readings on Sex, Pornography and the Internet*. Peter Lang, New York, 35–63.

Waskul, D. D. (2004b) Sex and the internet: old thrills in a new world; new thrills in an old world. In Waskul, D. D. (ed.) *Net.sexxx: Readings on Sex, Pornography and the Internet*. Peter Lang, New York, 1–8.

Weeks, J. (1995) *Invented Moralities: Sexual Values in an Age of Uncertainty*. Columbia University Press, New York.

Weitzer, R. and Ditmore, M. (2010) Sex trafficking: facts and fictions. In Weitzer, R. and Ditmore, M. (eds.) *Sex for Sale: Prostitution, Pornography and the Sex Industry*. Routledge, New York, 325–51.

West, R. (2005) *Adult Website Money: How to Build, Start and Market an Adult Website Business for Little to No Cost in 30 Days*. Clear View.

Whisnant, R. (2004) Confronting pornography: some conceptual basics. In Stark, C. and Whisnant, R. (eds.) *Not For Sale: Feminists Resisting Prostitution and Pornography*. Spinifex Press, Melbourne, 15–27.

Whisnant, R. and Stark, C. (2004) Introduction. In Stark, C. and Whisnant, R. (eds.) *Not For Sale: Feminists Resisting Prostitution and Pornography*. Spinifex Press, Melbourne, xi–xvii.

Williams, L. (1989) *Hard Core: Power, Pleasure, and the 'Frenzy of the Visible'*. University of California Press, Berkeley.

Williams, L. (1991) Film bodies: gender, genre and excess. *Film Quarterly* 44: 4, 2–13.

Williams, R. (1975) *Television: Technology and Cultural Form*. Routledge, New York.

Williams, R. (1977) *Marxism and Literature*. Oxford University Press, New York.

Williams, Z. (2014) Is there such a thing as ethical porn? *Guardian* [Online] 1 November. http://www.theguardian.com/culture/2014/nov/01/ethical-porn-fair-trade-sex

References

Wilson, E. (1983) The context of 'Between Pleasure and Danger': the Barnard conference on sexuality. Feminist Review 13, 35–41.

Wilson, E. (1992) Feminist fundamentalism: the shifting politics of sex and censorship. In Segal L. and McIntosh M. (eds.) Sex Exposed: Sexuality and the Pornography Debate. Long River Books, East Haven, 72–90.

Woodhouse, J. (2014) Extreme Pornography. Home Office, London.

Wyndham, S. (2012) 'Q+A'. The Sydney Morning Herald. 1 September 2012.

xhamster.com. (2012) Webcam models wanted. XHamster. [Online] http://xhamster.com/webcam_models_wanted.php

Young, A. (2008) The state is still in the bedrooms of the nation. Canadian Journal of Human Sexuality 17: 4, 203–16.

Young, H. (2013) Slaves in the supply chain: 12 ways to clean up business. Guardian [Online] 10 December. http://www.theguardian.com/global-development-professionals-network/2013/dec/10/how-to-tackle-supply-chain-slavery

Young, I. M. (2005) On Female Body Experience: 'Throwing Like a Girl' and Other Essays. Oxford University Press, New York.

Zillmann, D. (2000) Influence of unrestrained access to erotica on adolescents' and young adults' dispositions toward sexuality. Journal of Adolescent Health 27: 2, 41–4.

Index

Index

Index

Index

Index

Index

Index

Index